Reinventing Lean

Reinventing Lean

Introducing Lean Management into the Supply Chain

Gerhard Plenert

President
Institute of World Class Management

Lean Consultant
MainStream Management, GS, LLC

Adjunct Professor
University of San Diego
Supply Chain Management Institute

AMSTERDAM • BOSTON • HEIDELBERG • LONDON
NEW YORK • OXFORD • PARIS • SAN DIEGO
SAN FRANCISCO • SINGAPORE • SYDNEY • TOKYO

Butterworth-Heinemann is an imprint of Elsevier

Butterworth-Heinemann is an imprint of Elsevier
30 Corporate Drive, Suite 400, Burlington, MA 01803, USA
Linacre House, Jordan Hill, Oxford OX2 8DP, UK

⊗ Recognizing the importance of preserving what has been written, Elsevier prints its books on
acid-free paper whenever possible.

Library of Congress Cataloging-in-Publication Data
Application submitted

British Library Cataloguing-in-Publication Data
A catalogue record for this book is available from the British Library.

ISBN 13: 978-0-12-370517-4
ISBN 10: 0-12-370517-7

For information on all Butterworth-Heinemann publications
visit our Web site at www.books.elsevier.com

Printed in the United States of America
06 07 08 09 10 11   10 9 8 7 6 5 4 3 2 1

Dedication

To The Love of My Life–

Renee Sangray Plenert

Who makes my life worthwhile!!!

Contents

Part I
Integrating Supply Chain Management

Chapter 3

What Are the Tools of Supply Chain Management (SCM)?

Chapter 4

What Are the Measures of a Successful Supply Chain Management?

Chapter 5

What Does It Take to Create a World-Class Supply Chain Environment?

Part II
Developing a Lean Environment

Part III
Creating a Lean Supply Chain Management Environment

Acknowledgments

In order to give credit where credit is due, I would need to create a long list of individuals, companies, universities, and countries that I have worked with. In my most recent academic past I have had the pleasure of working with universities including the University of San Diego in its Supply Chain Management Institute, Brigham Young University, California State University, Chico, and many international universities. Professionally, I have had the pleasure of working with organizations such as MainStream Management as a Lean consultant, American Management Systems (AMS) as a senior principal in their Corporate Technology Group where I was the business practice leader on Supply Chain Management/ERP/EAM/DRP/Lean Principles in an eCommerce environment, and Precision Printers as executive director of Quality, Engineering, R&D, Customer Service, Production Scheduling and Planning, and Facilities Management. Other organizations that I have worked for include Hill Air Force Base, the California Department of Child Support Services (DCSS), Texas Attorney General's Office, Child Support Division where I was director of Change Management and Communications, Kraft Foods, and many more.

As you can imagine, it is challenging to "lean" out an office full of lawyers or accountants. But in some cases the results were a tripling of throughput using the same number of employees.

I have lived and worked in factories in Latin America, Asia, and Europe, I have co-authored articles and books, and I have worked with academic and professionals from as far away as Europe, Japan, and Australia. My broad exposure to a variety of manufacturing and service facilities all over the world has given me the background I needed to write this book.

I also need to recognize my family, my wife, Renee Sangray Plenert, and my children, Heidi Lynette Plenert, Dawn Janelle Plenert, Gregory Johannes Plenert, Gerick Johannes Plenert, Joshua Johannes Plenert, Natasha Ida Plenert, Zackary Johannes Plenert, and Chelsey Jean Plenert, who gave me the time I needed to make this book work.

Gerhard Plenert

Preface

There are two concepts in management that have become somewhat disassociated but that need to be integrated closely together. The first concept is Supply Chain Management (SCM). Integrating the linkages of the supply chain is an extremely complex task, especially if you are trying to integrate these linkages internationally. Supply chains can be as simple as going to a farmer to buy strawberries or as complex as involving thousands of suppliers, manufacturers, shippers, and retailers. But the failure of any one of the steps in this chain results in the failure of the entire supply chain. Customers do not care about why a product was late or why it was wrong; they only care that it was wrong, and they expected it to be correct.

Supply Chain Management (SCM) integrates networks of international companies into a structure that allows them to optimize performance as a collective unit. The integration starts with the vendor's vendor and ends with the customer's customer. Three key measures identify the successful performance of the international supply chain:

- Cycle time performance
- Operating cost minimization
- On-time performance and customer satisfaction

Information exchange within the supply chain is critical for its successful operation. This requires an openness and trust among all the entities of the supply chain. It also requires a mechanism for the efficient transfer of this information. Traditional methods of information transfer, such as fax, phone, or even e-mail, are too slow. Internet, intranet, and extranet information accessibility allowing all entities in the supply chain to monitor the performance of every other entity is critical to international competitive success.

The second concept that needs to be reassessed and that needs to be integrated in conjunction with SCM is Lean. Lean is a tool that facilitates the elimination of waste. And waste can be identified in a multitude of resource areas. Any, and probably all, of the resource areas identified as part of the supply chain contain waste. Lean is the methodology that identifies the waste and then utilizes a bag of tools to attempt to eliminate this waste. The more waste that is eliminated, the greater the value-added time, resulting in greater throughput, lower costs, increased capacity, and reduced cycle times. In the end, utilizing Lean principles provides a supply chain that is more efficient and more responsive to the customer, and therefore more competitive.

If every organization in the world worked in exactly the same way, this book would have been very easy to write. Unfortunately, however, no two organizations work alike. Even when the organizations are producing the same output and are right next to each other, they often operate differently because of management style and methods, or corporate influences. Therefore, it is impossible to come up with one book that can claim to be the perfect way to run all organizations. This reminds me of Newton's law for organizations: For every manager with a perfect solution there is an equal and opposite manager with a perfect solution.

This book contains simplistic SCM and Lean ideas that have proven to be enormously effective. Most of them will fit any organizational environment (and I have personally experienced some strange organizations), but they are not all intended to fit perfectly in every environment. This notion brings us to the purpose of this book: *this book is designed to be a starting point in discovering the power of leaning out your supply chain.* With that as our goal, we can now move forward in improving our supply chain performance.

Thank you.

Gerhard Plenert

Introduction

*We want to adopt proven and successful
business practices that have been used
in the commercial marketplace. We want
to do business like business does business.*
David Falvey, Business Systems
Modernization program manager,
Defense Logistics Agency

I recently went into a government attorney general's office of about 30 employees, many of them lawyers. Initially, I interviewed the office manager and the managing attorney. Then I performed a scan of the office personnel, going around the office and spending about 15 to 30 minutes with each employee. I asked questions about workflow, volume, and capacities. I was looking for the non–value-added content of their work and for bottlenecks—concepts that will be discussed in more detail later in this book. I spent most of the day performing these interviews. At the end of the day I met with the office manager and the managing attorney. I made specific recommendations about work assignments and workflow, and suggestions about work buildups and backlogs. The managers took these suggestions seriously (which is critical to any success) and implemented them immediately. Less than two weeks later, I received a call informing me that this office had tripled their daily output of work. This was accomplished without any hiring or layoffs and without cracking the whip on employees. It was accomplished by "leaning" out the paperwork and information flow process within the organization. Similar results can be achieved in any office or service environment. And it results from the effective use of Lean and supply chain tools and principles—the same tools and principles that you will learn about in this book.

Here's another example. I went into a high-tech manufacturer and within eight months was able to:

- Reduce a more than 14 percent defect rate to below 2 percent.
- Reduce production setup times from a maximum of 20 minutes to below 10 minutes and as low as 6 minutes in some cases.

- Reduce inventories by 40 percent.
- Significantly reduce the overall lead time.
- Reduce order preparation time from five days to less than one day.

All the tools used to accomplish these goals are described in this book. And you can accomplish them within your organization as well.

This book will discuss Lean tools and techniques, including

- Lean management
- Six Sigma
- Cycle time
- Value stream mapping and TAKT time
- JoHari window
- Spaghetti charting
- Value-Added vs. Non–Value-Added activities

This book will also discuss Supply Chain Management (SCM) tools and techniques such as

- Just in Time Management (JIT)
- Enterprise Resource Planning Processes (ERP)
- Distribution Requirements Planning (DRP)
- Advanced Planning and Scheduling (APS)
- Finite Capacity Scheduling (FCS)

The book will then discuss how to integrate these Lean tools with the SCM tools to form a world-class environment.

This book is divided into three sections, as follows:

Part I: Integrating Supply Chain Management   This first section discusses the foundation concepts of Supply Chain Management (SCM). It explains what the supply chain is and how it works. It discusses the tools that are available for managing a supply chain and describes the measurement systems that will monitor the performance of the overall supply chain. This section also discusses the need to become a world-class competitor. It defines what world class is, and it helps you rate your organization with the use of a step chart. Then it discusses the future state and shows how to develop the gap analysis that will help you identify needed improvements.

Part II: Developing a Lean Environment   This section delves into the detailed operation of a Lean environment. It discusses the cultural acceptance tools that are required to build acceptance of the lean process; the tools available to win acceptance; the technical tools used to identify non–value-added opportunities for improvement; and the improvement process.

Part III: Creating a Lean Supply Chain Management Environment   This section focuses on the integration of Lean and SCM. It discusses the need to focus your Lean efforts in the correct way in order to maximize the impact of these efforts. In the end, this section teaches you how Lean and SCM tools will help an organization achieve world-class goals.

The definition of Insanity is
  Continuing to do the Same Things and
    Expecting Different Results.
        Breakthrough Thinking,
        Nadler and Hibino

Part I

Integrating Supply Chain Management

Chapter 1

What Is a Supply Chain?

INTRODUCING THE FIRST ARTICLE LAB

Z Base is a military base with a high-tech laboratory facility that includes a chemical lab, a materials lab, an electronics lab, and a dimensioning lab. The dimensioning lab is referred to as the Quality Verification Center (QVC). The lab has achieved international recognition for its excellent, high-quality, professional performance. This facility's labs perform a number of services for the Department of Defense (DoD), including environmental investigations, failure investigations, and first article verifications. Recently, the author was tasked with identifying improvement opportunities in the supply chain for the processing of first article verifications.

Every part to be used on an aircraft must first be validated to ensure that it satisfies engineering requirements. Any failure can be disastrous. For example, recently the pins used to hold the wing in place on a war fighter aircraft were not fully validated. The aircraft was assembled, and the following day it was scheduled to receive a test flight. In the morning, when the pilot came out to the airfield to test fly the plane, he found the wing lying on the ground. The pins had sheered off overnight. Had the aircraft been flown with the faulty pins, the results would have been catastrophic.

Because of the high-level performance requirements for aircraft parts, inspections are required every time a vendor produces a part for the first time. The first production item is referred to as the first article and is thoroughly tested by the Z Base labs.

When I was initially introduced to the first article project, the following failure rates were reported for the inspected parts:

43 percent of the parts were accepted as meeting all engineering specifications.
28 percent of the parts were conditionally accepted, meaning that some minor issues will need to be fixed and that when those items are fixed the part is accepted for usage.
26 percent of the parts were rejected as not satisfying engineering specifications in some significant way, making them unusable.
3 percent had other issues; for example, they were shipped to the wrong lab for processing.

In order to validate a part, it is brought into the lab and receives all the appropriate tests specified on the engineering drawings. Included may be dimensioning tests where all aspects of the part are measured, or metallurgical tests that validate the metallic properties of the part, or chemical tests on coatings, or electronics tests that validate all the electronic functionality of the part. Tests may even include fit tests where the part is "tried out" in the aircraft to see if it will fit and function properly when installed. The requirement for thoroughness in the first article testing process for aircraft parts is obvious, since gravity makes failure disastrous.

First impressions would suggest that the first article testing process should be fairly simple: bring the part in and test it. But the reality of the situation is that the flow of this process is extremely complex. As seen in Chart 1.1, several layers of processing are required within the first article supply chain. There are material movement steps, where the material is manufactured and brought to the lab for testing; information movement steps, which include contracting, engineering, and testing documentation; and financial movement steps where the testing costs are allocated. This supply chain, like most supply chains, requires the optimization of three key resources: materials, information, and money.

As the facilitator to this process, I started by forming a team that proceeded to thoroughly investigate the supply chain in an attempt to clearly understand the full process. The team visited and interacted with all the organizations involved in the first article process, including the customer, engineering, contracting, and the Defense Logistics Agency (DLA). Through these meetings the team was able to develop a detailed map of the entire first article process. This map was then used to identify holes in the system and thereby determine opportunities for improvement. The team was also able to identify measures of process performance. Three main measures were targeted: flow days (process cycle time), jobs on hold that could not be processed because of incomplete information, and process travel time. A baseline for each of these measures was established. From there I followed the procedures for leaning out the supply chain that are documented in this book.

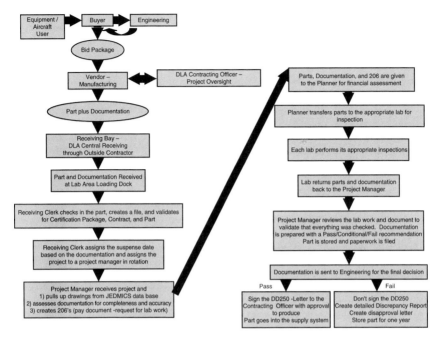

Chart 1.1 First Article Process Flow. For a more detailed view of this figure, please visit our companion site at: http://books.elsevier.com/companions/0123705177

We will visit the Z Base first article inspection process several times throughout this book and use it as an example of how to "lean" out a supply chain process.

DEFINING THE SUPPLY CHAIN

There are as many definitions of a supply chain as there are books in the marketplace. The definition finally chosen must at the same time be informative and restrictive. If the definition is too narrow, "improving a supply chain" will focus on efforts that are too limiting. If it is too broad, pulling any meaning out of the definition will become difficult. Therefore, our definition needs to be narrow enough to be informative, yet broad enough to encompass all the aspects of a global supply chain.

When attempting to define a supply chain, you will get definitions with terms such as integrating, connectivity, information exchange, communication, linkages, and logistics. All of these terms are appropriate when discussing a supply chain, but they are too generic to supply a meaningful definition to someone who does not already understand what a supply chain is. The DAMA (Demand Activated Manufacturing Architecture) Project created an interesting example of a supply chain, which demonstrates how complex the materials flow of a supply chain of something as simple as a bedsheet really is (see Chart 1.2 process maps courtesy of [TC]²).[1]

For the purposes of this book, we will start with a one-word definition of supply chain and will build on that one word to create a meaningful understanding. That one word is "movement"—supply chains are all about moving things around. Then, building on this one-word definition, we need to decide what movements we need to track. And the answer is "we need to track the movement of resources."

What resources are moved in a supply chain? Obviously, when we initially think of a supply chain, we think of materials or parts moving from one location to another and eventually ending up in the hands of a customer. For example, when we think of the supply chain for a television, we go all the way back to the mine that dug up the raw materials, then to the refinery where we process the steel or the chemicals, and next to the factory where we form the parts and assemble them into products such as circuit boards or screens. From the assembly plant that put the television together we go to the shipping company that packaged the product and delivered it to a warehouse, and finally to a retailer. The retail store puts the television on the shelf where the customer selects the product, purchases it, and takes it home. This process involves literally thousands of steps, and each step becomes critical to the success of the overall process. The customer interprets a failure in any of these steps as a failure of the entire supply chain.

As complex as the flow of the supply chain seems, when we look at the materials flow, we soon realize that this is a simplified view of the total supply chain. It is not just the flow of materials that defines a supply chain's success or failure, it is also the movement of two other key resources: information and money. Again, from the customer's perspective, a failure in the flow of either of these resources is a failure of the entire supply chain. And in the end, the customer's perspective is the only perspective that counts.

Look at an example of money movement. Failure in processing a payment, or charging the wrong amount, or collecting the incorrect amount is a failure in the supply chain. Or look on the information movement side. Failing to process the order correctly, supplying an incorrect product definition or shipment date, or distributing an incorrect materials list can result in a delay in completing the process or worse yet, shipment of an incorrect product to a customer.

---

[1] The bedsheet process map is the product of the DAMA (Demand Activated Manufacturing Architecture) Project, a joint project with the U.S. Department of Energy and the National Laboratory System. This research involved a large number of industry participants and several of the DOE laboratories that provided scientists and engineers who helped study, map, and measure performance in the traditional supply chain. Today, the supply chain may involve a similar number of steps, some of which may occur at disparate points around the globe. The DAMA project was managed for the industry by Jim Lovejoy or Jud Early at [TC]². Jim can be reached at jlovejo@tc2.com and Jud at jearly@tc2.com.

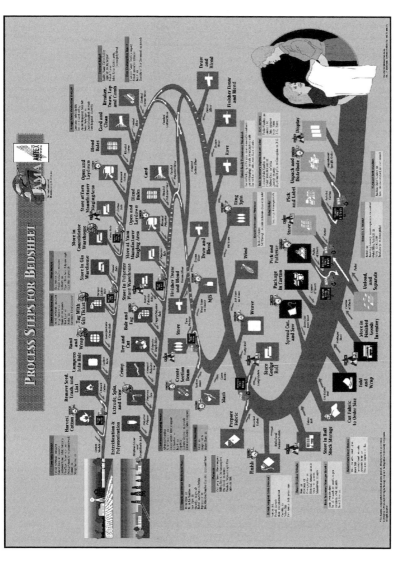

Chart 1.2 Process Steps for Bedsheet. For a more detailed view of this figure, please visit our companion site at: http://books.elsevier.com/companions/0123705177

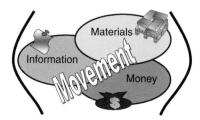

Chart 1.3   The Critical Driving Resources That Define a Supply Chain

We see then that three critical resources define the success or failure of movement within the supply chain: materials, information, and money (see Chart 1.3). One of these is not more or less important than any of the others; a failure of any is a failure of all.

Chart 1.3 shows the three "moving" resources as well as an area of overlap and interaction for them. None of these resources exists in isolation, and a change to any one of the resources often affects the performance of one or more of the other resources.

Examining this chart easily leads us to the conclusion that in order to optimize the supply chain process and thus make our supply chain a world-class supply chain, all we need to do is to optimize these three movements. But this conclusion is only partially true. As we have noted before, this model is far too simplistic to explain everything that goes on within a supply chain. When we seek to optimize the movement of these three resources, we also need to examine the forces that interact with these resources; the list of these forces can become quite long and complex. For example, time pressures such as holidays or work schedules, as well as technology availability and change, can affect the performance of the supply chain. An example of some of these forces and pressures exhibited against a supply chain can be seen in Chart 1.4.

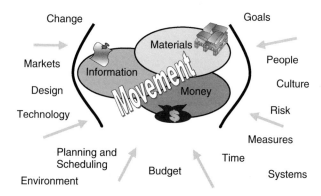

Chart 1.4   The Forces Affecting the Resources That Define a Supply Chain

The chart presents pressures such as risk, time, and budgets that need to become part of the optimization process of a supply chain. For example, timeliness can be prohibitively expensive and therefore impractical. Therefore, it is the balancing act of all these resources and pressures, optimized in conjunction with each other, that will optimize the total supply chain. Before identifying the perfect supply chain, however, let us take a short look at some of the history associated with the development of supply chains.

A LITTLE HISTORY

When studying the migration of productivity, quality, and delivery performance over time, we find that this migration was often driven by two key factors:

1. The capabilities of the available technology
2. The dominant concentration and cost of resources

For example, from Chart 1.5 we see that in the 1970s and earlier, the focus was on labor efficiency internal to the organization. At this time, labor still represented the highest concentration of cost for most types of manufacturing. In addition, the belief persisted that if people worked more efficiently and harder, more output would be generated. The production planning systems that would support labor-based strategies migrated from EOQ (Economic Order Quantity, which based all control on inventory levels) to MRP (Material Requirements Planning, which introduced the scheduling of labor, materials, and machinery) to MRP II (Manufacturing Resources Planning, which brought financial and marketing considerations into the production planning process) to ERP (Enterprise

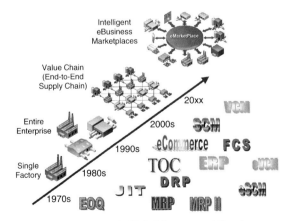

Chart 1.5 Supply Chain Management Migration

Resources Planning, which integrated all the information systems in an organization and looked at the enterprise, not just the manufacturing plant). Similarly, for distribution we have DRP (Distribution Requirements Planning). The focus was always internal, searching for improvements within the organization.

The 1980s demonstrated a fascination for substitute production planning philosophies such as JIT (Just in Time) from Japan or TOC (Theory of Constraints—initially called OPT or Optimized Production Technology) from Israel. These systems pulled some of the focus away from labor and shifted it toward materials and machine efficiency. But the direction of the focus was still internal. These new systems were simply adopted under the ERP wing and treated as subsets of the ERP planning and scheduling environment.

Through the 1980s, organizations were dominated by a fear of sharing too much information. As such, vendors and customers were "black boxes" where no information exchange was allowed. However, as we moved into the 1990s, organizations started to recognize the influence of external factors in overall profitability. Companies identified how customers, vendors, and partners played key roles in the performance of the overall supply chain. Organizations began to acknowledge how working with customers and vendors, and sharing information with these "outsiders," were critical in defining not just the external performance of the supply chain, but also the internal performance of the organization.

As significant as this new external supply chain perspective was, it failed to create harmony between the partners. Instead, a jockeying for power occurred, during which a financial kingpin in the supply chain attempted to control the entire supply chain. At times, as in the case of General Motors or Ford, we find that it is the manufacturer who tries to control and drive the performance of the supply chain. At other times, as in the case of Wal-Mart, we find that it is the retailer that controls the supply chain.

Now in the 2000s, we find organizations that realize that customers and vendors are not stupid and that they can add value. Working with customers and vendors as supply chain partners, and using their input rather than just dictating to them what is expected, brings an entirely new perspective into the management and control of the overall process and introduces the idea of a value chain. Today each participant in the process adds value to and receives value from the overall supply chain. As we see in Chart 1.5, the value chain (end-to-end supply chain) has been created and relationships are no longer fixed, controlled, and rigid. Suppliers can be interchanged based on the availability of resources within any of the vendors.

Using Dell computers, let me give you an example of a fully integrated, end-to-end e-commerce-based supply chain (eVCM or e-commerce value chain). In their purchasing process, customers go on-line and identify their customized configuration of the product they want to purchase. For example, if they want a laptop computer, they configure the computer out exactly the way they want it to look. Then, the on-line system gives them the pricing of their selected configuration. Everything we have described up to this point already exists. The next step is to blow this configuration out throughout the supply chain, to check product availability down to the vendor's vendor level, and if there is no product availability, to check for capacity availability. The eVCM system then allocates product and capacity for manufacturing and shipping at all these levels and comes back to the customers (while they are still on-line) and gives them a precise delivery date (currently, the system only offers the customer an approximate delivery date, which includes a buffer).

If the customer moves forward with the order by paying for it, all the inventory and capacity allocations become firm, triggering the production and delivery process for the laptop computer. From this example we can see a movement of the three resources in a supply chain: materials, money, and information.

We can see how an error in any one of these resources is a failure of the entire system. For example, if inventory records are incorrect, the production, shipping, and delivery schedules will be incorrect. Or if the cost or payment calculations are incorrect, the profitability of the entire supply chain will be affected. The performance of all three resources is interconnected, as are the forces that put pressure on these resources, notably time, planning and scheduling, or the systems used to make the eVCM work.

Chart 1.5 shows that eBusiness Marketplaces have also been started. These marketplaces represent an additional attempt to sever the link between specific customers and vendors by allowing everyone with an interest in buying or selling a specific product to go into a marketplace and place the order for it, regardless of which vendor will eventually take the order. Several attempts have been made to develop eBusiness Marketplaces in various industries such as the automotive or the agriculture industry, with varying success. Some efforts have succeeded very well, but others have failed miserably. It remains to be seen if eBusiness Marketplaces are truly an integration step of the future.

THE SUPPLIER[2]

Probably the single most discussed area of Supply Chain Management and of international operations management is the management of the supplier in the supply chain. The supply chain can best be described by the words movement, integration, and time.

---

[2]This section summarizes some of the material found in Plenert, Gerhard, *International Operations Management*, Copenhagen Business School Press, Copenhagen, Denmark, 2002. Reprinted in India by Ane Books, New Delhi, 2003. This book offers an extensive expansion of these fundamental SCM concepts.

We have already discussed the role of movement and of the resources that get moved. Integration refers to the vertical integration of all functions and activities that occur throughout the supply chain. It involves managing the suppliers' supplier all the way through to managing the customers' customer. The role of Supply Chain Management in all this is to minimize and eliminate all waste as we process through these functions. SCM focuses on incorporating only value-added steps in these areas.

Supply Chain Management also focuses on time. One of the primary goals behind the management of the supply chain is to help us achieve time efficiency throughout the entire supply network. Only by managing and optimizing the entire flow is it possible to shorten the cycle time.

In this section we will discuss the management of the supply chain by focusing on supplier sourcing and scheduling. In the next chapter we will look at the integration and waste elimination needs of the supply chain. Later in the book we will focus on cycle time efficiencies and logistics/wholesale management. To start this process, let's visit with a new company, N, Inc.

N, INC.

N, Inc. has manufacturing facilities all over the world. Its corporate office is in Dayton, Ohio, and the entire company is organized around two major marketing divisions, the domestic division and the international division. Despite some crossover and interface, the two divisions manage themselves independently. The international division comprises regions including the Austrial-Asia, the European, and the Latin American regions. The manufacturing section includes plants in Germany, several U.S. sites, Canada, Mexico, and Asia. The company's primary product line is point-of-sale terminals for the retail and banking industries and for small, medium, and large computers. N, Inc. also manufactures many of the computer components that other computer manufacturers utilize and install in their own equipment.

N, Inc. has encountered numerous difficulties in managing its supply chain. For example, it sources computer components from all over the world. In addition, it manufactures many of its own components and brings them into the production process when external resources become too expensive or difficult to access. However, its divisions are not required to purchase internally produced components; rather, they are required to be externally competitive.

N has a microelectronics manufacturing plant located outside of Dayton, Ohio, which produces and sells chips to other N divisions as well as to external customers. This division, like all divisions, is encouraged to be internally and externally competitive in all its processes. One of its primary customers is a terminal plant in Augsburg, Germany, that does its own board insertion work.

Sales to the Augsburg plant are about $1 million per year. Total annual sales are $10 million. However, the Dayton plant is not ISO certified, and it would cost about $500,000 to get certification. In addition, the Augsburg plant can get microelectrocircuitry from a competitive facility in Sweden for slightly more than the Dayton plant costs them. However, if Dayton adds in the certification costs into the parts sold to Augsburg, it is no longer competitive. The corporate office would prefer internal sourcing of components because of the control that gives to the supply chain and because of the additional political advantages of maintaining this method of sourcing. The microelectronics plant is worried that if it goes through certification, the Augsburg facility may not see things in the same light and may pull out. In addition, the Augsburg plant has become concerned about single sourcing the components and is wondering if it should not give the Swedish plant some of its parts demand simply to keep a backup supplier in the loop. What should Augsburg management do? What should Dayton management do? Should corporate management get involved?

The supply chain for the Augsburg factory is diagrammed in Chart 1.6, which shows how integration occurs from the vendor to the customer. This chart is extremely simplified, for it leaves out many of the vendors and retailers, as well as the distribution, logistics, and warehousing chain. We can see how the complexity increases and therefore how the management of the supply chain

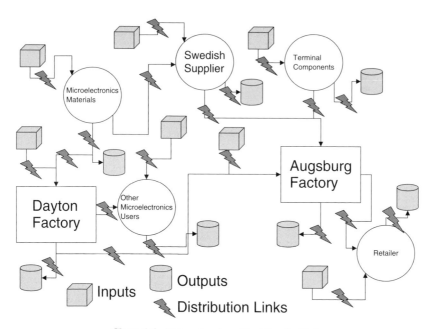

Chart 1.6 N, Inc. Augsburg Plant Supply Chain

becomes difficult. The chart shows some of the distribution and logistics points and reveals that in a simple two-factory model, management of the model becomes far more complex than can be managed by a simple system. However, this diagram helps us understand how a supply chain would work. For N, Inc., there is a lack of integrated information flow. For example, if inter- and intraplant information were to exist, the plants could be more efficient in their scheduling processes. Perhaps this communication would facilitate decisions and communication between Augsburg and Dayton.

The management of the supply chain is the second element of this case that needs consideration. How would you recommend that it be accomplished? What level or type of Supply Chain Management is needed in order to make a difference in N's effectiveness? How about its competitiveness?

WHAT IS THE ROLE OF THE SUPPLIER?

The focus words in Supply Chain Management are *integration* and *time*. With regard to supplier relationships, we focus on eliminating waste in all aspects of the supply chain, which we accomplish by focusing on these two issues. One of the best ways to discuss this topic is to take a close look at the traditional EOQ (Economic Order Quantity) model,[3] which the Japanese utilized in their development of the Just in Time (JIT) process. This process focuses on carrying cost reductions and order cost reductions, such as setup time reduction, which results in a decrease in the total cost of inventory and thereby reduces the order size. Therefore, reducing order cost can dramatically reduce inventory levels throughout the facility.

The entire discussion of inventory cost reduction and waste elimination basically touches on the philosophy behind JIT, which stresses that we should not assume anything to be fixed and constant. The strategy is to attack everything that is non-value added, and you end up with lower inventory costs across the board. We will examine this philosophy more fully when we discuss Lean in Chapter 8. The optimization of these cost reduction activities directly affects the international transaction.

Internationalization introduces some cultural variations in supply chain optimization, for example, the differences in the value of data collection. The United States believes that it has entered an information age, whereas much of the rest of the world sees it as an information obsession. For example, Activity-Based Costing is a tool for collecting data at points in the organization. It is assumed

---

[3] A detailed discussion of how JIT and EOQ interact and optimize flow in the supply chain can be found in Chapter 6 of Plenert, *International Operations Management*. This book offers an extensive expansion of these fundamental SCM concepts.

that more cost data will allow better management of costs. However, many countries believe the measurement of noncritical cost elements is a waste and prefer focusing on measuring the critical resource elements. For example, the JIT process does not include any shopfloor data collection. The recording of who did what and how long it took is not important. Rather, what is important is the efficient movement of the materials resource, which is more than 50 percent of the value-added cost content of the vehicle.

Another example of information waste is found in the nontrust systems established in most organizations. Every time an undesirable event occurs, a system is created to ensure that it will not happen again. As has been documented, in many companies the nontrust systems, and the cost of the data collection process that they have created, is much more expensive than the problem they are supposedly solving. It is this type of information obsession and lack of trust that is scoffed at internationally. In Japan, this is labeled information waste.

At this point we should have a feel for how the supplier relationship can be optimized for the benefit of everyone involved in the supply chain. We should also be getting an understanding of how some international considerations are treated differently, rather than using the more traditional approach of going wherever labor costs are cheapest. Some additional case examples of how these differences manifest themselves in the supply chain follow.

TAKING AN IN-DEPTH LOOK AT NAFTA'S EFFECT ON MAQUILADORA PLANTS

Next we will take an in-depth look at a specific case of international supply chain development. We will consider the case of the North American Free Trade Agreement (NAFTA), the United States, and the Mexican factories across the border from the United States that supply cheap labor for American manufacturers. This example will give you a sense of some of the issues faced by international operations management and Supply Chain Management.

Maquiladora plants sprang up in Mexico, right across the border from the United States, in an attempt to take advantage of the low-cost workforce available across the border. These plants were primarily assembly plants that performed all the technical functions across the border in the United States. After NAFTA was signed, however, new plants began moving deeper into the heart of Mexico. In addition, those plants that exist along the border are developing their own technical capabilities. This section discusses these changes through examples and considers how the new, post-NAFTA Mexican plant is priming to become a world-class competitor.

WHAT IS A MAQUILADORA FACTORY?

The term *Maquiladora* identifies Mexican assembly plants that are immediately across the border from the United States. A Maquiladora plant is a labor-intensive plant where the engineering, marketing, and technical functions are kept in the United States and the labor assembly work is performed in Mexico. It was established to take advantage of a special, pre-NAFTA tax arrangement that allows materials to be transferred into and back out of Mexico in a form of consignment program, without having to pay duties on the materials. Only the value-added labor component was taxed. Now there are approximately 320 of these assembly plants along the U.S.–Mexican border.

Ciudad Juarez is the home of the first Maquiladora plants. Approximately 600,000 Maquiladora trucks cross the border between El Paso, Texas, and Ciudad Juarez, Mexico, each year.

WHAT IS NAFTA?

The North American Free Trade Agreement (NAFTA) grew out of an agreement between the United States and its largest trading partner, Canada, in 1994. NAFTA incorporated Mexico into the initial U.S.–Canada trading alliance, allowing, for the most part, a duty-free exchange of goods among the three countries. The goal of such a trading partnership is to reduce tariffs for the benefit of consumers in the three countries by offering them lower priced goods. Mexico hopes that a lot of the industry that is being moved offshore to Asia or other locations will instead be relocated to Mexico, thereby taking advantage of both the lower labor costs and the reduced tariff costs. In the long term, Mexico hopes for a transfer of technology into Mexico, which will develop Mexico's technological strength.

PRE–NAFTA MAQUILADORA PLANTS

Prior to NAFTA, all businesses in Mexico had to have a primary Mexican ownership. At about the time NAFTA was implemented, and in conjunction with it, Mexican law was changed so that businesses could now be dominated by foreign ownership. The 1993 change in the ownership law was intended to encourage foreign plants to locate within the heart of Mexico, and, as we shall see, it has worked well.

Before NAFTA there was a region along the United States border where plants could be located and where materials could be moved from the United States into Mexico, converted into the finished product, and transported back out of Mexico. These were primarily assembly-only plants referred to as Maquiladora factories. The engineering, marketing, financial management, and other technical functions were kept across the border in the United States. The only tariff duties that needed to be paid were on the value-added content of the labor introduced into the product while it was in Mexico. These plants focused on products that had minimum value-added content, leaving the heaviest value-added contributions in the United States. As a result of NAFTA, the regional limits that had previously existed on the size of this border region have now been eliminated, as have the tariffs on the labor.

Often plants would be located deep in the heart of Mexico, closer to Mexico City with its more abundant labor force. Unfortunately, for many of these plants the border-crossing process could take days, weeks, or even months. The result was an enormous inventory holding cost associated with these items, which would often erase much of the benefit of Mexico's reduced labor costs. NAFTA has greatly shortened the border-crossing restrictions and has changed the process to one of having preclassified parts. The border crossings have become quicker, but many more lawyers are now employed to do all the paperwork.

Post–NAFTA Maquiladora Plants

NAFTA has greatly increased the number of products that can be transferred across the Canadian-U.S.-Mexican borders. Agricultural products are moving down to Mexico at a rapid pace, the speed of the transfers has improved, and tariffs have been reduced. As a result, the NAFTA consumer has the benefit of lower prices, and producers have lower costs, enabling them to be more responsive to the marketplace.

Since removal of the duties on Mexican labor, the consumer has netted a 3 to 4 percent price reduction net gain. However, the operations of the plants in Mexico have not changed much. What has changed, as noted earlier, is the amount of time that border crossings take.

Post–NAFTA plants, as we have already mentioned, are increasingly moving into Mexico's interior, but more importantly, these plants are bringing their design, purchasing, and marketing departments with them, giving Mexico the high value-added elements of the production process. The newer, post–NAFTA plants are incorporating EDI (Electronic Data Interchange) into the marketing and purchasing departments, and CAD/CAM (Computer-Aided Design/Computer-Aided Manufacturing) into their design elements. Companies such as General Motors and Motorola are establishing Technology Centers. Newer plants are focusing on Turn-Key Operations, where the designs are fitted directly to the customer's needs.

Mexican plants have changed enormously in their progressiveness, especially in the plants that I have contacted. They no longer see themselves as labor sweat shops. They are now searching for their own competitive edge, with quality programs, process efficiency improvements, and the like. Mexican plants such as Vitro are incorporating World Class Self-Directed Work Teams and Computer Integrated Manufacturing (CIM) technology that includes SMED (Single Minute Exchange of Die) principles to change dies in seconds rather than in minutes. Johnson and Johnson's Juarez plants incorporate JIT-focused cellular manufacturing processes with incentive-based teaming and employee empowerment. These processes already exist, and these companies are working on more improvements in the future.

The training and education process for plants in Mexico has also changed. For example, today six national conferences focus on productivity and quality improvements, and productivity and quality centers have been established all over Mexico. Schools such as the Monterey Technical University utilize innovative methods in teaching industrial technology. They have one of the most advanced CIM (Computer Integrated Manufacturing) labs in all of the Americas (including the United States and Canada).

The Mexicans are developing cooperative arrangements among government, unions, business, and civic groups (e.g., the local housewives group) in an attempt to focus on integrated growth. In addition, there are national and state-level quality awards through which the government is attempting to motivate new, competitive, integrative strategies in business.

NAFTA has encouraged an increase in trade and technology transfer. For example, General Motors is putting in a one million square foot warehouse that is totally automated. Similarly, UPS is setting up warehouses. Information and business systems have improved dramatically. Systems such as EDI (Electronic Data Interchange), JIT, and MRP (Material Requirements Planning) are common. This has required an impressive infostructure improvement, starting with changes in Mexico's telephone system.

The Johnson and Johnson plants in Ciudad Juarez, Mexico, right across the border from El Paso, Texas, have become leaders in the effective utilization of JIT processes. They utilize cellular manufacturing, teaming and team incentives, and empowerment, and are heavily involved in TQM (Total Quality Management) systems throughout all their plants. Johnson and Johnson employs about 3,700 personnel in Mexico. They have won Mexico's National Quality Award and have received the United States' Shingo Prize for manufacturing excellence.

One Johnson and Johnson Medical Inc. plant in Juarez, a surgical garment production facility, has about 1,800 employees and is ISO and EN 46002 certified (European certification for quality in manufacturing and quality in medical device production). It is the first Maquiladora plant to win the National Quality Award. As of March 1995, it had set a record 2,000 hours of no labor loss due to injury, and the record was still growing. They use cellular manufacturing with team motivators. The training required for the sewing processes can take as long as 12 weeks.

Elamax, a job shop in Juarez that builds custom electronic circuit boards, utilizes attendance and performance incentives. It has about 800 employees and gives approximately three weeks of training to each employee. The shop has water recycling systems to prevent polluted wastewater from going into the water systems. It returns all waste products, such as solder particles, to the United States rather than polluting the Mexican environment. Plants like the Johnson and Johnson or Elamax plants would be considered impressive operations no matter where they were located.

THE FUTURE OF THE RELATIONSHIP

Plants are now being built in which the design work is being done in Mexico and the assembly work in El Paso, Texas, with Mexican laborers. This arrangement therefore recognizes the technical potential of the Mexican engineer.

With Mexico's passage of the foreign investment law in 1993, U.S. investors can now own a Mexican company and can incorporate in Mexico. This investment policy has created a surge of interest from Japan. Japanese plants are flooding Mexico, taking advantage of the cheaper labor and at the same time gaining access to the U.S. and Canadian marketplace.

Today, the Maquiladora plants are the most efficient and productive plants in Mexico. Remarkably, these plants are no longer sweat shops; they are leading-edge technology movers. In an overall measure of customer satisfaction, the Maquiladora plants are rated as being more than twice as productive and customer quality conscious as the average, non-Maquiladora Mexican plant. The Maquiladora plants won out in every category in which the ratings occurred, including: customer satisfaction, employee satisfaction, information systems effectiveness, community relations, and results orientation. The Maquiladora and their followup plants that are moving into the heart of Mexico are becoming world-class international competitors.

Moving more technology into Mexico is certain to foster long-term economic growth. Although the United States is not rushing to Mexico with factories, Mexico's 1993 agreement to allow foreign ownership, as noted earlier, has triggered a Japanese migration of plants to Mexico.

Mexico sees itself as a major international competitor but also feels the pressures of losing contracts to other locations, especially Southeast Asia, where labor costs and transportation costs are higher but process costs are lower and quality is higher. The net effect is the Mexicans' concern that the Malaysian or Singaporian product is often selected over the Mexican product.

More infostructural support is forecast for the future. Phone systems are getting better, and schooling for the youth and for employees (minimum sixth grade education) is becoming more available. The future will also likely bring a focus on more comforts, such as air conditioning and employee transportation services.

In the short term, NAFTA has been a blessing for the United States and a struggle for Mexico. In the long term, it is expected to bring positive growth for all the NAFTA countries.

N, INC. REVISITED

The Swedish manufacturer N, Inc. is considering putting a plant into Mexico to move it within the NAFTA corridor. N, Inc. sees itself as a direct competitor of the Dayton microelectronics plant and feels it can underprice this facility. By producing in Mexico, it could take advantage of lower operating costs and still get enough product content to be able to move parts into U.S. markets, primarily to the half dozen N, Inc. plants that use these components. The Swedish manufacturer also feels that a move of this type will distract the Dayton plant from worrying about ISO certification and thereby give the Swedish plant a lock-in on the Augsburg production facility's need for chips.

Dayton is worried about the Swedish competitor. Not only is it threatened with the loss of one-tenth of its business in Augsburg, but now it may even lose some of its domestic business. N, Inc. is now considering building a plant in Mexico in order to offset costs. Suppose you are the plant manager in Dayton. What would you do? What analysis could be performed? What would be the basis of your decision to relocate to Mexico? Would you go ahead with the ISO certification and take on the Swedish plant on their own turf?

SUMMARY

The single most discussed area of international operations management is the management of the supply chain, which focuses on integration and time. In this chapter we discussed the supplier in the supply chain and learned how to develop appropriate relationships, eliminate waste, and make integration and time savings a reality.

A supply chain is movement, specifically the movement of three key resources: materials, information, and money. The movement of these resources is affected by a series of forces that interact with the overall supply chain. The objective is to make the entire supply chain as seamless as possible to the customer, while at the same time integrating all the operational complexities of the supply chain into an optimized, well-performing machine—which leads us to the next chapter's discussion of Supply Chain Management.

Chapter 2

What Is Supply Chain Management (SCM)?

Here at HP, 65 cents of every revenue dollar is consumed by the supply chain. Supply chain has a direct impact on customer perception, brand perception, and customer satisfaction. Supply Chain is ultimately responsible for the price of the products, product quality, lead times, and predictability. So it has a direct, I mean absolutely direct, impact on the customer, on the stock valuation, and on shareholder value.

Dick Conrad, Hewlett-Packard's Senior Vice President,
Global Operations Supply Chain[1]

Several excellent magazines provide examples of Supply Chain Management success stories. One of these, *CSCO: Insights for the Supply Chain Executive*, presents success stories like that of Owens Corning which wanted to develop an end-to-end supply chain solution. It started by working with a collection of unintegrated logistics folks, materials planners, schedulers, and so on. But a supply chain organization did not exist. Recognizing the need to develop a focused, integrated Supply Chain Management effort, it started this process with a focus on integrating customer relationship management software with an ERP (Enterprise Resources Planning) platform. Owens Corning could use this as the basis for developing a best-of-breed solution that it deemed critical to its business goals. The ERP platform it selected was SAP, a German Company, and it used this software to integrate all the supply chain aspects within its organization. It used CRM (Customer Relationship Management) to improve its integration with the customer, and its ultimate goal was to take the breaks out of the supply chain.

---

[1] Terry, Lisa, "Adapt or Die," *CSCO*, August 2005, p. 25.

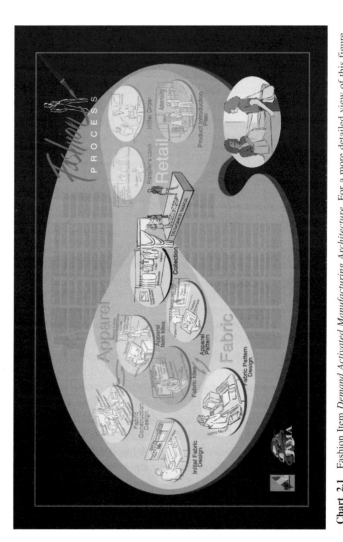

Chart 2.1 Fashion Item *Demand Activated Manufacturing Architecture*. For a more detailed view of this figure, please visit our companion site at: http://books.elsevier.com/companions/0123705177

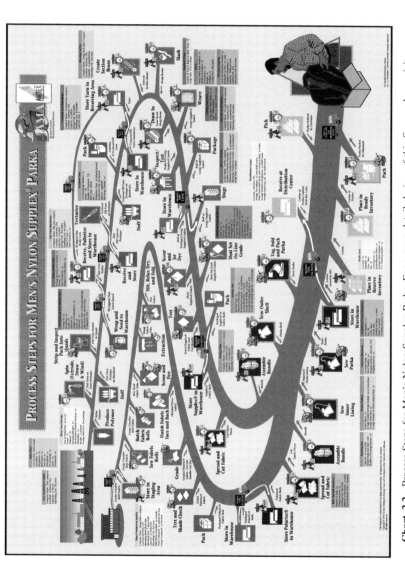

Chart 2.2 Process Steps for Men's Nylon Supplex Parka. For a more detailed view of this figure, please visit our companion site at: http://books.elsevier.com/companions/0123705177

have the final word, and they tell rather than ask. This type of manager is often referred to as the *Theory-X manager*.

Participative managers value employee opinions, and so they spend more time listening than talking during a meeting. They look for ideas from the bottom level of the organization, realizing that employees have the best understanding of day-to-day operations. These managers use these bottom-up ideas for top-down management and implementation of the ideas for change. They are concerned about employee job satisfaction and rewards. This type of manager is often known as a *Theory-Y manager*.[4]

There is a second type of participative manager. This manager tends to empower employees to make their own decisions and to implement their own ideas. This form of participative manager is known to as the *Theory-Z manager*.[5] In this management style, the top-down decision-making process characteristic of the Theory-X or Theory-Y management style is switched to a bottom-up, decision-making process characteristic of the Japanese management style. The Theory-Z style is heavily involved in teaming, much like the quality circles of old, and the teams develop, approve, and implement ideas.[6] Managers take on the role of facilitator, being responsible for implementing the approved ideas correctly and in a timely manner. These managers are no longer the decision makers and drivers of forward progress. Theory-Z managers keep their teams focused and present them with areas that need consideration and evaluation, but they let the team make their own improvement decisions. So are you a Theory-X, Theory-Y, or Theory-Z manager?

A third way to classify managers uses the Five C's: Cash, Crisis, Conflict, Cool, and Change Managers.

Cash Manager

Cash managers focus on costs and budgets and often come through the accounting or finance ranks. This type of manager tends to be risk-averse and looks toward stability rather than opportunity. Cash managers find it advisable to patch-and-repair old technology, as opposed to replacing it with new technology, because of the high expense of purchasing the new technology and the difficulty of absorbing all this cost in one or two fiscal years. This management style

---

[4]For more information about Theory-X and Theory-Y managers, including some very interesting examples, read the book: McGregor, Douglas, *The Human Side of the Enterprise*, McGraw-Hill, New York, 1985.

[5]Theory-Z management is explained nicely, including examples, in the following book and article: Pascale, Richard Tanner, and Anthony G. Athos, *The Art of Japanese Management*, Warner Books, New York, NY, 1982; Joiner, Jr., Charles W., "Making the 'Z' Concept Work," *Sloan Management Review*, Spring 1985, pp. 57–63.

[6]Quality circles are a Japanese methodology for empowerment and teaming.

is why we still have so many outdated factories in the United States, when we know they cannot be competitive in the long run. However, since the old factories are still demonstrating some minor profit levels, they are kept and maintained until they are totally unprofitable. Then the plants are transferred overseas, where labor costs are cheaper. The cash manager looks for short-term profitability rather than long-term competitiveness.

Crisis (or Crash) Manager

Crisis managers believe you should not fix anything that is not broken. This style of manager, like the cash manager, strives for stability, regarding problems as disruptions that need to be conquered rather than as opportunities for future improvements. These managers attack problems without considering the roots of the problems, thereby fixing only a symptom and not the cause. The fix often includes the installation of another "system" to monitor the problem and catch it if it happens again.

Conflict Manager

Conflict managers view the workplace as a battlefield of competing players. They always feel compelled to maintain the upper hand through whatever means necessary. Control is the primary tool of power, and intimidation is the primary motivating force. This type of manager is the reason unions were formed.

Cool Manager

Cool managers believe that the workforce is best motivated by giving it whatever it wants. These managers try to bribe their way into the hearts of their children, which is how they view their employees. They want to be everybody's best friend, and they want everyone to smile at them as they walk by. The cool manager often has a wishy-washy management style that results in more confusion than direction.

Change Manager

Change managers search for challenges in competitiveness. They thrive on positive, goal-focused changes, seeing them as the opportunities that make work exciting. Specifically, they regard a larger number of changes as more opportunities for growth and problems as opportunities for change. Rather than trying to fix problems, change managers spend time looking for the roots of the problems and attempt to generate the necessary changes that will make them disappear.

Using the five C's to define a management style requires integration with the other classifications. For example, you could have a manager who is sunrise, cool, and Theory-X; this would be a happy, smiley, bossy dreamer. Have you identified yourself yet? Let's add one more classification category before we integrate the management styles.

A last but important method for classifying a manager is to compare the "boss" to the "leader." A boss directs employee traffic, whereas a leader shows the way by using appropriate examples and by stepping out into the traffic in front of the employees. Bosses manage, but leaders tend to lead out and search for a difference. Bosses see themselves as "King of the Hill" and want to keep the hill for themselves, whereas leaders show and help everyone, by example, how to get to the top of the hill themselves. Bosses strive with a "Do as I Say" philosophy, whereas leaders use the "Do as I Do" technique. With leaders, employees tend to have a clear definition of what is expected of them because the example set by the leader has shown them their objective. Simply put, bosses provide stability and governance, whereas leaders open the door for innovation.[7]

The boss is someone who has to be there for the business to run correctly. Without the boss, the employees lose their decision-making ability. It is often a situation where "while the cat's away, the mice will play." Alternatively, leaders are people who, if they did not show up to work for a few days, would not be missed. All the employees would know how to keep the business functioning, and the leader's absence would hardly be noticed. Good leaders are people who manage themselves into obsolescence.

Insecure managers create complexity.
Real leaders don't need clutter.

John F. Welch, Jr.
Chairman and CEO,
General Electric[8]

---

[7]Many good articles discuss the role of leaders in a changing, growing organization. For example, Senge, Peter M., "The Leader's New Work: Building Learning Organizations," *Sloan Management Review*, Fall 1990, pp. 7–23. This article focuses on the need for an organization to be "continuously learning" through leadership.

See also Kotter, John P., "What Leaders Really Do," *Harvard Business Review*, May–June 1990, pp. 103–111. This article stresses that "good management controls complexity; effective leadership produces useful change." The article observes that "management controls people by pushing them in the right direction; leadership motivates them by satisfying basic human needs." This article offers three interesting leadership examples and is worth checking into just for the chance to read about the examples. They are: American Express, Eastman Kodak, and Procter & Gamble.

[8]Jack Welch's opinions about what makes a good manager (*business leader* is the term Jack prefers) is discussed in an interesting article: Tichy, Noel and Ram Charan, "Speed, Simplicity, Self-Confidence: An Interview with Jack Welch," *Harvard Business Review*, September–October 1989, pp. 112–120.

WHAT TYPE OF MANAGER ARE YOU?

Now it's time for you to classify yourself. You need to integrate the different types of management style in order to define your own personal style. What type of manager do you think you are? Are you a Theory − X = Sunset = Cash Manager, which would be a bean-counting, bossy, fire-fighter telling everyone what to do, how to do it, and when to do it, and insisting that no one do anything until directed? Or are you a Theory − Y = Sunrise = Cool Leader who loves everyone, likes to show rather than tell everyone how to do their job, and shares your schemes of grandeur with your employees? Figure out what type of manager you are. Remember;

> **Before You Can Figure Out**
> **How to Get Where Your Going,**
> **You Have to Know**
> **Where You're Starting From**

Use Chart 2.3 to evaluate yourself. Mark with an N, O, or Y next to each of the management types in order to get a clear picture of where you are now. Now that you have classified yourself, have your peers evaluate you. Use Chart 2.3 as a grading sheet to help them evaluate you. Next, have your employees evaluate you using some form of blind vote. You may be surprised to find out what kind of manager others think you are.

Now that you know what your management style is you know a little more about yourself. The next step to becoming a world-class SCM manager is to define your management style *goal*. After that, we need to devise a travel plan that will take you from where you are and get you to where you are going. We will spend the rest of the chapter doing that. But for now, let us take a close look at our target.

> The road to world-class leadership
> is not a journey,
> it's a race!

THE WORLD-CLASS SCM MANAGER

Another chart has been created in order to help you both to classify yourself in your present state and to help you clearly define your target. With four different methods for classifying management styles, a diagram representing all of the management options would require four dimensions. Unfortunately, a sheet of

In front of each management style indicate whether you (or the person you are evaluating) fit this description:

N – not really one of these
O – occasionally one of these
Y – definitely one of these

_____ Sunrise Manager – has a view toward the future, a dreamer full of wild ideas, progressive, leading edge, technology minded

_____ Sunset Manager – spends time fighting day-to-day fires, workaholic who is great at getting things done

_____ Theory-X Manager – secretive, has his or her fingers in everything that happens, always has the final word, tells rather than asks questions

_____ Theory-Y Manager – values the opinion of the employees, spends more time listening than talking, looks for ideas from the bottom-up but makes the final decision

_____ Theory-Z Manager – tends to empower the employees to make their own decisions and lets them implement their own ideas

_____ Cash Manager – cost and budget obsessive, looks toward stability rather than opportunity, prefers to patch and repair rather than replace because it is cheaper

_____ Crisis (or Crash) Manager – believes that you shouldn't fix anything that isn't broken, looks at problems as a disruption that needs to be conquered, attacks problems

_____ Conflict Manager – looks at the workplace as a battlefield of competing players, feels the need to take and maintain the upper hand

_____ Cool Manager – feels the workforce is best motivated by giving them whatever they want, wants to bribe their way into the hearts of their employees, wants to be everybody's best friend

_____ Change Manager – searches for challenges in competitiveness, thrives on changes, innovations, improvements, technology

_____ Boss – directs employee traffic, has self-image as "King of the Hill" and wants to have sole ownership of the hill, "Do as I Say" philosophy

_____ Leader – shows the way by using example and by stepping out into the traffic in front of the employees, not afraid to show everyone how to get to the top of the hill, "Do as I Do" philosophy

Chart 2.3   Find Your Management Style

paper limits us to two dimensions. Even the movie director Steven Spielberg has difficulty showing us four dimensions on a two-dimensional surface (the movie screen). Chart 2.4 breaks down the two most complex management style classifications and presents all sorts of mixes and matches of management styles. These mixtures of styles are detailed and explained in Chart 2.5.

World Class is being a Theory-Z Change Manager. Looking at Chart 2.4, we conclude that it doesn't matter where we find ourselves now; instead, we should strive toward Theory-Z change manager status. Now let us examine the last remaining two classification categories. As a world-class SCM manager, you would want to be a sunrise rather than a sunset manager, always looking for alternatives and options for improvement, but realizing that many of these options will fail. Also, as a world-class SCM manager you would want to be a

	Theory-X	Y	Z
Cash	Totally Impersonal Quick to Fire	Calculated but Sharing	Cost-Conscious Employees
Crisis	The "General"	Self-Directed Fire Fighting	Frustrated Employees
Conflict	The "Boss"	Confusion	WAR
Cool	Decision with Confusion`	Self-Directed Confusion	No Direction
Change	Enforced Improvements	Overriding Motivation	On the Right Track

Chart 2.4 What Type of Manager Are You?

leader rather than a boss, motivating and guiding your employees by your hard work and farsighted examples.

Finally, we know what a world-class SCM manager should look like. Such a manager should be a

Sunrise Manager—Possessing a long-term orientation looking for the "better way"

Theory-Z Manager—Having employees involved with and guiding the business process through participative and empowered team efforts

Change Manager—Guiding a dynamic, evolving business organism that capitalizes on change opportunities

Leader—Being a character-building, motivational example

The wicked leader is he who the people despise.
The good leader is he who the people revere.
The great leader is he who the people say, "We did it ourselves."

Lao Tsu

Having categorized world-class SCM managers and having determined how to categorize them, let us now decide why we want to fit into this slot. A world-class competitive stance will not allow us to be anything but world-class SCM managers. World-class SCM managers look to the future, a highly competitive future, a future full of changes. World-class SCM managers realize that their employees are the key to motivating successful change and that employees are led, not bossed.

Numerous organizations are attempting to move themselves toward world-class management status. For example, Tridon-Oakdale placed its management team in a hotel to get them away from the everyday bustle of fire

This chart explains and defines the categories listed in Chart 2.4. Here we see all sorts of mixes and matches of management styles.

Theory X Manager-Cash Manager   This manager is impersonal and quick to fire and bases all decisions on short-term financial reports.

Theory X Manager-Crisis Manager   The "General" charges his or her troops against the coming enemy, which is often a variety of problems, including the biggest problem of all, change.

Theory X Manager-Conflict Manager   The "Boss" expects the respect of employees and demands immediate response to his or her whims and wishes.

Theory X Manager-Cool Manager   The manager makes the final decisions, but in an attempt to keep everyone happy, many of the decisions are political and therefore contradictory. The result is more confusion than progress.

Theory X Manager-Change Manager   This manager forces change on employees, leaving them rebellious and resistant.

Theory Y Manager-Cash Manager   This manager wants the employees' ideas but will make the final decision in all cases based on short-term financial viability.

Theory Y Manager-Crisis Manager   This manager expects employees to be self-directed fire-fighters, maintaining the status quo.

Theory Y Manager-Conflict Manager   This manager listens to employees just to satisfy their egos and basically sees employees as a necessary evil requiring toleration.

Theory Y Manager-Cool Manager   This manager solicits the employees' ideas and says "yes" to everyone, leaving employees without any real guidance from the top.

Theory Y Manager-Change Manager   This manager wants employees to search for opportunities for change but reserves the right to override any suggestions, since the manager has the broader insight needed for all decisions made in the enterprise.

Theory Z Manager-Cash Manager   This management style has teams analyzing all changes on a financial basis.

Theory Z Manager-Crisis Manager   Here teams work on solving problems with a short-term perspective aimed at getting the problem fixed quickly.

Theory Z Manager-Conflict Manager   Here teams continually find themselves having to defend against a management that considers them ignorant.

Theory Z Manager-Cool Manager   This manager is completely employee oriented, but in the effort to keep everyone happy, ends up being an ineffective facilitator, causing frustration and a lack of direction.

Theory Z Manager-Change Manager   This manager facilitates change and motivates employee teams to search for opportunities for change. The teams see themselves as owners of the change, and they therefore attempt to implement the change and take pride in the results. Fire fighting is kept to a minimum, and fires are looked at as being caused by some "Root Problem" that needs to be identified and changed with a long-term perspective.[9] This is the management style of a world-class SCM manager.

Chart 2.5   The Two Most Complex Management Style Classifications

---

[9]Root cause identification is a theme of the book *Breakthrough Thinking*. This book helps Total Quality Management (TQM) teams identify opportunities for improvements—changes! A second, followup book expands on this theme. See Nadler, Gerald, and Shozo Hibino, *Breakthrough Thinking*, Prima Publishing & Communications, Rocklin, CA, 1990; and Nadler, Gerald, Shozo Hibino, and John Farrell, *Creative Solution Finding*, Prima Publishing & Communications, Rocklin, CA, 1995.

fighting. The goal given to these managers was to "work out a new vision for Tridon." The result was a complete turnaround in both management style and output performance. Some of the changes that occurred included the following:

An organization chart turned upside down with employee teams on the top
A new quality standard that far exceeded the standards of Tridon's competitors
"Legendary Customer Service"
Competitive pricing
Reduced inventory and lead times
A $6 million turnaround

Some of the keys to success included these efforts:

A new mission statement with a commitment to change
An improved focus on building relationships between all employees
Employee participation—"the goal is to have everyone speak"
Total Quality Control
Kanban—Just-in-Time Manufacturing[10]
"Smart Change" management focused on doing the right things
Group technology focused on technology improvements

Tridon has demonstrated that world-class management works, but it considers itself as just getting ready for the next wave of improvements.[11]

Now that we are in a constant state of change,
nothing will ever remain the same."

Don Green
Chairman, Tridon

A world-class SCM manager views the future as an opportunity. For this manager the here-and-now is adequate for the past but not good enough for the future. He or she views all aspects of the enterprise—systems, production philosophies, and even management styles that were in existence 20 to 30 years ago—as wholly deficient for today and especially inadequate for the future.

By their very nature, world-class SCM managers are risk takers, for change always involves risk. In addition, the long-term perspective of world-class SCM

---

[10]Later in this book we will discuss the Toyota production system as an example of continuous change and innovation. Toyota developed the Just-in-Time (JIT) production process, which uses a production control tool called the Kanban card. This card tracks and controls the quantity of products through the production process.

[11]An interesting article on Tridon, if you are interested in more details, is Tonkin, Lea, "Workshop Report: Canadian Region—Building on the Past at Tridon-Oakdale," *Target,* Summer 1990, pp. 34–37.

managers often makes them unpopular in the short run. World-class managers enjoy the excitement of being leading-edge innovators, despite the occasional failures they will suffer on this risky management road.

World-class management is the ability to *change yourself* faster than the *changes that are trying to affect you*. World-class SCM managers are in control of change rather than letting change control them. They are innovators and adventurers. They have the ability to listen when listening is wiser than talking, which is almost always.

World-class management is managing and motivating positive, goal-directed change. It is being in control of change, and it is using change to your advantage. But being in control of change is not a simple task. Many facets need to change, or it would not take this entire book to discuss them. To be effective users of change, we need to consider all these facets, plan for them, strategize their usage, and utilize them to our advantage.

Not all change is positive. Changing just for the sake of changing is foolish. Thinking through the consequences and effects of changes is therefore as important as implementing the changes. Changes need to make a positive contribution toward goal achievement, without sacrificing the value system (ethics and integrity) of the enterprise. However, not changing for fear of making a mistake is the same as deciding not to be world class.

To manage change, we need to be innovators and creators. An innovator searches for opportunities to change. An innovator sees opportunity in every problem and looks for ways to take advantage of opportunities. Innovators work with others, as team players, because they understand the synergistic ideas created by teamwork. The creator takes newly found opportunities and turns them into defined projects, activities, or programs that will take advantage of the recent discoveries.

The management of change also requires an adventurer and a general. The adventurer is not afraid to take a chance on change and looks for the opportunity to do battle, to take an idea and to drive forcefully forward. An adventurer despises the routine and mundane, and looks for opportunities to break away, always searching for new areas to discover. Generals know that they cannot win the battle alone. Even Michael Jordan, who was probably one of the greatest basketball players of his time, could not have won one basketball game without four other players on the court.

Two basic questions still need to be answered:

1. *Why should we go through the process recommended by this book?* Change is inevitable and will run you over if you are not ready for it. This book will teach you how to get ready for and manage change.
2. *Why is change necessary?* There are several reasons for change. The first reason is competition, whether from domestic or foreign competitors.

We need to improve to stay on top of our competitors. Another reason for change is to take advantage of technological advancements, such as automation or computerization. Yet another reason is the changing habits of our customers. Customer awareness programs, environmental conscious-ness, resource scarcity, governmental regulations, and economic swings affect the way customers think and act, and force us to change the way we manage.

To live is to change, and to be perfect is to have changed often.

John Henry Newman
English Cardinal, Writer

At this point, having a somewhat clearer view of the characteristics of a world-class SCM manager, we are ready to examine why change is such an important part of the lifestyle of this manager.

A DISCUSSION OF CHANGE

One day a man was leading his donkey down the street. After a short distance, the donkey decided he didn't want to travel any farther. He stopped in his tracks, put his rump on the ground, and wouldn't budge. The man tugged at the donkey's rope and tried to coax him to get up and walk. The coaxing soon turned to name calling and threats involving glue factories. Still the donkey didn't move. A neighbor was passing by and stopped to help the frustrated donkey owner.

"The only way you're going to get that donkey to move is by talking nice to it," the neighbor advised. Indignantly, the donkey owner challenged his neighbor to see if he could do any better with the stubborn critter. The neighbor picked up a two-by-four that was lying by the side of the road and proceeded to give the donkey a swift, hard wallop right between the eyes. Then he pulled on the rope softly and asked the donkey to get up. The donkey immediately stood up and followed the neighbor down the street.

"Didn't you say I should talk nice to the donkey?" the donkey owner protested.

"Of course! And I did," said the neighbor, "but first I had to get his attention."

Sometimes we managers are like donkeys. Sometimes we need to be hit by a two-by-four on the side of the head before we will start paying attention.[12] Often "change" brings out the donkey in all of us. Remember:

---

[12]Some of you may catch this pun on the best-selling book *Whack on the Side of the Head* by von Oech. The book stresses creativity and open-mindedness in our thinking. See von Oech, Roger, *A Whack on the Side of the Head*, Warner Books, New York, 1990.

Change and innovation are not stifled
By the way things are
But by the way we perceive things

Change is as old as time and as leading edge as the future. Even the rate at which changes are occurring is changing. But as prevalent as change is, we often want to resist it with all the effort we can muster.

Let us contemplate the two sources of changes:

1. The changes that come from us
2. The changes that happen to us

Treating the second source of change first, we need to be prepared for changes that will happen to us. We need to watch for these changes and manage them into opportunities. We need to become world-class SCM managers that watch for and use growth and development opportunities. This brings us to another thought:

It doesn't matter how far
in front of the pack you are,
If you're not moving fast enough,
you'll get run over.

Change is innovation; it is developing leading-edge competitive strategies; it is moving forward. Remember (this goes along with the previous thought):

It doesn't matter how fast you're moving,
If you're not moving in the right direction,
You'll never achieve your goal!

The first type of change, change that comes from us, requires us to originate the change. We are required to come up with the changes. For some managers, this type of change is a little harder to manage because of the effort involved in creating the changes. It suggests that we need to find and generate our own opportunities for change, our own innovations. This is harder to achieve because most organizations tend toward bureaucracy, which suppresses change. Most organizational structures are motivated by measurement systems that stifle and often punish change. We need measurement systems that motivate the discovery of change.[13] The search for change opportunities can mean a structural reorganization as well as a mental reorganization of your enterprise.[14]

This book focuses on systems that will facilitate both types of change. It also discusses how your organization needs these changes, not only to stay ahead, but also to survive in a competitive environment. The purpose of this book is to help you become a leader who can help your organization manage optimal change in your supply chain. It is to motivate you to find and implement positive changes in a goal-oriented direction and to turn you into a leader who motivates and directs changes in the supply chain. Finally, the purpose of this book is to help you become a world-class supply chain manager.

To get the most out of this book, carefully read the Preface, Introduction, and all the chapters. What you're doing is hunting for ideas. Mark the ideas that fit you best, and, after reading the book, reread those ideas that impressed you the first time through. Then search for ways to implement these ideas into your management style. The last step in the use of this book is to TQM (Total Quality Manage) the review process by repeating this process every six months to one year. As your goals and job function change, so will the information and tools you need to help you through the change process. Reviewing this book regularly

---

[13]Other organizations and authors have wrestled with this issue. One of the more interesting can be found in the work by Eli Goldratt and Bob Fox who strongly support a Socratic process for the discovery, creation, and stimulation of change. They believe in the participative development of change (a team process), and they believe that imposed change is ineffective change. In addition, an incorrectly developed measurement system will block rather than motivate the change process. Some additional reading by these authors includes: Fox, R. E., "Theory of Constraints," *NAA Conference Proceedings*, September 1987; and Goldratt, Eliyahu M., and Jeff Cox, *The Goal*, North River Press, Croton-on-Hudson, NY, 1986. Goldratt, Eliyahu M., *The Haystack Syndrome*, North River Press Inc., Croton-on-Hudson, NY, 1990; Goldratt, Eliyahu M., and Robert E. Fox, *The Race*, North River Press Inc., Croton-on-Hudson, NY, 1986; Goldratt, Eliyahu M., *What Is This Theory Called Theory of Constraints?*, North River Press, Croton-on-Hudson, NY, 1990; Plenert, Gerhard J., "Bottleneck Scheduling for an Unlimited Number of Products," *Journal of Manufacturing Systems*, 9, No. 4, pp. 324–331; and Plenert, Gerhard J., and Terry Lee, "Optimizing Theory of Constraints When New Product Alternatives Exist," *Production and Inventory Management Journal*, 34, no. 3, Third Quarter 1993, pp. 51–57.

[14]Articles discussing change and change management are endless. Here are a few of the better ones: Schaffer, Robert H., and Harvey A. Thomson, "Successful Change Programs Begin with Results," *Harvard Business Review*, January-February 1992, pp. 80–89. (This article stresses that we focus on results, not activities). Kanter, Rosabeth Moss, "Change: Where to Begin," *Harvard Business Review*, July–August 1991, pp. 8–9. This articles encourages the following steps: (1) Begin with use-directed, action-oriented information. (2) Be willing to build on platforms already in place. (3) Encourage incremental experimentation that departs from tradition without totally destroying it.

See also Beer, Michael, Russell A. Eisenstat, and Bert Spector, "Why Change Programs Don't Produce Change," *Harvard Business Review*, November–December 1990, pp. 158–166. This article focuses on the idea that "effective corporate renewal starts at the bottom, through informal efforts to solve problems."

have, for a long time, been successful in beating out the big guys, both foreign and domestic, in competition and quality.

And the examples go on endlessly.

We have defined world-class management in terms of the style of management and the role of change. Let us now take another look at world-class management, this time addressing the role of innovation and creativity.

INNOVEERING

A world-class organization is an innovative, creative, goal-oriented organization. A world-class SCM manager motivates the positive innovative and creative thinking process referred to as *innoveering*, which means, "creatively innovated changes." Changing just for the sake of changing only creates turmoil. Changing in order to move positively forward toward a goal without sacrificing the integrity of the organization is world class.

Recently, the topic of creative thinking has become very popular. Books such as *Breakthrough Thinking* and *A Whack on the Side of the Head* have stressed the importance of imagination in the change process.[16] For example, Roger von Oech stresses the need for creativity to discover new solutions to problems and to generate new ideas when old ones become obsolete.[17] Stephen R. Covey, in his book *The Seven Habits of Highly Effective People*, focuses his second habit on creativity.[18] Tom Peters, Robert Waterman, and Nancy Austin, in their search for eight common characteristics of excellent companies, emphasize employee innovation within the corporate value system.[19]

---

[16]Numerous other works are available on creativity, such as Stimson, Judith A., "Unleashing Creative Thinking for Change," *APICS 37th International Conference Proceedings*, October 30–November 4, 1994, APICS, Falls Church, VA, pp. 665–666; and Abair, Robert A., " 'Dare to Change': Revolution vs. Evolution," *APICS 37th International Conference Proceedings*, October 30–November 4, 1994, APICS, Falls Church, VA, pp. 40–41.

[17]We have already listed von Oech's book *A Whack on the Side of the Head*. Another good book by the same author is *A Kick in the Seat of the Pants*, which also deals with building creativity in the reader. It can be found in most bookstores under von Oech, Roger, *A Kick in the Seat of the Pants*, Harper & Row, New York, 1986.

[18]Covey's book has been a worldwide best-seller. I have encountered it as far away as Malaysia. It can be found in any bookstore. See Covey, Stephen R., *The Seven Habits of Highly Effective People*, Simon & Schuster, New York, 1989. Another excellent Covey book that discusses important issues related to the lifestyle and habits of a leader is Covey, Stephen R., *Principle-Centered Leadership*, Summit Books, New York, 1991.

[19]There are two books in this vein: Peters, Tom, and Robert Waterman, *In Search of Excellence: Lessons from America's Best Run Companies*, Harper & Row, New York, 1985; and Peters, Tom, and Nancy Austin, *A Passion for Excellence*, Harper & Row, New York, 1985.

Innoveering is innovative change engineering. It is change that uses technology, integration, and innovative strategies and focuses on a continuous improvement model. Again, change in and of itself is not necessarily good. When we have positively directed, goal-oriented, innovative, creative change, we have innoveering. That's when we become world class.

One of the best examples of innoveering is the Toyota Just-in-Time production system, a production planning philosophy developed in Japan to minimize waste through inventory reductions. JIT did not exist before being developed by Toyota. JIT was not copied; it was innoveered. Here's a brief summary of its development history.

World War II had ended, and Japan was trying to rebuild its devastated industry. The Japanese tried copying Western (primarily U.S.) production methodologies, which were considered the best in the world, but they soon encountered four problems:

1. The Japanese lacked the cash flow to finance the large in-process inventory levels required by the U.S. batch-oriented production systems.
2. The Japanese lacked the land space to build large U.S.-style factories.
3. The Japanese lacked the natural resource accessibility that the United States had.
4. Japan had a labor excess rather than a labor shortage, which meant that labor efficiency systems were not very valuable.

The Japanese innoveered these problems into opportunities. Realizing that their competitive problem was a process problem, not a product problem, they proceeded to copy product technology and worked diligently to innovate *process technology* oriented around materials efficiency rather than labor efficiency. The result was the flow-through JIT production methodology for which Toyota has now become famous. But Toyota will be the first to admit that it was not easy. Toyota officials scoff at U.S. attempts to copy JIT after two or three years of implementation, for as they will readily admit, it took them 30 years to develop JIT. But they got into this position one innoveering change at a time.

The result was that the Japanese "leaned" out their process. They built smaller factories (about one-third the size of those of their U.S. counterparts) in which the only materials housed in the factory were those on which work was currently being done.[20] In this way, inventory levels were kept low, investment

---

[20] This statement is a little idealistic. In reality, the Japanese work with single-digit batch sizes (one to nine units), whereas U.S. batch sizes can range in the hundreds of units. For each batch, only one item in the batch is worked on at a time; the rest of the batch is inventory. Therefore, a batch of 100 units creates a continuous, ongoing inventory of 99 units. Unfortunately, the batch is often not being worked on and is just idle inventory. This batch size difference between the United States and Japan creates a tremendous difference in inventory levels.

in in-process inventory was at a minimum, and the investment in purchased natural resources was quickly turned around so that additional materials were purchased.[21] The focus was on materials (inventory) efficiency rather than labor efficiency.

The Toyota innoveering process has not ended. It continues, focusing on "Lean"-oriented changes and improvements, in both the product and process areas. Toyota is working on its innoveering through a continuous improvement process called *waste elimination*. The company views waste as anything that does not add value to the product. Waste can occur in labor, materials, machinery processes, or any other aspect of the company. Toyota's "Lean" strategy consists of seven key areas of waste elimination:

1. Waste of overproduction—reduced setup times, process synchronization, visibility
2. Waste of waiting—balance uneven workloads
3. Waste of transportation
4. Waste of processing—why is the product made?
5. Waste of stocks—inventory reduction
6. Waste of motion—motion for economy and consistency
7. Waste of making defective products[22]

Toyota is determined to continue to improve. Innovative change is constant. Integration involving all levels of employees is critical.

However, we in the United States, or any other part of the world, are past the point of trying to copy Japan. We need to innoveer beyond what we can copy from anyone if we are to stay competitive. As long as we are playing copy-cat, the best we can ever do is to get caught up, and that's just not good enough![23] The only way we can get ahead is by innoveering. The Japanese will only stay ahead as long as we, by focusing on copying rather than innoveering, allow them to do so.

Imagination is more important than knowledge.

Albert Einstein

---

[21]Numerous books detail the Toyota production philosophy JIT. See Shingo, Shigeo, *Study of the Toyota Production System from the Industrial Engineering Viewpoint*, Japanese Management Association, Tokyo, 1981 (Shingo has worked with Toyota and has an insider's viewpoint); and Wantuck, Kenneth A., *Just in Time for America*, The Forum, Milwaukee, 1989.

[22]More detail is available from Hall, Robert W., *Attaining Manufacturing Excellence*, Dow-Jones-Irwin, Homewood, IL, 1987.

[23]This concept of innovating yourself out ahead rather than copying someone else is the theme of another one of my books, Plenert, Gerhard, *International Management and Production: Survival Techniques for Corporate America*, Tab Professional and Reference Books, Blue Ridge Summit, PA, 1990.

HOW DO WE MANAGE CHANGE?

The biggest struggle in learning to manage change is identifying where, when, and how to begin. One purpose of this book is to provide the answers to these questions.

1. "Where do we begin?" With you, the reader!
2. "When do we begin?" IMMEDIATELY
3. "How do we begin?" By carefully laying out a "Lean" plan for innovation and change. This plan is developed by:

   A. Deciding on a focus or a vision for our change efforts
   B. Developing strategies for change that focus on our vision
   C. Solidifying each of the strategic areas around the vision (here we discuss how each of the strategies is defined and implemented):

      a. Quality vs. productivity
      b. Global management
      c. Timely technology
      d. Integration and measurement
      e. Value-added processes
      f. Training

   D. Discussing the characteristics, abilities, and traits that a world-class SCM manager should have to motivate innoveering, including a discussion of the specific change tools available to the manager:

      a. Change models
      b. Management traits
      c. Management skills
      d. The role of teaming
      e. The integration of the manager in the enterprise
      f. The manager, the enterprise, and the environment
      g. The changes that affect the manager and the enterprise through time

   E. Providing a wrapup of whether or not you are working toward becoming world class

Let's move forward and learn about ***World-class Supply Chain Management***, which uses goal-oriented, positive-change leadership to motivate and direct the change process. Let's evolve into effective masters of the change process. Let's change, innovate, and improve ourselves, our family environment, our working environment, and our enterprise.

> *The definition of insanity is continuing to do the same things and expecting different results.*
>
> Breakthrough Thinking
> Nadler and Hibino

THE PEOPLE

Do we know anyone who resists change? We probably see them every day, every time we look in the mirror. So where does this stubborn streak come from? Tradition! The greatest resistance to change comes from what we already know and from what we already believe. Just look at the small child who is not yet hindered by tradition. The child will learn and believe anything. I'm not asking you to be gullible; I'm just asking you to be open minded, like the little child. Learn and understand before you hastily condemn.

Change is especially hard for managers. As we have learned from our quotes, the only thing certain in life is change. But we don't want change to happen to us; rather, we want to utilize and control change to our advantage. A well-known anonymous axiom is:

> People like things to change,
> but they don't like to be changed

Stated differently, this means that people like changes, if the changes are benefiting them. However, people do not like changes imposed upon them.

Federal Express (FedEx), a 1990 Malcolm Baldridge Quality Award winner and a master of supply chain optimization, is the brainchild of founder and CEO Frederick W. Smith who virtually invented the air express industry.[24] The key objective of the FedEx quality program is to achieve 100 percent customer satisfaction through continuous improvement and change. The continuous improvement process involves the customer in the change process through a Survey–Feedback–Action (SFA) program.

FedEx has based its quality program on precepts, like: Customer satisfaction starts with employee satisfaction. In order to make this precept effective, FedEx has implemented a program call the Guaranteed Fair Treatment Program (GFTP) whose aim is to maintain a truly fair working environment. Anyone with a

---

[24]The Malcolm Baldridge National Quality Award (MBNQA) is the U.S. government's national award for quality. [There's an oxymoron for you: "Government Quality."]

grievance or concern about his or her job, or who feels mistreated, can have these concerns addressed through the management chain, all the way to Fred Smith if necessary.

FedEx considers its employees to be its most important resource and so wants to provide a fair and equitable process for handling grievances. The GFTP philosophy provides an atmosphere for employees to discuss their complaints with management without fear of retaliation. An employee is given 7 days to submit a grievance, after which time management has 10 days to respond. If the employee does not agree with the manager's decision, the employee has 7 days to appeal the decision up the chain of the review process.

A key element of the GFTP program is the evaluation of managers from both directions, from the top down and from the bottom up. The manager's boss evaluates the manager's ability to implement change through innovation and improvements, whereas the manager's subordinates evaluate the manager's responsiveness to the employee's needs. To get promotions, raises, or bonuses, a manager must receive favorable ratings from both directions.[25]

The FedEx quality program emphasizes both change (SFA) and the management–employee relationship aspects of how change is implemented (GFTP). FedEx managers state that FedEx is the most challenging, and at the same time the most rewarding company they have worked for because the FedEx program puts the manager into the challenging position of attempting to install change while at the same time not allowing the manager to be excessively forceful in implementing the change. The best managers would be those who implement change by giving the employees ownership in the change.

I want workers to go home at night and say, "I built that car."

> Pahr G. Gyllenhammar
> Chairman, Volvo

At this point we have established that change is inevitable; therefore, it is important that change become a part of our lives and the life of our enterprise. We have also learned that change management needs to be participative, not forced. But why is a chapter on people the second chapter in this book? Because, like Steve Young of the San Francisco 49ers football team, you cannot complete one touchdown pass without the linesmen to protect you and the receivers to catch the ball and run with it. You need the rest of your team! You can't become world class alone!

---

[25]FedEx offers a nice document called the *Quality Profile* which outlines their various quality programs including the GFTP and the SQI. For more information contact: Federal Express Corporation, Public Relations Department, 2005 Corporate Avenue, Memphis, TN 38132, (910) 395-3466.

So what do managers need in order to be effective motivators of change? What do we need to do to become world class in people relations? Here is a list of nine key points:

1. The circle
2. Goal setting
3. Leadership
4. Values and ethics
5. Adding social value
6. Continuous learning
7. Innovation and change creation
8. Measuring/rewarding
9. Stakeholders

The Circle

You can make more friends in two months by becoming interested in other people than you can in two years by trying to get other people interested in you.

Dale Carnegie

The term *circle* refers to a group of cohorts working together to achieve a common purpose and is variously named the quality circle, management circle, family circle, and so on. In order to be a world-class SCM manager, we need to define our circles and make them as effective as possible. The first quality circle in the life of any manager should be the family circle.

The family is the first and highest priority circle in anyone's life, serving as your reward structure, your reason for working. Essentially, it is what brings quality into your life. A disastrous home life destroys your work life, whereas a disastrous work life is tolerable if you have a successful home life. It is self-destructive to let your work life become your reason for living because "change" can destroy that life in minutes.

Another important circle of everyone's life is the society to which they belong. In the United States, success is measured by individual earning power; in most other parts of the world, however, success is measured by one's ability to contribute to society. Far too many of us are not contributing (adding value) to society; rather, we are only self-gratifying (trying to fill our own pockets at the expense of others). In reality, your own personal value is increased only by how much you work with and help others.

The third circle important in each of our lives is the circle in which we work; this circle is often called the team. But are we really forming teams or are we just grouping? A group is a collection of people thrown together in a room for the purpose of making a decision. A team is a collection of individuals who have worked together over a long period of time and have developed a creative harmony and synergy. Teams are characterized by sharing, not domineering as we see in groups.

In all the circles in our lives, we need to establish quality. This is not the equivalent of "quality time" a phrase often used in referring to our children. This phrase has become a kind of excuse for spending as little time as possible with them. There is no "quality time" if an insufficient amount of time is spent, whether with children, spouse, or employees. The biggest challenge of a world-class SCM manager is to prioritize his or her time in order to achieve sufficient "quality time" that will make a difference in the circles important in the manager's life.

Goal Setting

If you don't know where you're going,
    You'll probably get there.

If you cannot see a target, how can you expect to hit it? Unfortunately, far too many people and companies go through life without targets to shoot at. They permit changes to affect the road they take in life without ever identifying why they are traveling down the road to begin with. If we are working only for money, then money is all we will ever get out of our work. However, if we are working for some greater purpose in life, such as having a successful family and marriage or becoming the best at whatever we do, we will view the money as a nice added benefit, and we will have a lot more fun doing it.

We need goals at many levels and in many time frames. Here are just a few areas in which we should have long-range (20 years +), midrange (5 years +), and short-range goals (1 year):

Family Goals: Sit down with your spouse and children and determine what is important to the family.

Personal Goals: What do you want out of life? What will give your life meaning?

Career Goals: Where do you want your career path to go, realizing that most people change professions an average of about four times during their lives?

Corporate Goals: What are the goals outlined in your company's business plan?

Job Function Goals: What do you want to accomplish in the job function you are performing? Are you hoping to build better relationships in your "circles"? Do you want to become world class? Far too often I have encountered people who, when asked; "How do you decide what areas of your job function you want to perform well in?" I get an answer like "Whatever it takes to keep my job and get a raise." My reaction is "I'm glad you don't work for me!"

After you have collected these goals, you need to do two things:

1. Develop an action plan that will work toward achievement of the goal.
2. Communicate the goal to all involved. For example, I have encountered numerous organizations where the corporate goals are pretty much kept secret among top management. Yet the employees are expected to achieve these goals. You can never overcommunicate your goals.

Your personal success needs to be defined. Even playing the lottery requires selecting numbers and purchasing a ticket. Most goals, such as family or work goals, need a clearly defined game plan. A number of good books have been published on the development of life and work goals, especially the Covey and von Oech books.[26]

Recently, we have discovered a slight reversal of the goal-setting process in organizations. Previously, the trend had been for top management to define the vision and mission of the organization. In a clear reversal of this process, the employees are defining the mission of the organization, and then a top management vision statement is developed from this employee-defined mission statement. For example, Tridon-Oakdale brought a team of managers together and had them establish the mission statement of the corporation. This gave the managers an ownership in the goals and an added commitment in achieving the organization's goals.

Goals define success. Without defined goals, how will you ever know if you were successful in achieving them?

Leadership

The power of example has always been the most powerful teaching tool. Every parent has learned this principle the hard way: "The children always seem to 'do as I do' rather than 'do as I say.'" This principle is just as relevant in the

---

[26]The following books provide excellent lessons on goal setting (and numerous other principles discussed in this chapter). Covey's books focus on the characteristics of leadership, whereas von Oech's books deal with creativity and the "meaning of life." See Covey, Stephen R., *Principle—Centered Leadership*, Summit Books, New York, 1991; Covey, Stephen R., *The Seven Habits of Highly Effective People*, Simon & Schuster, New York, 1989; von Oech, Roger, *A Kick in the Seat of the Pants*, Harper & Row, New York, 1986; and von Oech, Roger, *A Whack on the Side of the Head*, Warner Books, New York, 1990.

workplace as it is in the home. If you are grumpy about changes that are being passed down to you, do not expect your employees to be motivated by changes you pass on to them.

Tinothy Mojonnier states that top management's role in fostering positive organizational change has four essential elements:

1. Create a detailed vision statement. This is done with a vision and mission statement, as well as a strategic plan.
2. Assess your current organization's total culture. This is done as part of the core competency assessment and vision statement process.
3. Develop a strategy for achieving your vision.
4. Establish midpoint goals to mitigate your troops. Midpoint goals are part of the short-term strategy and plan of operation.[27]

The leader runs his or her organization using respect, whereas the manager drives his or her people by intimidation. Just ask yourself which work environment you would prefer and then give your employees the same level of respect. A leader positively influences and motivates changes and helps to position an organization for success.

Values and Ethics

The integrity of men is to be measured by their conduct, not by their professions.

Junius

Values provide the glue that keeps us together. We need a value system built on virtue, integrity, and ethics if we want to grow old feeling good about what we have done in life, whether or not it was successful. It would be helpful to define some of the terms we are using here:

Values: Worth; that which renders anything useful or estimable; excellence
Virtue: Worth; moral excellence
Integrity: Completeness, wholeness; honesty, sincerity
Ethics: Standards of right and wrong; system of conduct or behavior, moral principles[28]

---

[27]This model comes from Mojonnier, Timothy M., "Top Management's Role in Fostering and Managing Positive Organizational Change," *APICS 37th International Conference Proceedings*, APICS, October 1994, pp. 49–51.

[28]*Webster's New Dictionary*, Russell, Gebbes & Grosset, New York, 1990.

The lack of ethics and integrity in the United States has resulted in the creation of so many nontrust systems that often the nontrust systems are more complex than the systems they are trying to protect. A nontrust system is a system established specifically for the purpose of making sure that the original system is not abused. For example, antifraud systems such as financial auditing systems exist in every organization. Another example is the extensive employee monitoring systems like security cameras, sign-in and sign-out sheets, and time logs, all designed and put in place to make sure employees stay on task. Most of these systems were created because of the employee who is the "exception," but the systems affect the morale and attitude of all employees, including the trustworthy good performers.

From a psychological perspective, we develop nontrust systems to protect us from having others do to us the types of things we ourselves are likely to be guilty of. Otherwise, we probably would not have thought of setting up the nontrust system in the first place. It has been estimated that the nontrust systems now in existence are costing us more than if we were to just absorb the occasional fraud that might happen. Our lack of ethics and integrity leaves us morally and financially bankrupt.

We can get into a long, drawn-out discussion about whether a bribe is less ethical than a tip, but it is not really that complicated. If we feel good about ourselves, and if the results leave everyone involved in a win-win situation, chances are the activity was ethical. It's like pornography; we have difficulty defining it, but we know it when we see it.

Internationally, ethics gets very confusing. U.S. citizens seem to see everything in life as black or white in the decision-making process, whereas most of the rest of the world sees a lot of gray. For example, recently Malaysia and Thailand were having a border dispute in a region where a large reserve of oil had been discovered. Whereas the American solution would have been to battle it out, there has to be a legal, documented solution. The Malaysia–Thailand solution was to draw a line around this region and to bring in a private developer to develop the oil reserve. Then both countries shared equally in the profits. So which is more ethical, the U.S. way or the Southeast Asian way?

In the United States we are obsessed with the legalistic. The handshake is worthless because our legal system has declared it as worthless in court. Technically (on the books), the handshake has value, but in practice (in the courts) it has no worth. This has destroyed our ability to trust each other. If it is not written down and spelled out in fine print, it legally does not have to happen. This brings to mind another interesting ethics example from the Southeast Asia region. Both North America and Southeast Asia have a free trade agreement. North America has NAFTA, which binds three countries, the United States, Canada, and Mexico, in a free trade arrangement. Southeast Asia has the Association of Southeast Asian Nations (ASEAN) which involves six countries in a trade agreement: Indonesia, Malaysia, Singapore, the Philippines, Brunei, and Thailand. The NAFTA agreement is 2,200 pages long, whereas the ASEAN agreement, with twice as many countries, is only 16 pages long. This example makes it pretty obvious that our lack of integrity and ethics has made us obsessed with nontrust systems. Show your employees a little more trust and respect and they may surprise you by trusting and respecting you in return.

Levi Strauss considers its most important asset to be its people's "aspirations." This organization is widely known for combining strong commercial success with a commitment to social values and to its workforce. In 1987 it developed its famous Levi Strauss Aspirations Statement, a major initiative that defines the shared values as a guide to both management and the workforce. The statement is reshaping occupational roles and responsibilities, how performance evaluations are conducted, how training is handled, and how business decisions are made. With its focus on "people" and their values, this document has been credited with making Levi Strauss a flexible and innovative company. More importantly, the company has an exemplary record on issues such as workforce diversity and worker dislocation benefits.

Levi Strauss's Aspirations Statement identifies a new type of leadership that encompasses:

New Behaviors: Directness, openness, honesty, commitment to the success of others, willingness to acknowledge problems and errors.

Diversity: Diversity (in age, sex, ethnicity, etc.) in the workforce.

Recognition: Financial and nonfinancial recognition for individuals and teams that contribute to success. "Recognition must be given to all who contribute."

Ethical Management Practices: "Leadership that epitomizes the stated standards of ethical behavior."

Communications: Employees must know what is expected of them and receive timely and honest feedback.

Empowerment: Leadership should increase the authority and responsibility of those employees closest to the products and customers.

Levi Strauss has demonstrated the importance of people values and ethics and has taught that these values are critical to world-class management (leadership) status.[29]

---

[29] A detailed discussion of the Aspirations Statement can be found in Howard, Robert, "Values Make the Company: An Interview with Robert Haas," *Harvard Business Review*, September–October 1990, pp. 133–144.

A company's values—what it stands for, what its
people believe in—are crucial to its competitive
success.

Robert Haas
CEO, Levi Strauss & Co.

Adding Social Value

Being world class involves two opposite but equal activities: eliminating all waste and focusing on value-added functions. Identifying non–value-added activities on a factory floor has always been relatively easy, but how do we identify non–value-added activities in our own lives? Here are a couple of guidelines:

Does the activity help achieve any of the goals that we established earlier in this chapter?

Does the activity we are engaged in benefit society or our family (our "circle") in any way?

Let me tell you a story that will help your understanding of this concept. One time when I was working overseas I got into a discussion of "what is wrong with the United States?" Outsiders always have lots of ideas about what Americans should be doing differently, and sometimes, as in this occasion, these insights can be thought provoking. The answer was: "The economic decay of the United States is being caused by the fact that you are graduating more and more non–value-added graduates than you ever did before." So I asked for a definition of a non–value-added graduate, to which the answer was "Anyone working in a profession that does not increase the output of the nation." Individuals who work at professions that simply move the existing resources of the nation around—placing some of them in their own pocket during the process without adding any value—are non-value added.

On a smaller scale, many of our activities only benefit our own pocket books in the short term; we are not creating anything of value to society. And if we are engaged in activities that add no value, then we are actively engaged in creating waste. In our private or corporate life, we need to redirect our activities, and the activities of our employees, toward adding value. We need to eliminate non–value-added processes and to add value to society as an enterprise, through the efforts of our employees.

Continuous Learning

It is only the intellectually lost who ever argue.
Oscar Wilde

The Oscar Wilde quote tells us that you cannot learn if you have your mouth open; you can only learn if you have your ears open and your mouth closed. In this section, we focus on people learning or sharing with each other.

Many people are filled with good ideas, and indeed we need to listen to them if we are to benefit from their wisdom. In addition, being world class means realizing that improvement only comes about if we open ourselves to change in the form of new ideas. We need to learn new ideas in order to incorporate them into what we do. World class means giving everyone in the organization opportunities and the appropriate motivation to learn and develop through education and training. We need to build a learning organization.

This category encompasses the need for self-renewal, which is otherwise known as vacation time. Creativity is improved when pressure is removed, and drudgery is relieved. Employees need time to "get away from it all," and they need to be encouraged to get away from it often.

Innovation and Change Creation

Chaos often breeds life when order breeds habit.
Henry (Brooks) Adams
American Historian

World class is breaking out of the ritualistic, mundane things in life. It is the realization that

Professionals built the Titanic—*amateurs the Ark*
Frank Pepper

Just because an employee is not an expert at something does not mean he or she does not have valuable ideas. And the expression of all ideas, whether by the professional or the amateur, needs to be encouraged. The trick in managing ideas is to make sure egos do not get wrapped up in the innovation process. Every idea has to be considered valuable, even if you really think it stinks. Remember, you are a prejudiced observer, and you do not want to discourage the creative process. You also need to be careful that the "professional" is not offended if the ideas of an amateur contradict his or her opinion.

World class is also the ability to laugh at yourself.

For the Wisdom of the World is foolishness with God
1 Corinthians 3:19 (NT)

Von Oech and Nadler and Hibion, listed earlier, state that the ability to laugh at yourself is critical to the creative process. Allow your ideas to be destroyed—in fact, do your best to destroy them yourself. How else can you be sure they are foolproof?

Employees need to be involved in and to understand the change process in order to effectively initiate changes. This process is explained in many models but is similar to the following:

1. Identifying/recognizing the need or opportunity for change, which is the first step in making any change
2. Defining the problem or opportunity that needs to be addressed
3. Identifying the current company position relative to the problem: you have to know where you're at before you can determine where to go.
4. Identifying alternative destinations
5. Identifying the desired destination
6. Defining a road map to get you where you want to be
7. Unfreezing the organization and preparing it for change, including training and empowerment
8. Changing implementation
9. Stabilizing the organization under the new order, including the establishment of a new feedback mechanism that will monitor the new status quo

With an understanding of the change process, organizations and their employees are now ready for innovation and change creation.[30]

This brings us to a critical element of world-class employee innovation and creativity. We need to develop empowered people who will work together as teams, not groups, and have the authority to implement their ideas. Creativity works best through the synergy of effectively developed and empowered teams. We saw an example of this earlier in this chapter in the Levi Strauss story. Another example is the Antilock Braking Systems Division (ABS) of General Motors in Dayton, Ohio (formerly Delco Products Company). ABS did what it was told was impossible: it developed a world-class empowerment program called employee involvement (EI), starting with a traditional United Auto Workers (UAW) contract. A covenant was established between the union and ABS. They felt this was the only way they would be in business in two years and that this was necessary if they were to stay even with the continuous improvement programs of their competitors.

ABS supervisors were given new responsibility based on communication and training, and so they established a system of trust with the workers. This trust is at the core of the EI program. Based on this trust, a set of guiding principles were established, which included the following.

1. We will establish and maintain innovative systems that can compete in a world-class climate.

---

[30] Another interesting example of the change process is found in the textbook by Bell, Robert R., and John M. Burnham, *Managing Productivity and Change*, South-Western Publishing Co., Cincinnati, Ohio, 1991, pp. 10–11.

2. We will enact cultural change necessary to ensure profitability and job security at the Dayton plants.

3. We will run the business as a joint activity seeking contribution from and sharing benefits with all.

4. We will provide mechanisms and incentives that promote continual improvement in customer satisfaction.

5. We will approach this covenant as a living agreement, continually reviewing our progress and proactively adjusting to maximize our competitiveness.

ABS's world-class empowerment program is worthy of much study and wide emulation.[31]

Measuring/Rewarding

Innovation and creativity need to be stimulated. Recently, I was working for a company that had established an elaborate Total Quality Management (TQM) program. (TQM is a tool designed to implement change in an organization.) However, the TQM program was failing, and the company could not understand why. After reviewing their measurement system, I quickly learned that it was evaluating employee performance based on units per hour efficiency. Bonuses were being paid when employee performance exceeded the standard rates of production. Why would any employee want to spend time implementing changes through TQM if (1) they were being rewarded based on historical rates and historical methodologies; (2) there was no reward for implementing the change; and (3) changes would, in effect, decrease their productive output in the short term and therefore reduce their bonuses.

With regard to point number three, when change is implemented, the first result is a dropoff in efficiency. As we see in Chart 2.6, we are working away at a certain level of output, and immediately, as change is introduced, productive output declines. Then, through the process of the learning curve, employees slowly become better and better at the new process, eventually achieving a new, higher (hopefully) level of output. Unfortunately, in the short term, efficiency suffers, and so does the pay check.

This company was asking the employees to sacrifice their paychecks in order to implement changes. The company didn't want to lose output but still wanted the employees to initiate improvements. It was giving the employees mixed signals, and the signal that motivated the employees the most was the paycheck

---

[31] For details on the ABS EI program, see the following article Powell, Jr., Cash, "Empowerment, The Stake in the Ground for ABS," *Target*, January–February 1992, pp. 7–17.

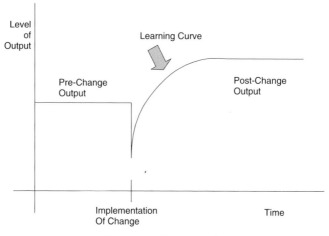

Chart 2.6   Change Function

signal. To understand this concept completely, here is a "hang on your wall" statement:

A Measurement System Is Not for Management Information It's for Motivating Employees

Any measurement system that exists simply for accounting or information-gathering purposes is probably countereffective and is destructive to the company's ability to achieve its goals. A measurement system that does not focus on the goals of the organization is distracting employees from those goals. This is because, whether or not it is true, employees believe they are being graded by what they are being measured on. And they will focus on those areas they are being measured on. So, a company should select its measurement systems wisely; otherwise, it may motivate the wrong actions.

Stakeholders

As a world-class SCM manager, you need to identify ALL the people involved in your circles. These include family, friends, employees, peers, bosses, customers (both internal and external), vendors, and the community.

Taking it from the top, can you satisfy your spouse's needs? Are you making him or her happy? Does he or she enjoy being with you? How about your children? How about your friends?

Do the people you work with come to you for help, or do they avoid you like the plague? Do your customers consider you as someone who can get things done or as someone who puts things off or who seeks to affix blame? Do you identify both your immediate customer (the one you pass product to) and your final customer (the eventual end user) as someone who needs satisfaction?

Do you get involved? Do you reach out to help your fellow employees and your family and friends, or do you avoid challenging situations? Are you willing and eager to change? Simply put: **are you world class?**

SUMMARY

In Hawaii the native population has a sense or feel for each other that supersedes the words of conversation. They refer to this as the "ha," which can best be translated as the "breath of life." When Westerners started to visit the islands, that "ha" didn't seem to be present. The warmth of the relationship which is a comfort, or a knowing where the other person was coming from, was not there. The Hawaiians started to refer to these people as "ha-ole," which is translated "without ha." They felt alienated from these foreigners because of their lack of feeling for each other. This lack of feeling ultimately created a lack of trust. Today's SCM manager must learn what Hawaiians already know well: they must learn to have "ha."

This section described past and future management styles and showed how competitive markets have forced rapid decision-making processes. This speed has in turn forced decisions to be made at operational levels of the organization rather than strategically. This section stressed the importance of strategic goal setting.

Without people who are willing and motivated to change, no world-class organization is possible. It is "We the People"—you the manager, your bosses, employees, customers, and vendors—that makes an enterprise world class, and just like Steve Young or Michael Jordan, you cannot get there without your "circle."[32]

Man is here for the sake of other men.
                                          Albert Einstein

---

[32]You can do further reading on effective world-class people relations in Boyst, Jr. III, William M., "HRM—Key to the Integrated Management Revolution," *APICS 34th International Conference Proceedings*, APICS, Falls Church, VA, 1991, pp. 354–357; Wallace, Thomas F., *World Class Manufacturing*, OMNEO, Essex Junction, VT, 1994 (the section of the book that is of interest is titled "Part III—People"); and Plenert, *International Management and Production: Survival Techniques for Corporate America*.

GOALS

There are numerous ways to address the identification of goals and goal setting. One technique that has been demonstrated to be successful is to start by identifying what a world-class supply chain environment would look like. This process can be accomplished using two tools: benchmarking and step charting. In benchmarking, we start by going to the literature (books, journal and magazine articles, conference proceedings, web site postings, etc.) to identify what the "best practices" are as related to SCM for your particular industry. Once you have created a list of best practices, they are categorized into the four classifications of a step chart. Chart 2.7 provides an example of a Supply Chain Management step chart. It is not intended to be all-inclusive, nor will it fit your specific industry. In addition, step charts are date stamped so that what is world class today will not be world class one year from now. However, we can use Chart 2.7 as an example of what a step chart should look like.

The four categories in Chart 2.7 are as follows.

- *Clerical*   The clerical organization is one that operates in a foundational mode. It is dictatorial, top-down directed, and has a militaristic style. It generally contains some type of dominant authority figure. This organization is generally a manual operation that is not receptive to leading-edge concepts and opposes change.
- *Mechanical*   The mechanical organization recognizes the need to introduce a minimal level of technology. This organization is still missing integration and organizationwide direction. The focus of the organization is departmentalized, and the emphasis is on the performance of the individual department. There is only minimal communication beyond the organization to the customer or the vendor.
- *Proactive*   The proactive organization feels the need for integration within the organization. It establishes company goals, and the various departments attempt to align themselves with these goals. It recognizes the need to interface with vendors and customers, but these relationships are still arms-length. Some teaming exists. Quality optimization and some levels of automation are being introduced.
- *World Class*   This is the ideal, perfect world for your industry. It contains a high level of integration with customers and vendors both within and external to the organization. It contains automation and leading-edge, sophisticated management, planning, and scheduling systems. Appropriate, goal-based metrics and the supportive data collection systems exist. Change is a goal and is a natural part of the organization.

With Chart 2.7 in mind, we are now ready to rank the current state of our organization. The hard part is being honest with ourselves, for we tend to

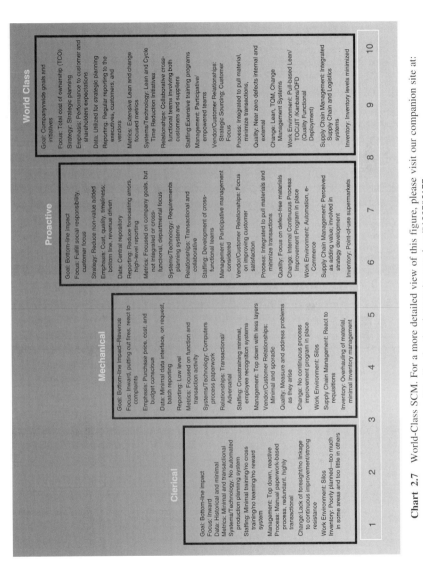

Chart 2.7 World-Class SCM. For a more detailed view of this figure, please visit our companion site at: http://books.elsevier.com/companions/0123705177

Clerical

| 1 | 2 | 3 | 4 |

Goal: Bottom-line impact
Focus: Inward
Data: Historical and minimal
Metrics: Minimal and transactional
Systems/Technology: No automated production planning system
Staffing: Minimal training/no cross training/no teaming/no reward system
Management: Top down, reactive
Process: Manual paperwork-based process, redundant, highly transactional
Change: Lack of foresight/no linkage to continuous improvement/strong resistance
Work Environment: Silos
Inventory: Poorly planned—too much in some areas and too little in others

---

Mechanical

| 3 | 4 | 5 |

Goal: Bottom-line impact–Revenue
Focus: Inward, putting out fires, react to complaints
Emphasis: Purchase price, cost, and budget conscious
Data: Minimal data interface, on request, batch reporting
Reporting: Low level
Metrics: Focused on function and transaction activity
Systems/Technology: Computers process paperwork
Relationships: Transactional/Adversarial
Staffing: Crosstraining minimal, employee recognition systems
Management: Top down with less layers
Vendor/Customer Relationships: Minimal and sporadic
Quality: Measure and address problems as they arise
Change: No continuous process improvement program in place
Work Environment: Silos
Supply Chain Management: React to requisitions
Inventory: Overhauling of material, minimal inventory management

---

Proactive

| 6 | 7 | 8 |

Goal: Bottom-line impact
Focus: Fulfill social responsibility; customer focus
Strategy: Reduce non-value added
Emphasis: Cost, quality, timeliness; bottom line, revenue driven
Data: Central repository
Reporting: Reduce forecasting errors, high-level reporting
Metrics: Focused on company goals, but not integrated or cross-functional, departmental focus
Systems/Technology: Requirements planning systems
Relationships: Transactional and collaborative
Staffing: Development of cross-functional teams
Management: Participative management considered
Vendor/Customer Relationships: Focus on improving customer satisfaction
Process: Integrated to pull materials and minimize transactions
Quality: Focus on defect-free materials
Change: Internal Continuous Process Improvement Program in place
Work Environment: Automation, e-Commerce
Supply Chain Management: Perceived as adding value; involved in strategy development
Inventory: Point-of-use supermarkets

World Class

| 8 | 9 | 10 |

Goal: Companywide goals and initiatives
Focus: Total cost of ownership (TCO)
Strategy: Strategic planning
Emphasis: Performance to customer and shareholders expectations.
Data: Utilized for strategic planning
Reporting: Regular reporting to the executives, customers, and vendors
Metrics: Extensive Lean and change focused metrics
Systems/Technology: Lean and Cycle Time Reduction Initiatives
Relationships: Collaborative cross-functional teams involving both customers and suppliers
Staffing: Extensive training programs
Management: Participative/empowered teams
Vendor/Customer Relationships: Strategic Sourcing; Customer Focus
Process: Integrated to pull material, minimize transactions,
Quality: Near zero defects internal and external
Change: Lean, TQM, Change Management Systems
Work Environment: Pull-based Lean/TOC/JIT /Kanbans/QFD (Quality Functional Deployment)
Supply Chain Management: Integrated Supply Chain and Logistics systems
Inventory: Inventory levels minimized

| 1 | 2 | 3 | 4 | 5 | 6 | 7 | 8 | 9 | 10 |

overrank ourselves. Simply because one of our 10 departments has MRP does not mean that we are proactive. We need to look at our organization as an outsider would and to evaluate our performance realistically. If, for example, we have some but less than half of the characteristics of a mechanical environment generally applied throughout our organization, we should not be ranked more than a 4. If we have about half, we would probably rate about a 4.5. We would use similar rankings for all categories of organizations; this gives us our "current state ranking."

Again looking at Chart 2.7, we should now consider where our organization is heading, and again, we must be careful to be meaningful. We do not want to know where you personally think the organization is heading. Rather, we want to know where the rhetoric and actions of the organization's leadership seem to be guiding us. And again, we want to carefully and realistically rank the future state of the organization on the scale of 1 to 10. This assessment will give us the future state ranking.

Often it is helpful to assess current and future states graphically. As can be seen in Chart 2.8, the current state is in red (a ranking of 3.9) and the future state is in yellow (a ranking of 7.1) (See web version to view colors.). This ranking process clearly delineates where we are now and where we project ourselves to be in the future. We are now ready to develop a strategy for the future, which will be covered in the next section of this chapter.

Before we examine strategy, however, let us see a more detailed classification of each of the four categories for ranking Supply Chain Management proficiency. This detail is behind some of the categories found in Chart 2.7, and it will help you identify your true ranking.

Clerical

1. Goal: Bottom-line impact: overhead
2. Focus: Inward
3. Strategy: None, reactive, focused on immediate need
4. Emphasis: Convenience and expediency, focus on paycheck
5. Data: Historical and minimal
   - Back pocket lists/no sharing
6. Reporting: Very low level, no empowerment
   - Minimal with routine followup
7. Metrics: Minimal and transactional
   - Focused on sales/profits
8. Systems/technology: No automated production planning system
   - Informal and not integrated, primarily manual
   - Planning performed at the department level
9. Relationships: Personal/self-centered
10. Staffing: Minimal training/no cross training/no teaming/no reward system

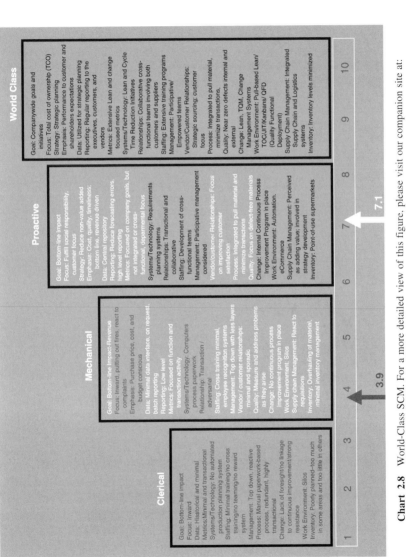

Chart 2.8 World-Class SCM. For a more detailed view of this figure, please visit our companion site at: http://books.elsevier.com/companions/0123705177

11. Management: Top down, reactive
12. Vendor/customer relationships: No collaboration between SCM members
    - Often adversarial/don't see need for partnerships
13. Process: Manual paperwork-based process, redundant, highly transactional
14. Quality: Not emphasized/minimum measurements
15. Change: Lack of foresight/no linkage to continuous improvement/strong resistance
16. Work environment: Inbound and outbound work in silos
    - Control system focus—Confirm the actions of others
    - Departmental relationships
    - Pull environment
17. Supply Chain Management (SCM): Viewed as little or non-value added, "order placers"
    - Paper/phone communication with supply chain
18. Inventory: Poorly planned—too much in some areas and too little in others
    - Manual shortage lists/buying cards used

Mechanical

1. Goal: Bottom-line impact — revenue
   - Not defined clearly
2. Focus: Inward, putting out fires, react to complaints
3. Strategy: Reduce transactions, share supply base
   - Minimal, react to requisition release, last buy basis
4. Emphasis: Purchase price, cost and budget conscious
5. Data: Minimal data interface, on request, batch reporting
   - Limited availability, based on history
   - Manual data used to measure SCM
6. Reporting: Low level
   - Report to logistics/warehouse/transportation manager
   - Available for completed transactions
7. Metrics: Focused on function and transaction activity
   - Minimal and inconsistently monitored
   - Group metrics by department
   - No metrics to measure success of SCM policies
   - No benchmarking
8. Systems/technology: Computers process paperwork
   - Multiple MRP (Material Requirements Planning) systems
   - No shopfloor control, simplistic ERP (Enterprise Resources Planning) systems
   - Exception reporting, not integrated, shortage lists
   - Stand-alone procurement system
   - Technology deployed too late without looking at the process

9. Relationships: Transactional/adversarial
10. Staffing: Cross-training minimal, employee recognition systems
    - Reward system based on internal performance
    - Employee selection and training informal
    - Departmental teams to implement SCM
11. Management: Top down with fewer layers
12. Vendor/customer relationships: Minimal and sporadic collaboration
    - Recurring interaction between buyers and suppliers
    - Emphasis on unit price
    - Limited supply base/single sources/proliferation of sources
    - No strategic sourcing teams in place
    - Minimal customer involvement
13. Process: Transactional focus, fewer transactions and approvals
    - High expediting
    - Push with some simple pull processes
14. Quality: Measure and address problems as the arise
15. Change: No continuous process improvement program in place
    - Done only when necessary
16. Work environment: Work as individual silos
    - Local and national operations
17. Supply Chain Management: React to requisitions
    - Not involved in the front end of the business/key source selections
    - React to requisitions
    - Common logistics provider
    - Organization investigating the SCM process
    - Engineering data communicated to suppliers through mail or hand delivered
18. Inventory: Overhauling of material, minimal inventory management
    - Replenishment decisions based on historical demand

Proactive

1. Goal: Bottom-line impact—profit contributor
2. Focus: Fulfill social responsibility, customer focus
3. Strategy: Reduce non-value added
    - Supplier relationships, focus on value-added activities, best value analysis, early identification of issues
4. Emphasis: Cost, quality, timeliness; bottom line, revenue driven
5. Data: Central repository
    - Bar coding
    - Real-time data available internally within functional unit
    - Large degree of data interface

- Information flow laterally
- Self-generated, standard reports with some customization
- Information and engineering data communicated to suppliers through traditional methods, electronic data exchanges such as EDI (Electronic Data Interface) and PDM are being considered

6. Reporting: Reduce forecasting errors
   - High-level reporting
7. Metrics: Focused on company goals but not integrated or cross-functional, departmental focus
   - Measures focused on quality and timeliness
   - Benchmarking utilized on a limited basis
8. Systems/technology: Requirements planning systems
   - Align DRP and master plan
   - Shopfloor control system
   - One integrated MRP system with capacity planning
   - Initial ERP integration
   - Interface with tier 1 suppliers only
9. Relationships: Transactional and collaborative
10. Staffing: Development of cross-functional teams
    - Cross-training programs/SCM training programs
    - Employee empowerment
    - Employee Selection and Training Criteria and Expectations defined, focused on functional development
    - Reward program in place to promote better performance
11. Management: Participative Management considered
12. Vendor/customer relationships: Focus on improving customer satisfaction
    - Long-term contracts/vendor relationships/supplier development
    - Customer involvement, active source selection
    - Competitive bidding/active source selection
    - Strategic sourcing teams
    - Supplier Relationship Management system considered
    - Customer focus—slogans and posters
    - 3PL and outsourcing is initiated
    - Competitive Bidding, Supplier Partnerships and Agreements, Supply Base Reduction; Primarily Domestic; International sources considered
13. Process: Process and systems integrated to pull materials and minimize transactions
    - Pull Systems and Just in Time considered, some Kanban exists with vendors
    - Documented operating procedures
14. Quality: Focus on defect-free materials
    - Considered to be an order winner, improvement ongoing

15. Change: Internal Continuous Process Improvement Program in Place
16. Work environment: Automation, e-Commerce
17. Supply Chain Management: Perceived as adding value; periodically involved in strategy development
    - Inbound and outbound logistics
    - Plan for recurring requirements
    - Accurate SCM measurement systems
    - Supplier selection, classification, commodity management, and planning are integrated but not fully aligned to the SCM strategy
    - Minimal internal goals are aligned with the objectives of the supply chain
    - Cost drivers affecting the entire SCM process begun to be identified and monitored
    - Logistics managed and tracked through manual methods
18. Inventory: Point-of-use supermarkets
    - Managed and some reduction realized

World Class

1. Goal: Companywide goals and initiatives
   - Internal goals are aligned with the objectives of the supply chain
   - Shingo Award winner
2. Focus: Total cost of ownership (TCO)
   - Outward toward the extended enterprise and beyond; functional to process
   - Minimal cash to cash cycle time integrated across the whole supply chain
   - Environmentally conscious
3. Strategy: Strategic planning
   - Supplier partnerships, focus on value add activities, total cost analysis, risk management, and time to market
4. Emphasis: Performance to customer and shareholders expectations
5. Data: Utilized for strategic planning
   - Self-managed for customization, integrated into supply chain
   - Minimal paperwork
   - Data and paperwork are moved using the Pull system
   - Information and engineering data communicated to suppliers through electronic data exchanges such as EDI and PDM
   - Real-time data utilized and shared with suppliers and customers alike. Information is shared frequently, freely, formally and informally
6. Reporting: Regular reporting to the executives, customers, and vendors
7. Metrics: Extensive lean and change focused metrics

- Integrated with cross-functional goals and value-added activities with stakeholder accountability
- Minimal number high-level business focus
- Reward and measurement system in place supporting SCM through all supplier tiers

8. Systems/technology: Lean and cycle time reduction initiatives
   - RFID and UID
   - Bar coding fully implemented
   - Integrated MRP II (Manufacturing Resources Planning)/ERP (Enterprise Resources Planning) with vendor and customer interfaces
   - Advanced Planning and Scheduling (APS) systems
   - Finite Capacity Scheduling (FCS) systems

9. Relationships: Collaborative cross-functional teams involving both customers and suppliers

10. Staffing: Extensive training programs
    - Employee mentoring, employee empowerment
    - Employee selection and training supports best in class philosophies
    - Skilled in applying world-class SCM tools to supply base
    - JIT (Just in Time)
    - TOC (Theory of Constraints)
    - Self-motivated. Employees are empowered and decision makers

11. Management: Participative/empowered teams
    - Integrated risk management

12. Vendor/customer relationships: Strategic sourcing
    - Supplier partnership alliances
    - Collaborative planning and scheduling
    - International interfaces in place
    - 3PL (third-party logistics providers)
    - Leverage supplier technology
    - Early involvement in product designs
    - Commodity teams/commodity strategies
    - Suppliers ISO certified
    - Customer focus: Mission, values, and goals embody voice of customer; developed by employees and management
    - Total integration from R&D (Research and Development) to customer; Supplier's supplier through customer's customer

13. Process: Process and systems integrated to pull material, minimize transactions, and support NPI cross functionally
    - Standardized best practices

14. Quality: SPC (Statistical Process Control) or TQM (Total Quality Management) used to manage all quality processes
    - Near zero defects internal and external

15. Change: Lean, TQM, Change Management Systems
    - Done proactively as part of business; realized as part of continuous improvement
    - Continuous Improvement systems
    - Agile, six sigma initiatives
16. Work environment: Pull-based Lean/TOC/JIT/Kanban/QFD (Quality Functional Deployment)
    - Extensive e-integration throughout the supply chain
    - Extensive use of event management
17. Supply Chain Management: Integrated supply chain and logistics systems
    - Reports at the executive level; fully integrated in strategic planning and operations; cross-functional integration, minimal management layers, practice participative management
18. Inventory: Real-time trace ability of materials
    - Supplier Managed Inventory (SMI)
    - Inventory levels minimized
    - Buffers used strategically only
    - Matches demand; right parts, right quantities; real-time traceability
    - Managed centrally

At this point you have a fairly detailed example of what a Supply Chain Management step chart should look like. What you still need to do is to customize the step chart for your organization. Chart 2.9 presents an example of the customization of this step chart for the logistics operation of a large manufacturer. From this example you should be able to better understand what is expected in order for you to develop your own organization-specific step chart.

At this point you should have (1) customized the step chart to fit your organization, (2) identified your "current state" ranking on the step chart, and (3) identified your "future state" ranking on the step chart, which now becomes the goal of your organization. You are now ready to move forward in developing a strategy for implementation. First, however, we need to consider some optional supply chain models.

A MODEL

The purpose of considering optional/alternative models is to facilitate your thought process as you attempt to develop your own Supply Chain Management step chart. The foundational model was presented in Chart 1.4. These additional models offter a more sophisticated look at the supply chain process. For example, Chart 2.10 shows an SCM puzzle built from the critical components of every supply chain process.

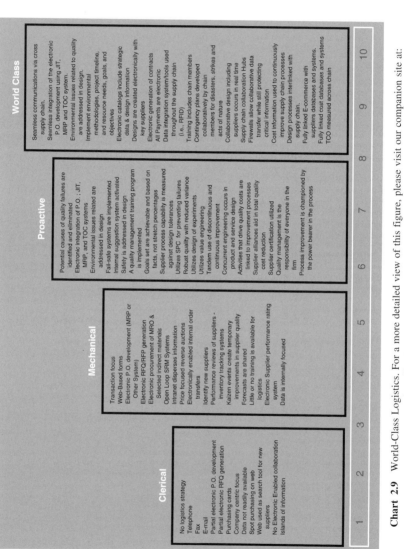

Chart 2.9 World-Class Logistics. For a more detailed view of this figure, please visit our companion site at: http://books.elsevier.com/companions/0123705177

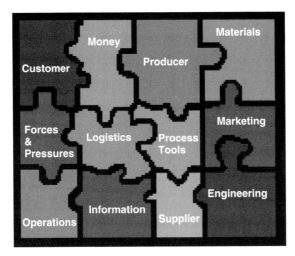

Chart 2.10 The Supply Chain Model

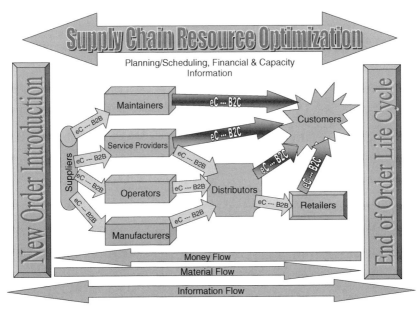

Chart 2.11 Supply Chain Resource Optimization

Another model, which focuses more on the flow and optimization of the supply chain, can be seen in Chart 2.11. In this model we see the materials, money, and information flow that occur in a supply chain, as well as all the steps that occur in this process and that move the product from inception (new order introduction) through completion (end-of-order life cycle) and delivery to the customer.

A third example of a supply chain model can be seen in Chart 2.12. This model keys in on the planning process that occurs within the supply network and shows how the process is cyclical and integrated. The process starts with Demand Planning, which is triggered by forecasts and customer orders. Next, the long-term planning process becomes a short-term Supply Scheduling process in which materials, information, and money are initially scheduled and then moved through the process starting with the supplier, through to the producer, and on to the finished product. The third stage of the process is Demand Fulfillment, in which the delivery system kicks in and the customer product is delivered.

Each of the three models has a story to tell us about the supply chain. It would be valuable, at this point, for you to consider your own story and to create your own supply chain model that focuses on elements and processes critical to your organization.

A STRATEGY

Having goals such as the "future state" on your step chart is not enough. You need to develop a strategy for achieving that goal, and the step chart helps you in developing that strategy. Referring back to Chart 2.8, note that the items highlighted in yellow are the items around which you would now need to develop a strategy or plan of attack (See web version to view colors.). These yellow items identify the "gaps" in your organization, and they incorporate what is commonly referred to as the gap analysis. The strategy is now developed around these gaps.

To develop a strategy, take each item in the gap and develop a plan around it. For example, using Chart 2.8, we select the yellow item "Data: Central Repository" and we develop a plan around that item. The plan should, at a minimum, include

1. *Performance measures* (How do we measure the success or failure of the plan?)   In this case, we could measure the number of independent systems that exist which are not linked to the central repository.
2. *Time stamp* (What is the time frame within which the goal must be achieved?)
3. *Resource requirements* (What does this project require in terms of cost, people, equipment, etc.?)
4. *Interface effects* (What effects will this repository have on existing users, customers, vendors, and the performance of the organization?)

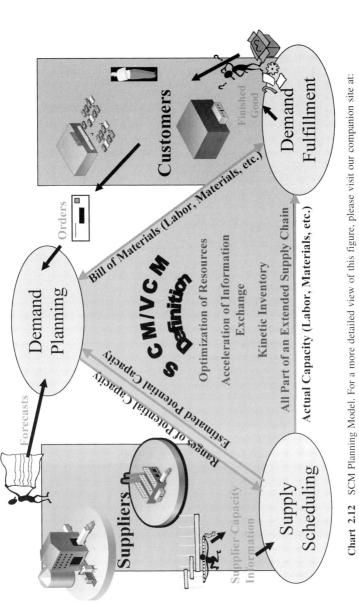

Chart 2.12 SCM Planning Model. For a more detailed view of this figure, please visit our companion site at: http://books.elsevier.com/companions/0123705177

5. *Cost/benefit* (Is this worth doing? Is it in line with the long-term goals and objectives of our organization?)
6. *Organization* (Who should be in charge? What should the team that will be involved with and responsible for this implementation look like?)

Once you have resolved these issues for each yellow "gap" item on your step chart, you can put all these pieces together and consider how they link and interrelate with each other. Once you feel good about the overall integrated plan of attack for your "gaps," you will have the makings of a strategy.

After formulating a strategy, your next step is to incorporate the strategy into a detailed plan of attack that is often referred to as an operating plan. This is where we define specific tasks and assign workloads. Do you have the resources available to accomplish your strategy? This is where the actual work on implementing the change begins.

A STRUCTURE, THE MANAGED, THE MANAGING

These last three characteristics of management are fairly basic and do not relate directly to the theme of this book; they are therefore included in one section. To start with, what is the ideal organization structure? There seems to be an infinite number of ways to run an organization. Two factories, sitting side by side, with the same number of people and producing the same product, can have entirely different structures and still be successful to varying degrees. One can be authoritarian, and the other can participate in their management styles. One can be clerical and the other proactive in their step chart rankings. So what is the ideal structure for your organization? The first thing to consider is that if you plan to become a proactive or a world-class organization, then you cannot adopt a clerical management structure. The management structure must fit the environment that you are managing.

When we talk about the managed and the managing, we see from the step chart in Chart 2.3 that the further you move to the right, the less time you spend managing and the more time you spend leading. Managers push their ideas and direction into an organization. Leaders recognize that many of the best ideas are hidden within the ranks of the organization, and they focus on pulling these ideas out of the organization by creating the participative environments that motivate the employees to eagerly share their ideas. A pull management style turns employees into idea generators and organizational designers. Ricardo Semler's book *Maverick* is an extreme example of total employee participation. The book discusses the company Semco, where the employees basically run the organization, and managers exist just to facilitate the ideas of the employees. It is an example of total participation and management pull. There are many successful organizations of this type, and we can learn lessons from each of them.

"The managed" refers to a collection of employees who are "in the dirt" of the process. Whether the process is a service, producing a product, or the logistics of moving a product around, the people who actually do the work are the managed. And they look to those doing "the managing" to give them meaningful guidance in the form of schedules, training, and priorities. The managed are often quite capable of performing their process. What they need is the guidance of a well-structured supply chain manager to help them optimize their throughput.

EDUCATION

Education is critical for the successful supply chain manager. A supply chain manager needs to be familiar with numerous tools, though rarely are all of these tools applicable to a specific situation. However, if the supply chain manager is not familiar with these tools, he will not know when, how, or what to use to fix specific supply chain issues when they arise. There are numerous MBA programs in Supply Chain Management. One of the best, by far, is the program at the University of San Diego (USD), School of Business, Supply Chain Management Institute (SCMI). This program is designed for the executive student and is web based so that the student can, and often does, take the course from locations all over the world. It is a project-based MBA program where the students are expected to engage in a supply chain improvement project within their own company. This project is expected to generate a return for the company that is significantly greater than the cost of the program.

Dr. David Burt, the grass-roots founder of the USD-SCMI program, has outlined a set of Supply Chain Management competency areas. He feels that all successful supply chain managers should have a basic understanding of these concepts.

Functional Competencies

1. Supply Management
   - Requirements generation
   - Strategic sourcing
   - Global sourcing
   - Cost and price analysis
   - Negotiations
   - Value analysis and engineering
   - Relationship management
   - Subcontract administration
   - Supplier development

2. Operations
   - Systems evaluation
   - Process modeling
   - Productivity/quality
   - Planning systems
   - Scheduling systems
   - Forecasting
   - Lean, Six Sigma, JIT, ERP
   - Inventory systems
   - Measures/motivation
   - Technology (RFID)
3. Logistics
   - DRP
   - Routing/freight
   - Warehousing
   - Transportation
   - International effects
   - Logistics systems
   - Integration
4. Information technology
5. Supplier integration
6. Communications

Process Competencies

7. Leadership
   - Leadership skills
   - Collaboration
   - Strategy development
   - Goal setting and performance management
   - Change management
   - Project management
   - Value network management
8. Legal
9. Ethics
10. Finance
11. Marketing

The goal of a supply chain manager, as we learned in Chapter 1, should be to optimize the supply chain. This can only be accomplished if the manager has a well-founded background in supply chain tools and principles. With that foundation, the manager can generate optimized results.

N, INC.

N, Inc. (see Chapter 1) moved forward with its plans to build a plant in Mexico. After these plans were implemented, it found the plant to be extremely effective and efficient. However, the plant did not generate the desired overall cost savings. In the new facility, yields had dropped from 75 to 60 percent, but some of this decrease could be explained by a learning curve. N, Inc. performed a detailed cost comparison analyzing the before and after environments and discovered that transport costs and inventory carrying costs had jumped dramatically. In addition, the supply chain had become enormously complicated. The materials that previously came from companies like C, Inc. now had to be moved across borders, which meant more distribution layers, resulting in increased cost.

In the meantime, the Swedish supplier had successfully demonstrated its location and performance advantage over the Mexican plant and had strengthened its relationship with the Augsburg plant. It was now supplying about 25 percent of the demand. However, the Dayton plant maintained its operations under the assumption that international demand would increase. Since the capacities were now balanced between the Dayton and Mexico plants, and since demand had decreased in Augsburg, the corporate office was in a dilemma. How should it effectively utilize the excess capacity? One approach could be a vigorous marketing effort. At this point, the capability for external marketing for chip production was weak because in the past the internal demand had been so strong. However, now the corporate office faced the dilemma of growing a segment of the business that was not considered to be within the core competency of N, Inc.

The distribution of component materials currently passes through the Dayton facility, which has kept the quality inspection process centralized and container-izes all the materials for transport to Mexico. The Mexican facility opens the containers, produces the product, containerizes the product, and sends it back to Dayton where final inspection occurs. Then the product is packaged and shipped to the customers.

The Swedish manufacturer also opened its Mexican facility. However, through extensive marketing efforts, which was one of its core competencies, it was able to sell nearly all its capacity in Mexico and Canada. It ended up not needing to compete with N's Dayton facility for N's domestic capacity. It is even considering an expansion program that will permit addressing even more customers, including ultimately the N, Inc. market in the United States.

Consider that you are the SCM manager and that you are again given the assignment of developing an SCM strategy for N, Inc. Once again it would be valuable to look at each of the perspectives:

N's corporate office
N's Dayton plant

N's Mexico plant
N's Augsburg plant

What would be an appropriate strategy? What would you do?

SUPPLY CHAIN MANAGEMENT INTEGRATION[33]

Supply Chain Management focuses on time-efficient movement of resources and on the integration of the various functions and pressures that play on those resources. In this section we will focus on the integration.

AN INTEGRATION SUPPLY CHAIN STRATEGY

We have already discussed strategy development in earlier chapters. We will now address the development of an integrated supply chain strategy, which is a component of the overall international production, operations, logistics, and distribution strategy. This section addresses the international factors involved in successful Supply Chain Management and centers on the integration of the supplier, logistics system, manufacturing, and customer service of total Supply Chain Management. It focuses on the following key issues:

The strategic framework
Cycle time and response time as the key strategic issue
The global supply chain
Information integration
Risk management
Logistics management

THE STRATEGIC FRAMEWORK

The strategic structure that provides the foundation for Supply Chain Management is critical in defining corporate performance, as is witnessed by the increasing number of CEOs who are coming from the ranks of operations. Running a company strictly by the financial numbers has proven to be short sighted. Operational measures of performance are being used more frequently.

Strategically, managing the supply chain requires looking at management from a broader perspective. In Chart 2.13 we see how an ever broadening supply chain

---

[33]Portions of this material were taken from the author's book: Plenert, *International Operations Management*. This book offers an extensive expansion of these fundamental SCM concepts.

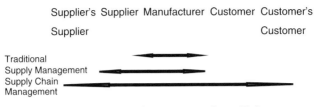

Chart 2.13 Supply Chain Management Span of Influence

perspective requires broader levels of management. We see that traditionally we were only concerned with the environment immediately around us. Later we broadened that perspective through tools such as Electronic Data Interchange (EDI) to include the management of the supply source. We felt that managing the source would allow us to run a leaner production environment with lower inventory levels. More recently we have recognized the need for an even broader perspective, examining the management of the entire source supply through the entire demand/customer network. This is the management of the entire supply chain. However, it is broader than management in the traditional sense. Managers do not take over the responsibility of everyone in the supply chain; rather, they integrate the information network so that all elements of the supply chain can uniformly interact and extract information from the same supply network. The Internet has become the tool for the interchange of Supply Chain Management activity. It moves us away from a traditional point-to-point information exchange to a more connected, interactive information exchange in which all elements of the supply chain can continuously monitor the performance of the overall supply network. This includes a lot more elements than are diagrammed in Chart 2.13.

Chart 2.14 presents the diagramming of a simplistic two-supplier, two-customer supply chain network. From this we can see that it would be nearly impossible to manage the exchange of information using traditional

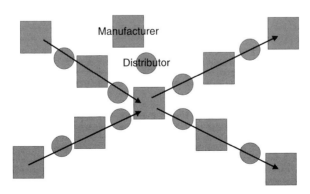

Chart 2.14 Managing the Supply Chain

point-to-point data transfer methodologies. Not only do the suppliers and customers need to be kept informed, but also the distribution and logistics network, which includes transportation and warehousing, needs to be kept in the information loop. This network of information exchanges can now be effective through the use of some type of Internet connectivity.

Traditionally, we would take a slightly different approach to the supplier to customer relationship. The line for vendor to customer was more linear and direct; the process was more simplistic and more controlled. It was difficult to manage the logistics and sourcing process in any other way than by having the producer control the entire process. However, more recent supply chain environments look more like that in Chart 2.15 where we see the Supply Chain Management approach. In this process we see the sharing of information and a form of integrated interdependence. It is integrated in the sense that all the components are connected to the information network, but it is independent in that a level of trust must exist between the organizations which allows each of them to manage its own piece of the relationship.

The benefits of this type of integration are many.

Greatly reduced inventories since the supply chain manages inventory movement

Lower safety stock levels

Greatly reduced cycle times

Increased customer responsiveness

A more participative management approach

Greater information accessibility at all nodes in the supply chain

Significant cost reductions

More price and delivery competitiveness, which is extremely important when dealing with products that are at the mature stage of the product life cycle

Fewer middlemen and promotional costs in the sales transaction

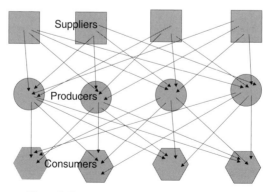

Chart 2.15 Supply Chain Management Approach

More direct customer problem responsiveness and problem resolution

Better quantitative indicators for all elements of the supply chain

The disadvantages of Supply Chain Management include the following:

Loss of direct control of internal information

Loss of information secrecy

Ineffectiveness of the remainder of the supply chain to integrate

Loss of management control of the overall process

Often more catastrophic failure in the supply chain because of the elimination of inventory buffers at each step in the supply chain

In developing a strategy that focuses on Supply Chain Management, the methodology of information integration becomes critical. The connectivity and relationships between sources and customers also become critical. This strategy would not work well in a management environment that emphasizes control and authoritarianism.

The next strategic element that needs to be managed is time. The supply chain network reacts quickly to changes. For example, in the Toyota supply chain, a customized car can be ordered in the morning and come rolling off the production line later that same day. This type of integrated SCM network responsiveness requires the integrated management of not just the facility but of all suppliers.

From this discussion, we have seen that a supply chain approach to international industrial management affects all the competitive strategic priorities, notably:

Cost Reduced because of reduced inventory levels and lower sales costs

Service Increased because of shorter cycle times, which increases customer responsiveness

Flexibility Through shorter cycle times, more flexibility in product customization and product mix performance

Quality The supply chain approach is closer to the JIT flow because of reduced cycle times, which means that product defects or errors are caught more quickly, thereby allowing corrective action to be quicker. More importantly, the supply chain approach integrates not just time, quantity, and delivery information, but also quality specifications and standards so that everyone is on the same page with regard to customer expectations.

CYCLE TIME AND RESPONSE TIME AS THE KEY STRATEGIC ISSUE

Time is critically important in a global strategic supply chain network. (We will revisit this measure in the discussion of Lean, later in this book.) Time is the key to competitive success. Supply Chain Management together with Lean methodologies reduces cycle time and therefore increases response time to customer concerns and expectations. Because of these reasons, an organization that is not part of an integrated supply chain will not be an effective competitor in the next decade.

THE GLOBAL SUPPLY CHAIN

So far we have focused on the operational workings of the three resources in a supply chain. We will next focus on some of the forces that affect the performance of the supply chain.

Political forces—Government restrictions and expectations that you will need to work with

Technology forces—Technological changes both in product technology (which product is competitive and where is the product on the product life cycle) and process technologies (what are the best shipping methods, warehousing methods, or manufacturing methods). The costs of these technologies and their level of development vary all over the world. Some costs, like labor prices, levels of education, or capital equipment costs, are regionally dependent, and others are not regional. For example, if we are shipping by container, the shipping cost from Los Angeles to San Francisco is nearly the same as the cost of shipping from Singapore to San Francisco because the majority of the cost comes in handling the containers, not in moving them.

Market forces—Market interests and demands can vary significantly from region to region. For example, the demand for crosses in Saudi Arabia is somewhat limited, but in Italy the demand would be very strong. Demand will also vary significantly as countries migrate from underdeveloped to developing and then to developed status.

With all of these considerations, we can easily come up with a long list of some of the increased complexities of integrating into a global supply chain network. These include the following.

Geography—Distance tends to slow down the supply chain. For example, trucking products in China is quite different from trucking them in the United States. In addition, some areas have infrastructures, such as poor roads, poor power, or poor telephone landlines, that are difficult to access.

Information—Not all areas of the world have information structures that are effective enough to facilitate Internet access.

Training levels, including language skills—Not all areas have the same standards and expectations from their employees. For example, the education levels in India are, in some regions, higher than in the United States. In addition, specifications and documentation can be misinterpreted if language skills are lacking. For example, the United States' insistence on using inches has more than once caused confusion when other countries mistook an inch measure and produced the product as a metric measure. Even NASA has encountered unit of measure discrepancies in some of their flights.

Demand forecasting becomes more challenging—Demand trends cannot be patterned after the United States in different cultures and environments. And often there is no local demand history on which one can base forecast estimates.

Economic factors—Exchange rate variations can significantly affect the profitability of a transaction. A minor variation in the exchange rate can destroy profit margins. Therefore, it becomes important to standardize the supply chain on a common, stable currency. However, the negative effect of this standardization is that the local manufacturer may be driven out of business because the exchange rate variations can drive his or her operating costs up substantially. There is a level of economic risk associated with the international supply chain transaction that did not previously exist in a strictly domestic supply chain.

Technology—Levels vary significantly from region to region and from country to country.

Quality—The expectations for quality can vary significantly. Germany wants engineering while the United States wants economy.

Financial resources—The financial capability to gear up for increased production demand can affect a supplier's performance.

An example of a global Supply Chain Management process has been included in the discussion of NS, Inc. later in this chapter.

INFORMATION INTEGRATION

As mentioned earlier in this chapter, EDI, as a traditional SCM information integration tool, has been replaced by the Internet. Using the Internet, individuals can now do much of their demand shopping through a computer terminal. For example, if you need a book, you go on the Internet and type "Amazon.com" and you have immediate access to a bookstore that is much more complete than anything available to you by direct shopping. The prices are competitive because they avoid the overhead that a normal bookstore requires. Moreover, they can direct ship the book of your choice to you in only a few days. This does not replace the need for someone to occasionally go to a Barnes and Noble in search of a new book on a subject of interest. Sometimes it is fun to just go shopping. But the Internet saves a tremendous amount of time in the area of demand shopping.

As a consumer, you can purchase products from all over the world through the Internet. You have the ability to access suppliers that had previously been completely out of your reach. You can also evaluate and compare products in ways that had previously been impossible. And you can do it without the cost of travel, sales and marketing costs, and the like.

The retailing benefits are just a small part of the potential benefits of the Internet. In the area of Supply Chain Management, we have already discussed how the Internet allows integrated information access between suppliers, manufacturers, distributors, retailers, and even the end consumer. This information integration opens up a new world of information sharing between these links of the supply chain, which should also build confidence between the various elements.

The Internet does not eliminate the need for internal, intranet systems. Internal production processes still need to be managed using the traditional management tools. These tools need to be carefully evaluated to satisfy the requirements of the local operation. It is the input and output of these internal systems that require access to the Internet for information exchange. For example, a customer's placement of an order would trigger all of the following:

1. Open a purchase requisition at the customer's site.
2. Open a sales order at the retailer's location.
3. Open a purchase requisition at the retailer for a purchase from the manufacturer.
4. Open a sales order at the manufacturer for the retailer's product.
5. Open a shipment requisition with the shipper for the scheduled due date.
6. Open a purchase requisition at the manufacturer for the materials needed to build the product; this could be several requisitions for several sets of materials.
7. Open a work order for the production process to begin when all the materials become available.
8. Open a sales order with each of the respective vendors.
9. Open a shipment requisition for each of the materials to be shipped to the manufacturer.
10. Open a materials requisition at each supplier location for the materials needed at each location.

From this example it is easy to see the interconnectivity that occurs with the placement of an order. All of this information is needed to drive the internal information mechanisms.

RISK MANAGEMENT

The global supply chain transaction requires a great deal of trust—trust in the reliability of the information, trust in the logistics mechanisms, trust in the political stability, trust in the financial mechanisms, as in the exchange rate fluctuations, and so on. This trust is built up over time; it is not automatic. Internationally, we often find that relationships are more important than contractual agreements. In some countries, the spoken agreement is more legally binding than the signed document. Failure in any of these trusts creates transactional risk, and this risk needs to be assessed. Basically, organizations are willing to engage in an entire gradient of risk levels, where they go from Risk Averse to Risk Taking. Generally, the reason for taking on an increased level of risk is for the increased potential level of gain that comes with the risk. In this section I will discuss several areas of risk and how these risks can be managed. However, this discussion is not intended to be a comprehensive discussion of all the elements of risk assessment. That would be a textbook all by itself.

Political risk is assessed and measured in several international data banks. For example, the CIA evaluates the political stability of a country and assigns a risk value to this assessment. Similarly, international monetary organizations such as the World Bank and the IMF (International Monetary Fund) evaluate and assess the financial risk of all the countries in the world. These risk assessment values are extremely valuable in international transactions. But these are the easier risks to assess because we have individuals and organizations developing these assessments for us. It is more difficult to assess the risks associated with markets and their reaction to issues like foreign products, and international trends. For example, there is a defined trend that shows how markets in the United States follow the trends in London, and how Japan follows the trends of the United States. The books by Dent and Naisbitt discuss some of these international market trends. This information can be used to initiate some market planning. However, reactions to your product are often extremely difficult to predict. For example, competitive, government, vendor, or customer reactions have been known to dramatically affect product acceptance. We hear of stories such as the difficulty of selling a very successful American car, the Nova, in Mexico, because, in Spanish the name means "no go." Or the reverse, when a Mexican producer tried to sell a very popular Mexican sandal in the United States, people were offended by the name "Jesus shoe."

The objective of managing risk is to minimize the exposure to unforeseen and unplanned-for risks destroying profitability. If you are a risk-averse organization, you need to minimize all the excessive risk factors. If you are a risk-taking organization, you want to identify and account for as much of the risk as possible so that your financial returns are sufficient to justify the risk taken. The importance of risk and risk assessment strongly affects operational performance and should be carefully considered.

LOGISTICS MANAGEMENT

Logistics management, which includes the transport of goods and the warehousing of them, is an extremely large piece of the Supply Chain Management puzzle. Without the efficient flow of the logistics process, all the gains of manufacturing efficiency are erased. For example, Toyota can manufacture a car in four hours. Then it takes weeks and sometimes months to move the product to the overseas retailer. That is why the flow of this logistics process has become so critical that the supply chain can be ineffective without properly managing it.

Now let us take a look at some of the struggles of an organization that is developing its supply chain.

SUCCESSFUL CHANGE MANAGEMENT

The business functions of an organization have, for a long time, given greater attention to stability than to change. For example, accounting, finance, personnel, the legal department, most upper management, and marketing would love nothing more than to have a steady stable growth. Traditionally, operations loves a perfectly balanced operation with just the right amount of inventory, just the right workforce, and no problems. However, one of the competitive lessons we have learned is that stability breeds failure. If we try to stay where we are, we will get run over. Just ask the American passenger railroads.

Operations has learned the new competitive lesson, which the remaining functional areas are just waking up to:

The only way
    to competitive success,
        Is through
            change management!

The function of the operational organization has changed from one of seeking stability to one of managing change—change in products and their components, change in demand, changes in resources and their availability, changes in operational technology, changes in competitive product makeup, and changes in competition. This is a lesson that needs to be shared with the remainder of the organization.

Continuous improvement (change) is critical in a global economy.[34] Changes should include product innovation, process innovation (what the Japanese are good at), technology innovation, time-to-market innovation (as seen in Taiwan), marketing innovation, and many others.

But uncontrolled and undirected change can be as disastrous as no change. What we need is to be able to stay ahead of the change process; we need to change ourselves faster than external forces have a chance to change us; we need the change to be focused on a target; and we need to maintain our corporate integrity as we institute change.

To manage change we have to incorporate change models into our business which facilitate the change process. Some of these change models, such as Total Quality Management and Process Re-engineering, will be discussed in this chapter. The problem with the change models is that they are often thought of as just another fish story.

Company (and change models)
are like fish—
after three days
they stink.

Most change models contain some label of quality in them. Quality has become the flag behind which the battle for continuous change is most often fought. But "quality" does not fully define everything that the change process entails. Nevertheless, the terms Total Quality Management (TQM), Quality Functional Deployment (QFD), and the like are change processes that appear to focus on quality, but, in reality, like all change models, they focus on positive, goal-directed changes in all the measurement areas, including quality, productivity, efficiency, and financial improvements. In this chapter we discuss and compare several of the "trendy" change models (some are not really change models, even though they get credit for being one). These include Quality Functional Deployment, Total Quality Management, Process Re-engineering, and ISO 9000.

Before we discuss some of the change models specifically, let us first examine some of the psychology behind change.

SOME MODELS FOR CHANGE

Remember the change function shown in Chart 2.6. We start by operating at a steady-state, stable level of operation, and then change is implemented.

---

[34] Kobu, Bulent, and Frank Greenwood, "Continuous Improvement in a Competitive Global Economy," *Production and Inventory Management*, Fourth Quarter, 1991, pp. 58–63.

The level of efficiency drops, and a new learning curve kicks in. The growth stage is the most critical stage because this is the time when many changes are dropped. If the growth stage takes too long, the change may be dropped. This is what has occurred with Florida Power and Light and in many JIT, TQM, or Process Re-engineering implementations. Unfortunately, when a change process is dropped during the growth phase, the organization wastes the growth that has occurred and that would have brought them to a newer, higher level of performance. Most U.S. companies do not want the growth stage to take more than a few months, and often, with larger changes, this short time span is impossible.

Eventually, after the growth has leveled out, we start to see a return on the change process. The final phase of the learning curve has kicked in. Finally, we have once again achieved stability, and hopefully at a higher level of output.

Another model for change shows us as having to work our way through the phases of growth in a change process. They are:

Phase I: Recognize the need for change. Invest in new technology or processes. Motivate innovation and experimentation. Encourage learning about new technologies just for the sake of learning.

Phase II: Learn how to adapt technology beyond the initial sought-after results. Keep the ideas flowing.

Phase III: The organization goes through structural changes as process changes occur.

Phase IV: The broad-based implementation of change occurs, affecting all aspects of the organization.[35]

The Japanese model for the continuous change process is called *Kaizen*. It suggests that every process can and should be continually evaluated and continually improved. The primary focus of the improvements is on waste elimination, for example:

Reducing process time
Reducing the amount of resources used
Improving product quality

Kaizen problem solving involves: (1) observing the situation, (2) defining the changes that need to take place, and (3) making the changes happen. One example of the implementation of the Kaizen continuous improvement process is at the Repair Division of the Marine Corps Logistics Base in Barstow, California.

---

[35]Gibson, Cyrus F., and R. L. Nolan, "Managing the Four Stages of EDP Growth," *Harvard Business Review*, January–February 1974, p. 76.

Utilizing the Kaizen focus on continuous improvement, it ran a pilot project and received results like the following:

63 percent reduction in final assembly lead time
50 percent reduction in work-in-process inventory
83 percent reduction in the distance material traveled
70 percent reduction in shopfloor space requirements[36]

The process and the system which controls it
represent the real problem facing business today, not
the people who work within the boundaries set for
them by management. . . . The improvement efforts
and their supporting systems must be directed at the
process and not the individual.

H. James Harrington[37]

The focus of any change model should be on continuous improvement in the broad sense, which includes both the Japanese incremental step perspective and the U.S. breakthrough business process improvement perspective. The need for change is rarely argued. What is different between the various change models is the speed of the change and the depth at which the change occurs. This is where the Japanese and the U.S. change methods bump heads. Here is a comparison of the two models.

The U.S. model

Fast change
Fast return on investment
Radical and dramatic change
Deep and extensive changes in response to the felt need to redefine the whole process
On the hunt for the one big change that will fix all the problems
Process Re-engineering, which is characterized by rapid/radical changes and focuses on change implementation and high-tech solutions
Slower to get around to making any change because the change process is viewed as being extensive, dramatic, and upsetting. The result is that there is more resistance to any change process.
Change ownership belongs to some change "hero" who quite often is the CEO.

---

[36] Szendel, Timothy N., and Walter Tighe, "Kaizen American-Style, Continuous Improvement in Action," *APICS 37th International Conference Proceedings*, APICS, October 1994, pp. 496–497.
[37] H. James Harrington, Ernst & Young, made a presentation titled "Continuous Improvement or Breakthrough Dilema" in Guatemala in November 1994 where these comments were made.

Implementing and using QFD is not an easy process.
A great deal of commitment throughout the company
is required for the process to be successful. The
results of effective implementation are well worth the
effort. Reduced product development time, increased
flexibility, increased customer satisfaction, and lower
start-up costs are just a few of the benefits that can be
expected through the use of QFD.

Gregg D. Stocker[38]

QFD has been widely recognized as an effective tool for focusing the product and the process on customer satisfaction. A lot has been written on the subject.[39] However, as discussed earlier, QFD is a Japanese approach to change and therefore emphasizes extensive analysis, utilizing the philosophy that we need to:

Make sure we are doing the right things,
Before we worry about doing things right!

Detailed analysis through the matrices is time
consuming, conceptual planning time is much
extended by QFD. However, the overall design-to-
market time should be cut because the design effort
focuses on the most important areas.

Dave Henrickson

TOTAL QUALITY MANAGEMENT (TQM)

Simply put, TQM is a management approach to long-
term customer satisfaction. TQM is based on the
participation of all members of an organization in
improving the processes, products, services and the
culture they work in.

Karen Bemkowski[40]

---

[38] Stocker, Gregg D., "Quality Functional Deployment: Listening to the Voice of the Customer," *APICS 34th International Conference Proceedings*, APICS, October 1991, pp. 258–262.

[39] Another excellent article, like the Stocker article, on the QFD procedures is that by Dave Henrickson, manager of the Western Region, Motorola Education and Training Center. In addition, the Wallace book listed earlier has two sections worth looking at: I-3 "Linking Customer to Strategies via Quality Functional Deployment (QFD)" by Thomas F. Wallace; and II-6 "Quality Functional Deployment: Breakthrough Tool for Product Development" by William Barnard Henrickson, Dave, "Product Design as a Team Sport," *Target*, Spring 1990, pp. 4–12.

[40] Bemkowski, Karen, "The Quality Glossary," *Quality Progress*, February 1992, pp. 19–29.

As mentioned earlier, Total Quality Management (TQM) focuses on careful, thoughtful analysis. However, the analysis should be creative, innovative, and innoveering. The carefulness enters in when it comes time to implement. We want to make sure that we are implementing positive, goal-focused changes before we move a muscle.

TQM is much broader than QFD; TQM is enterprisewide. Some people define it in general terms as simply making the "entire organization responsible for product or service quality." This is the way TQM is defined in many organizations, and it encompasses everything and anything. However, there is also a specific, proceduralistic version of the definition of TQM. Perhaps the best way to understand this change model is to examine this TQM process closely. Afterward we will consider the significance of TQM and its process.

The TQM Process

TQM is not just a tool; it presents an entire philosophy about how businesses should be run. The philosophy of TQM is filled with ideas and attitudes, such as:

Attitude of desiring and searching out change
Think culture—move from copying to innovating
Do the right things before you do things right
Focus on the goal
Measurement/motivation planning
Top to bottom corporate strategy
Companywide involvement
Clear definition and implementation of quality
Education, training, and cross training
Integration and coordination
Small, step-by-step improvements

In TQM, the philosophy behind change is that we become excited about changes. We look for opportunity to change, especially because change should mean that we are becoming better. To be a TQM organization is to become an organization that wants to be the best, and to realize that there is always room for improvement.

TQM's success stories can be found in settings all over the world and are measured in terms of the successful implementation of change. This change can take the form of implementing new technology or correcting and improving old technology. Often, a successful TQM project leads employees to work more effectively together. The result is that the measurement of TQM success tends to be an internal success story, and not always externally comparable.

Success in TQM can be found in large organizations such as PETRONAS, the national petroleum corporation of Malaysia, where TQM implementation is moving forward on a companywide basis. TQM, through its systematic implementation of changes, won the Deming Award, the prestigious Japanese quality award, for Florida Power and Light, a U.S. producer of electricity. TQM is receiving nationwide attention in Mexico through a sponsoring organization, Fundameca, the Mexican national productivity and quality improvement organization. Many other Latin American countries are also placing national attention on TQM implementation: one specific example is Guatemala's II Congreso Nacional Y I Cetroamericano De Calidad Total meeting. Specific individual companies, like Solectron, have had much success with TQM.[41]

Operationalizing TQM involves several points of importance:

The TQM coordinating team (quality council)
The three-"P" teams—cross-functional teams
The TQM project implementation steps
Training programs
Measurement and feedback
Showcasing
Team building
Systematic Problem Solving (SPS)

TQM implementations start with a *coordinating team*, which is often referred to as a quality council. This team is composed of high-level corporate leaders from all functional areas and is appointed by the CEO, operating under his or her direction. The quality council is responsible for organizing and measuring the performance of the other TQM teams within the organization. It oversees the installation, training, performance, and measurement of the other teams and focuses specifically on the corporate goal/vision and definition of quality.

The quality council organizes three different teams referred to as the cross-functional *three-"P" teams*: process, product, and project teams. The process teams are ongoing, continuous-improvement teams set up at different levels of the organization. They look for improvements in the organization's functioning processes. These teams should be made up of both insiders and outsiders: the insiders know and understand existing functions and operations, whereas the outsiders challenge the status quo.

The product teams, though cross-functional, focus on a specific product, product line, or service. They are customer and vendor interface teams that are

---

[41]Ramalingam, P. Rama, "Making TQM Pay Off: The Solectron Experience," *APICS 37th International Conference Proceedings*, November 1994, pp. 472–476; Bao, Quang, and E. B. Baatz, "How Solectron Finally Got in Touch with Its Workers," *Electronic Business*, October 7, 1991; Grant, Linda, "Six Companies That Are Winning the Race," *Los Angeles Times*, January 17, 1993; and "Solectron Corp.," *Business America*, October 21, 1991.

specifically oriented toward developing new products and improving existing ones. Their life span is the same as that of the product they represent.

The third of the three-P teams, the project teams, are limited-life teams set up for a specific project, such as the construction of a new plant or a computer installation. These teams may be the result of a specific process or product that is being targeted, or they may be formed to research something that the general management team wants to develop or improve.

The TQM *project implementation steps* are as follows: identify problems (opportunities); prioritize these problems; select the biggest bang-for-the-buck project; develop an implementation plan; use operations research and MIS tools where appropriate; develop guideposts and an appropriate measurement system; conduct training; carry out implementation; perform feedback—monitoring—control—change; after successful project implementation and ongoing status, repeat cycle.

The first function of any of the three teams is to identify its function and charter. If you are a member of one of these teams, your team's charter is laid out for you by the quality council; if you are the quality council, this charter is laid out for you by the CEO and is aimed at the organization's stated goals. After understanding their charter, the team will then search for and identify problems that exist and that prevent the organization from achieving this charter. The word "problems" has a negative connotation; a better wording would be to say that we search for "opportunities for improvements." We are not just trying to correct negative effects; we are looking for techniques or tools that will allow us to become better and possibly even the best.

Next we take these problems (opportunities) and prioritize them based on their effect on the charter of the team (which should be focused on the goals of the organization). We do a type of ABC analysis (80–20 Rule or Parieto principle) to determine which change would have the greatest effect. Then we select the biggest bang-for-the-buck project and develop an implementation plan for this project. This implementation plan needs to contain guideposts that are based on an appropriate measurement system that points the team toward achieving its charter. The book *Breakthrough Thinking* does an excellent job of discussing opportunity identification techniques.[42]

Training of the implementers and users is critical; otherwise the planned project is doomed to failure. This training makes future users comfortable with the changes. It also offers a bit of ownership since the planned users will now feel comfortable with the changes.

---

[42]Nadler, Gerald, and Shozo Hibino, *Breakthrough Thinking,* Prima Publishing and Communications, Rocklin, CA, 1990. See also Nadler, Gerald, Shozo Hibino, and John Farrell, *Creative Solution Finding*, Prima Publishing and Communications, Rocklin, CA, 1995.

The next step is implementation. The implementation should be a trivial process, if all the planning and training steps are performed carefully. Part of the implementation involves installing feedback, monitoring, and control mechanisms, as laid out in the implementation plan. Careful monitoring allows corrective changes to occur whenever necessary.

After the project has been successfully implemented and the ongoing status of the project is functioning correctly, the team repeats the implementation cycle, looking for other new opportunities for change. If this process is performed correctly, the list of change opportunities should become longer with each iterative cycle. This means that your team is now open for newer and broader opportunities for change.

Training programs need to exist before and after project selection. In the before case, the TQM team needs to understand what tools are available to them. This training involves an understanding of tools and techniques. Initial training could include programs in areas such as operations research/management science tools and techniques, motivational/philosophical training, semitechnical and technical education, the operation of the systems approach, and so on. Training programs instituted after TQM team implementation should be user training focused on the changes being implemented. These programs need to be defined (and often conducted) by the TQM team that has the best understanding of the change.

The issue of *measurement and feedback* has already been discussed several times. It is critical to realize the motivational role of the measurement system and to recognize that the proper implementation of an effective feedback (reporting) mechanism will assure the ongoing success of the changes implemented.

Showcasing is one of the best techniques for expanding implementation time. The quality council can be used to develop and implement a "sure thing" TQM implementation project. We are attempting to demonstrate the successes of an organizationwide TQM implementation. In the United States, where short-term, quick benefits need to be demonstrated, showcasing becomes a critical part of TQM's selling job.

Several types of *teams* are required in a TQM environment—for example, the quality council and the three-P teams. Understanding which teams need to be organized is just a small part of the problem of team construction. A much bigger problem is making the team effective. For example, team training and team relationship building are necessary for effective interaction and for the synergy of the team.

One of the biggest drawbacks of a TQM system, as far as the United States is concerned, is the implementation lead time of changes—that is, how long it takes to implement the change. Often a decision is made to change, but then the worry arises about how to implement the change. *Systematic Problem Solving (SPS)* is a procedurization of the change process. Although there is no one perfect model for how this change procedurization should be set up, a few good examples exist. We will consider three of them here. The first is the one used by Florida Power and Light when it won the Deming Award; the second is the AT&T SPS process; and the third is a generalized SPS model called the T-Model.

Systematic Problem Solving (SPS) at Florida Power and Light

In the Florida Power and Light (FP&L) case, the SPS process it used when it won the Deming Award was referred to as its Quality Improvement Story. This is a series of steps that are standardized and used to organize and document the change process. The steps are as follows:

1. *Team Information.* A Team Project Planning Worksheet is developed which lists the team members, the meeting schedules, and an outline of activities in Gantt Chart format. The Gantt chart lists each of the following "Quality Improvement Story" steps and timelines them.
2. *Reasons for Improvement.* This is a graphic and flowcharted look at why an improvement is desirable. FP&L will analyze which issues are being addressed, and which are not, in light of a specific goal it is trying to achieve. It follows the repeated "Why?" questioning process in order to determine the root problems.
3. *Current Situation.* Here FP&L will apply Parieto principles to focus on the area that will maximize benefits with the least amount of effort. It graphs performance history in order to get a better handle on the problem. It defines targets and goals for the corrective action that is being planned.
4. *Analysis.* Here the primary tools are fishbone (cause-and-effect) diagrams that analyze the possible reasons for the problems being considered. FP&L will develop a Root Cause Verification Matrix in order to verify that it is truly working on the root causes of the problems.
5. *Countermeasures.* Here FP&L will develop a Countermeasures Matrix and an Action Plan. This is when the change takes place.
6. *Results.* FP&L will use Parieto diagrams and Before and After graphs to validate the occurrence of the changes. It uses these to monitor the performance of the implemented changes.
7. *Standardization.* This section establishes a documented procedure for the ongoing operation of the change using graphical and systems flowcharting tools.
8. *Future Plans.* This is a review of what was learned by this change process. It follows a philosophy of Plan–Do–Check–Act.

Plan is what you plan to do with regards to this change in the future. For example, are you going to look for even more improvements?

Do is what will be done next.

Check is a look at what the feedback mechanism will entail. What do you want to watch for?

Act is what action is next to be taken by the team. For example, are we now going to look at the next highest Parieto contributor to improvements?

SYSTEMATIC PROBLEM SOLVING (SPS) AT AT&T

AT&T uses a methodology that includes tasks performed in four distinct stages.

Ownership: Provide team responsibility for the activities

Assessment: Clearly define the process

Opportunity selection: Analyze how process problems affect customer satisfaction and rank them in order of opportunity for improvement

Improvement: Implement and sustain the change

The ownership, assessment, and opportunity selection stages are considered management processes. Then, based on the overall four stages, grouped under management and improvement, AT&T has developed a series of steps called the Management and Improvement steps which focus on the SPS process.

1. Establish process management responsibilities.
2. Define process and identify customer requirements.
3. Define and establish measures.
4. Assess conformance to customer requirements.
5. Investigate process to identify improvement opportunities.
6. Rank improvement opportunities and set objectives.
7. Improve process quality.

Note that the AT&T process follows the Japanese model closely. More detailed information about this process is available through publications issued by AT&T.[43]

---

[43]The following publications and additional information are available from: AT&T's Customer Information Center, Order Entry Department, P.O. Box 19901, Indianapolis, Indiana 46219, 1-800-432-6600. AT&T Bell Laboratories, *AT&T's Total Quality Approach*, Publication Center of AT&T Bell Laboratories, 1992; and AT&T Bell Laboratories, *AT&T Process Quality Management & Improvement Guidelines*, Publication Center of AT&T Bell Laboratories, 1989.

*Quality excellence is the foundation for the
management of our business and the keystone of our
goal of customer satisfaction. It is therefore our
policy to:*
* *Consistently provide products and services
that meet the quality expectations of our customers.*
* *Actively pursue ever-improving quality
through programs that enable each employee to do
his or her job right the first time.*

Robert E. Allen
Chairman and CEO, AT&T

THE T-MODEL

The T-Model is a systemized model for change that has a philosophical as well as a procedural aspect which follows systems analysis principles. Philosophically, this model looks for rapid, continuous improvement, change implementation. Procedurally, the T-Model follows a series of basic rules, or steps:

1. Define area of change.
2. Define the purpose of the change; don't ask why the change should be made and don't do an analysis of the change and its requirements. The purpose of the change needs to be defined first.
3. Evaluate the purpose: does it eliminate waste and improve the value-added component of the product?
4. Define the constraints—environmental, customer, cultural.
5. Evaluate the techniques available for solving the problem.
6. Implement the change.
7. Perform monitoring, feedback, and data collection.
8. Take corrective action—here we are reacting to the feedback. If the feedback is not what we want, then we return to step (2) above and rethink our corrective action.

The T-Model is more general than the Florida Power and Light example because it is not applied to a specific situation. There are no specific tools assigned to each step. However, as the T-Model is applied to a specific example, such as in the FP&L situation, it would become more focused, detailing specific tools and procedures that should be used.[44]

---

[44]Plenert, Gerhard, and Shozo Hibino, "The T-Model: A Systematic Model for Change," *National Productivity Review*, 13, No. 4, Autumn 1994, pp. 543–549.

THE GOOD NEWS ABOUT TQM

TQM marked the first stage in realizing our need to take "quality" (or the search for positive change) out of the quality department and make it a companywide program. TQM is a strategy directed toward continuous, corporatewide change, it is a philosophy, it is an operationalized process, and it is a fad. It becomes a fad if we expect quick results and become disenchanted because we are not "like the Japanese" in the first two months. TQM is a strategy toward becoming leading edge and world class.

TQM differs from the other quality tools TQC, SPC, or ILQC in that it is not as directly focused on a specific procedure. Rather, TQM is a continuous search for problems (opportunities) that eliminate waste and add value in all aspects of the organization. It makes these improvements one small step (5 to 10 percent improvements) at a time.

In spite of its slowness, TQM has been extremely successful internationally and is getting ever-increasing attention. References to TQM and its leadership abound.[45] It is a very specific process improvement step in a drive toward world-class status.

PROCESS RE-ENGINEERING

Wisely, and slowly. They stumble that run fast.

William Shakespeare
Romeo and Juliet

Process Re-engineering (PR) is rapid, radical change. It is not downsizing, which many companies are using it for; rather, it is work elimination. It is positive, growth-focused change, ever seeking opportunities to eliminate waste and improve value-added productivity, often through implementing technology such as image processing.

In 1994, $32 billion was invested in re-engineering, but two-thirds of the re-engineering projects will fail. Why? The primary reason for failure is that the

---

[45]The organizations that I have referenced in previous appendices are filled with publications and conference information that will help you implement a TQM environment. Some additional readings include Costin, Harry, *Readings in Total Quality Management*, Dryden Press, Fort Worth, TX, 1994; Ross, Joel E., *Total Quality Management: Text, Cases, and Readings*, St. Lucie Press, Delray Beach, FL, 1993; Omachonu, Vincent K., *Principles of Total Quality*, St. Lucie Press, Delray Beach, FL, 1994. Articles of interest on TQM include a couple from the Wallace book listed earlier: IV-1 "Total Quality Management (TQM)" by Joseph Colletti and IV-2 "Tools for Total Quality Management (TQM)" by Bill Montgomery.

change process builds up a lot of resistance, thereby forcing its failure. Second, because PR is used as an excuse for downsizing, often the downsizing results in eliminating critical employees who will be difficult to replace. When the downsizing process is rushed through without careful thought the results are disastrous.[46]

However, as is true of any tool, some extremely positive aspects of process re-engineering make it worthy of our attention. PR focuses on change implementation at the top of the corporate hierarchy. It generates more of a top-down change culture, and it focuses on process-oriented changes.

PR's focus on the process emphasizes that the process, not the products, is behind the most dramatic improvements within an organization. PR focuses on an "all-or-nothing proposition that produces impressive results." PR has been defined as the "fundamental rethinking and radical redesign of business processes to achieve dramatic improvements in critical, contemporary measures of performance, such as cost, quality, service, and speed."[47] The principles of re-engineering include the following: organize around outcomes, not tasks; have those who use the output of the process perform the process; subsume information processing work into the real work that produces information; treat geographically dispersed resources as though they were centralized; link parallel activities instead of integrating their results; put the decision point where the work is performed, and build control into the process; capture information once and at the source.

The three R's of re-engineering are:

Rethink: Is what you're doing focused on the customer?
Redesign: What are you doing? Should you be doing it at all? Redesign how
  it can be done.
Re-tool: Reevaluate the use of advanced technologies.

In Process Re-engineering, several jobs are combined into one; workers make the decisions (given them empowerment); job steps evidence a "natural order" sequencing; there are multiple versions of processes depending on the need; work is performed where it makes the most sense; checks and controls are reduced; reconciliation is minimized; an "empowered" customer service representative is established; and hybrid centralized/decentralized organizations are organized.

---

[46]Plenert, Gerhard, "Process Re-Engineering: The Latest Fad Toward Failure," *APICS—The Performance Advantage*, June 1994, pp. 22–24.
[47]Hammer, M., and J. Champy, *Reengineering the Corporation*, Harper Business, New York, 1993.

Like TQM, re-engineering focuses on the team. Departments are replaced by empowered process teams, executives change their role from scorekeeper to leaders, organizational structures become flatter, and managers change from supervisors to coaches.

PR features the following steps or phases in the change management process:

1. Mobilization

   Develop a vision.
   Communicate the vision.
   Identify champions and process owners.
   Assemble the teams.

2. Diagnosis

   Train and educate.
   Perform current process analysis.
   Select and scope the process.
   Understand the current customer.
   Model the process.
   Identify problems.
   Set targets for new designs.

3. Redesign

   Create breakthrough design concepts.
   Redesign the entire system.
   Build prototype.
   Employ information technology.

4. Transition

   Finalize transition design.
   Conduct implementation phase.
   Measure benefits.
   Use communication to avoid resistance.
   You cannot overcommunicate.

PR shares many of TQM's procedural characteristics, but it is more philosophical than TQM. PR focuses on being competitive via the rapid and the radical, and it stresses the process as the key to successful change. Numerous books are available that discuss the PR philosophy. The best is still the original, written by the gurus of Process Re-engineering, Michael Hammer and James Champy. In addition, SME/CASA has issued an excellent booklet focusing on manufacturing processes that can be re-engineered, and *OR/MS Today* has an excellent article that discusses first- and second-generation re-engineering programs.[48]

ISO 9000

The ISO 9000 model is often advertised as a model for change and improvements, but its process tends to focus on stability. The ISO standard was developed in Europe in an attempt to standardize the quality of goods coming into Europe. For many companies the ISO 9000 model appeared to act like a trade barrier in its attempt to keep companies out of Europe. The reason for this impression is that ISO 9000 focuses on quality in the internal process of the organization, ensuring that what was designed is what is actually built. It does not focus on the customer. Nevertheless, the ISO standard has become an international standard for quality and systems performance that many companies are utilizing.

ISO has come to define quality, not change. It is a set of standards for quality based on two main foundations: (1) management responsibility and commitment to quality, which should be expressed in a formal policy statement and implemented through appropriate measures; and (2) a set of requirements that deal with each aspect of company activities and organization that affects quality.[49]

ISO can be used as a standard for improvement, and the ISO quality system requirements can become the focus of change systems. In this way, ISO criteria

---

[48]Hammer, M., and J. Champy, "The Promise of Reengineering," *Fortune*, May 3, 1993, pp. 94–97; Hammer, M., "Reengineering Work: Don't Automate, Obliterate," *Harvard Business Review*, July–August 1990, pp. 104–112; Jason, R., "How Reengineering Transforms Organizations to Satisfy Customers," *National Productivity Review*, Winter 1992, pp. 45–53; Marks, Peter, *Process Reengineeering and the New Manufacturing Enterprise Wheel: 15 Processes for Competitive Advantage*, CASA/SME Technical Forum, Society of Manufacturing Engineers (SME), Dearborn, MI, 1994; Harbour, Jerry L., *The Process Reengineering Workbook: Practical Steps to Working Faster and Smarter Through Process Improvement*, Quality Resources, White Plains, NY, 1994; Cypress, Harold L., "Re-engineering," *OR/MS Today*, February 1994, pp. 18–29; Ravikumar, Ravi, "Business Process Reengineering — Making the Transition," *APICS 37th Annual International Conference Proceedings*, APICS, October 1994, pp. 17–21; Miller, George, "Reengineering: 40 Useful Hints," *APICS 37th Annual International Conference Proceedings*, APICS, October 1994, pp. 22–26; Melnyk, Steven A., and William R. Wassweiler, "Business Process Reengineering: Understanding the Process, Responding to the Right Needs," *APICS 37th Annual International Conference Proceedings*, APICS, October 1994, pp. 115–120; Boyer, John E., "Reengineering Office Processes," *APICS 37th Annual International Conference Proceedings*, APICS, October 1994, pp. 522–526; Stevens, Mark, "Reengineering the Manufacturing Company: 'New Fad or for Real'," *APICS 37th Annual International Conference Proceedings*, APICS, October 1994, pp. 527–530.

[49]The Wallace book mentioned earlier contains an article by Robert L. Jones and Joseph R. Tunner titled "ISO 9000: The International Standard for Quality." ISO information can be obtained from any of the quality and productivity organizations mentioned in earlier chapters. The ISO organization, International Organization for Standardization, is located in Geneva, Switzerland.

can be integrated into a change process. However, in and of itself, ISO is not a change model, as is frequently believed.

NS, INC.—A GLOBAL SUPPLY CHAIN NIGHTMARE

NS, Inc., a health food supplement company located in Provo, Utah, conducts international research into natural substances that have medicinal properties. It packages these substances into pills and capsules, and sells them over the counter at health food stores. It initially limited its market to the Utah area but quickly spread sales all across the United States and Canada. In its early stages, NS dealt mainly with products that utilized domestically available materials. However, it soon found that in order to complete its product line it needed to source herbs and plants from all over the world. It therefore searched for international producers throughout Asia and Latin America and in many cases found that it needed to develop its own suppliers. It contracted with growers for its entire crops several years in advance just to lock up the availability of the plants. This made NS not just a producer, but also an agricultural manager of the harvest. If the harvest fell short, it would need to find additional sourcing. If the harvest overproduced, it would find itself purchasing products that were not needed. NS found it necessary to make a variety of arrangements with these growers. For example, some growers wanted to get a base value for their crops, plus extra if they overproduced, whereas other farmers wanted a fixed price regardless of the output. This concerned NS because it could not be assured that the farmer would put as much effort into the crop if it was already sold. In addition, NS had to deal with the risks of government regulatory changes, where taxes and tariffs could be changed after commitment to the product prices had already been made. Risk management became a critical part of the supplier management process. In addition, exchange rate fluctuations would often increase the cost of the initial arrangement, since most of the farmer contracts needed to be negotiated in local currencies.

NS experienced many of the struggles associated with Supply Chain Management, but found that it lacked information integration. Many of the farmers NS worked with had never even seen, let alone used, a computer. Therefore, it became necessary for someone to visit the various farms to evaluate the anticipated levels of crop output. This required travel and transportation costs and became quite expensive. However, NS felt that it could not rely on local sources for evaluating the crop outputs. Next came the issue of product movement through the logistics process. The infrastructure was often inadequate, often requiring days, weeks, and months to get the product to the plant in Utah.

As NS grew, extensive international interest in its products developed. The company opened up the European marketplace, after complying with the ISO requirements. Success in Europe led to a move into Latin America and many Asian countries, there by opening an entirely new can of worms in the supply chain process. For example, should NS use distributors who would purchase the product from NS and then resell the product? This would eliminate many of the supply chain issues and greatly simplify NS's involvement. However, this would also consume a large portion of the margin that NS was hoping to earn. In addition, the capital investment in trucks and the like forced many distributors to go in and out of business fairly quickly. If a truck broke down, a distributor could be out of business for quite some time until it found the capital to make the necessary repairs. As another alternative, NS could deal directly with the retail outlets, but to do that NS would need to establish its own distribution supply chain within each country. In some countries, Singapore, for example, this was fairly easy to do, but in countries such as China, it was much more difficult. In addition, the international transaction risks became more complicated as NS became more involved in directly managing the vertically integrated process. Maintaining financial returns could not be assured since NS was entering into new, unproven market areas and the risk of failure could be quite high.

Certification of a medicinal product also became an issue in many countries whose legal requirements forced extensive documentation of the process, even more so than was required by ISO certification. Often, localized chemical testing was required to certify the contents of the pills.

Here is the challenge for the reader. What would you do? Would you go for the low margins of distributor relationships, or would you attempt to manage the vertical supply chain yourself? And how about the farmers? Would you trust the locals to evaluate the farm production? What would change in their current operations?

SUPPLY CHAIN TECHNOLOGY TRANSFER TO THIRD WORLD COUNTRIES

Now we will consider some of the specific issues associated with technology transfer supply chain strategies in developing country settings. Numerous lessons can be learned from these countries. For example, why do Western production planning and control systems, including information systems such as MRP and JIT, enjoy little or no success in Third World countries? Haven't we in the West already learned the best methods of production control? Shouldn't these same control systems be transferable to factories in other countries? We need to discuss the key differences that exist in installing production planning systems in developing environments and to explore what these experiences teach Western manufacturers about their plants.

Western countries are failing in their factory implementations in Third World countries. Developing environments cannot seem to understand that "profits" are the key to success—or are they? Production control methodologies that seem to be effective in the United States, Japan, or Europe have been disappointing. The search for the reasons behind this phenomenon has involved studies in numerous countries and factories. The problems revolve around several key differences:

1. Goals
2. Data/information obsession
3. Goal communication
4. Resource planning

What we learned from our visits to developing countries came back to haunt us at home. Many of our own inefficiencies are simply magnified when we view them in these Third World environments.

GOALS

When we study developing countries, we quickly find that financial goals are strictly a phenomenon of the United States, Canada, and Europe. Even Japan does not believe in financial goals; in Japan the primary goal is employee job security. Other countries stress the goal of customer satisfaction. In developing countries the goals often revolve around (1) full employment, (2) improved balance of trade, (3) improved throughput, and (4) technological independence. These countries consider these four goals much more important than the profitability of one organization. A Western manager will often ask, "How can a company survive if it loses money?" It cannot do so, any more than a company that has profit as its primary goal can survive by beating up its employees. The important question here is "What is the Primary Goal?" The United States is by far in the minority in its financial focus; only a few selected companies, primarily found to be the Baldridge, Shingo, or NASA award winners, have moved successfully in new directions.

DATA/INFORMATION OBSESSION

The standard answer for academics and consultants who do not know how to approach and deal with a particular production problem is to declare that not enough "data" exists to properly define and solve the problem. If only they had enough "information." The result is that management installs several additional staff functions and adds more computing systems in an attempt to come up with this magical answer. Unfortunately, this simply builds an unnecessary level of complexity into the operation. Additional data is not the answer; focused data is! Focused data is data collected only from those areas that will help the organization operate better.

The obsession with data collection accompanies another enormous hazard. It sends a false message to the employees of the company. Employees assume that whatever areas data is being collected from must be important to the management of the company.

GOAL COMMUNICATION

I asked the managers of several factories I visited how they communicated their goals to employees. They talked about newsletters and memos. Then I asked them what their measurement system on the factory floor contained. They talked about job sheets that recorded labor start and stop times and compared them to labor standards that measured efficiencies. I then asked them if they felt that the plant's goals were in harmony at the operational and strategic levels. They looked at me as though I were speaking a foreign language. So I reworded the question: "Do you feel that by making your employees more efficient at the expense of stockpiling inventory at each workstation you will in fact improve profitability?" They answered, "Of course." Not only was that the wrong answer, but they were not getting the whole message. What I was trying to stress was that the plant should not measure employee efficiency unless this measure helped it achieve its goals. By measuring employee efficiencies, they were sending a message to their employees about what was important to management: that they should be labor efficient no matter the cost, because that was what they were being evaluated on. Chapter 4 will discuss measures and motivation in more detail.

I helped install a production control system in Mexico for a U.S. manufacturer. At that time both the Mexican national goal and the plant goal was full employment. Yet the company wanted to install a production control system based on labor efficiency. Why would one want to be concerned about labor efficiency when the national goal was to hire as many employees as possible, regardless of the labor efficiency level? Fortunately, this company is no longer under U.S. influence and has removed this contradiction. Expecting employees to work toward the goals of the company and then (1) giving them too many and often conflicting goals; (2) not communicating the goals to them at all; and (3) sending improper messages by focusing on unrelated resources is like expecting them to use one arrow to hit several targets at once and then blindfolding them for added fun.

RESOURCE LEARNING

We run our factories as if only two resources were of any importance: labor and materials. Everything else is pigeonholed into something called *overhead*. In reality, labor is often less than 10 percent of the value-added cost component of the products we manufacture. Materials are typically between 30 and 60 percent. Overhead is left with from 30 to as much as 80 percent of the value-added cost component. If the goal of our factory is profitability, would it seem more reasonable to strive for a 10 percent improvement in labor or in overhead? Overhead is the answer, of course. Then why do Western production control systems like MRP still emphasize labor efficiency measurements? We are not focusing on the most critical resource.

We find that Third World countries need to prioritize their resources, categorizing them by their effect on their primary goal. Then they build the appropriate control systems around that goal. For example, if the goal is to improve the balance of trade, the primary control resource may be to focus on reducing imported materials.

Developing environments cannot afford to be as trendy as the United States. They can ill afford to jump from one three-lettered fad, such as TQC (Total Quality Control) or TQM (Total Quality Management) or JIT (Just in Time) or MRP II (Manufacturing Resource Planning) or ABC (Activity-Based Costing) or CIM (Computer Integrated Manufacturing) to another every other year. For this reason, focusing on resource and data collection becomes even more important for them.

A multitude of production planning and control systems focus on optimizing a specific resource. For example, MRP (Material Requirements Planning) is almost always used as a labor efficiency measurement tool through its use of labor-based routings and industrial engineering-generated labor standards. This labor efficiency is achieved at the expense of stockpiled materials in front of each workstation and machinery standing idle. JIT (Just in Time) production control methods out of Japan have changed that focus to emphasize materials efficiency at the expense of labor or machinery efficiency. OPT (Optimized Production Technology) from Israel focuses on machine efficiency. And the list goes on. However, it is important to realize that specific resource-oriented production planning control systems exist, and if they do not exist, then modifications to systems like MRP can be made to change the resource focus.

WHAT'S THE BEST WAY?

Up to now, this discussion has demonstrated that there is not one best way to manage an organization or run a factory. We should realize that the United States' labor-oriented method of management is in fact inappropriate in many instances. In developing countries, where we often have problems of high unemployment, labor efficiency is near the bottom of the priority list. A lack of jobs is a prevalent situation, and this encourages make-work environments throughout the country.

Most production systems outside the United States do not fall into the U.S. or Japanese models. Most developing countries have specific problems that they must resolve, such as space restrictions, untrained workforces, or distribution restrictions. Often, simply obtaining electricity or installing a telephone system may require years.

To enable us to better understand some of the difficulties that exist in developing countries, I will review two specific examples, one in Mexico and one in Indonesia. These will highlight a few of the problems that developing countries have in their factories, such as differences in system installations, technology transfer, production methodologies, production objectives, logistics problems, and communications.

T IN Q, MEXICO[50]

The city Q is the home of T and is a major industrial city north of Mexico City. T is a division of a major U.S. manufacturer that employs approximately 6,000 people. It is a discrete manufacturer (both fabrication and assembly) of transmissions for automobiles, buses, and small trucks. It also has a small satellite facility a few blocks away that produces forklifts and front-end loaders.

The top levels of management at T are primarily U.S. citizens. The second and third levels of management are, for the most part, Mexicans trained in the United States or heavily indoctrinated in the U.S. way of doing things. In addition, there always seems to be a sufficient number of U.S. "advisers" sent by either the home office or one of the U.S. automobile manufacturers. These advisers work on the factory floor and try to keep production running smoothly.

The workforce on the factory floor is largely unskilled. The average employee even has difficulty filling out his or her time sheet. Most of the production that is scheduled is done by the expediting method, which means it is not scheduled at all. Management has tried to implement educational programs and even has a staff of full-time instructors and classrooms, but the need for a more complete education of the workforce far exceeds the capacity of these facilities.

An adversarial relationship has developed between the average worker and the rich Mexican boss. The average worker also resents the non-Mexican who has

---

[50]The next two international cases were taken from the author's book: *International Operations Management.* This book offers an extensive expansion of the fundamental SCM concepts.

(followed by work-in-process and then finished goods). If inventory must be stored, it should be stored as cheaply as possible—as raw materials.

In machinery, we have already established that T should avoid automation. We also recognize the need for scavenging as a means of keeping needed equipment in operable condition. Although this system seems foolish to the typical U.S. manager, let us consider its advantages:

1. The employee knows where to find the part without a lengthy catalog search.
2. The employee can see how it is supposed to look and how it should fit into the machine.
3. The equipment used is generally old and was most likely purchased second-hand from the United States. Keeping an extra machine strictly for spare parts may not be too costly.
4. Very few individuals are needed with the ability to order spare parts. These individuals would spend their time rebuilding the "spare parts" machines after pieces have been taken out. Ordering parts is much easier since you now have a machine to look at. The pressure to get the machine operational is off since it is only a spare parts machine.

Which of the three areas of emphasis (materials, labor, and machinery), is the most critical to manage in the T environment? Not labor, since to have excess labor is advantageous and fits the goals of both the company and the country. Not machinery, since having extra spare parts machines is also advantageous. However, inventory is costly because of high interest rates, and currently, inventory levels are out-of-hand. Several inventory-oriented management systems exist, like JIT, and any one of them would offer better production management than what T is now experiencing.

N IN B, INDONESIA

B is a city on the island of Java in Indonesia. It is the home of N, a military aircraft manufacturing facility. N is a discrete manufacturer involved primarily in assembly, with plans to expand the level of vertical integration to include the fabrication of all necessary components.

The top levels of management are primarily foreign-trained, with many of them holding Ph.D. degrees from major universities in the United States. The workforce is largely unskilled and uneducated, but the relationship between the employer and employee is much closer than that in the Mexican facility. The labor force is easier to manage than that of T.

Problems similar to those of T are found in the source and quality of raw materials. The infrastructure problems are even worse than those of T because good roads are practically nonexistent in Indonesia. Tanks as well as cars and trucks share those that do exist.

The market for N's products—small planes and helicopters—is entirely within Indonesia. N hopes to produce parts for foreign markets, such as Boeing in the future.

At N, an interesting conflict in technology and labor force utilization has arisen. N wants to do sophisticated design work, yet the majority of its labor force has a limited ability to read and write. The primary national goal in Indonesia, as in Mexico, is full employment, and automation would defeat this objective. Indonesia has a very limited, highly trained technical workforce, but the abilities of these technicians need to be increased with advanced technology. The solution appears to require the introduction of high-tech disciplines such as CAD (computer-aided design) along with as *little* automation as possible in the production area.

With regard to the management of labor, materials, and machinery, many of the same conclusions can be reached as with T. However, the spread between the educational levels of the employees and management is much broader. So, an educational program for the employees must be more extensive.

A management system installed here would also have to consider the infrastructure problems more so than at T. These will have a significant effect on lead times.

Both T and N are examples of the types of management problems encountered in industry in a developing country. They provide examples of how the international manager involved with such situations needs to resolve management problems differently than in a U.S. environment.

SOME ADDITIONAL THOUGHTS

In developing countries, manufacturing facilities such as T and N need to establish company goals and objectives before a management or production control system is selected. For example, the United States assumes that its "get rich" philosophy appeals to everyone, whereas in the case of T, family time is more important than money. Consideration needs to be given to a number of factors, including

1. Location of plant
2. Resource differences
   - Energy
   - Land availability
   - Infrastructure

3. Market differences
   - Traveling distances
   - Tariffs and quotas
4. Management expertise
5. Economic potential
   - Country
   - Company
6. Workforce
   - Education
   - Motivation
   - Goals
7. Availability of machinery
   - Levels of automation
8. Inventory
   - Problems with inventory sources
   - Lead times
   - Financing costs
9. National goals and guidelines

For example, in reference to N, the problem of blending high-tech engineering, no factory-floor automation, and an excess workforce that is idle much of the time frustrates traditional production management philosophies. However, this is necessary when trying to satisfy the goals of the nation as well as those of the company.

Once we have evaluated the climate of a particular production or management environment, how do we develop an appropriate system? A unique system can be developed for each new environment, but this approach is not always practical. However, if we realize that every country of the world was a developing country at some time, then we see that it is appropriate to look at countries that have already developed production systems under conditions similar to the country under study. (This should be one of the primary applications of this book.)

Referring again to N or T, we see the need for a management and production planning and control system that will work under conditions of:

For T
   - No factory-floor automation
   - Limited paperwork
   - High worker–manager interface
   - Overemployment
   - A restrictive union

For N
- Poor infrastructure
- High technology in engineering
- No factory-floor automation
- Limited paperwork
- High worker–manager interface

By looking for a management system that satisfies these and other needs, a smoother-operating, more effective plant will be the result.

For developing countries, a few additional considerations should be mentioned. (Some were evident in the T and N examples.) Governmental relations are critical. Investigate the structure and procedures within the "system." It is important to work with the systems and not fight with the individuals in power. They should be given the respect that is due them. If you treat them as bureaucratic nuisances, they will recognize your attitude and treat you accordingly.

Border-crossing considerations are important in materials sourcing and product shipments. The distribution process is often critical to the product's effectiveness. In addition, acquiring spare parts will be important in keeping machinery operational.

Search for local trends and attitudes and maintain harmony with them. One good way of doing so is by utilizing as few "foreigners" as possible in the factory. Foreigners are often considered intruders. When they are brought in, they should always have a local "adviser" on hand to make sure that consistency with local thought and traditions are maintained. The Japanese follow this policy when they install a factory in the United States, an environment with which they are familiar.

Find technology that is "appropriate" for the local environment, not technology that is "familiar" to the manager. This includes management methods, production methods, and the types of machines that are selected. Work within the limitations of the assumptions that have been established.

Develop appropriate measures of performance. Measure those areas that will motivate the labor force using their own goals and standards, not ours.

Individual performance standards are degrading and humiliating to many cultures, and only help to alienate workers. Team or companywide performance standards may be much more effective. In addition, the front-office, authoritarian-management style tends to alienate. A more participative, involved, walk-around management style develops a relationship between the employer and employee. The visibility of management is important in many cultures, even if it seems like a waste of time to the managers; it builds a binding and lasting relationship and will help to avoid confrontations.

The amount of time the employee of a developing country facility should spend in training will typically be much larger than that of his U.S. counterpart. Several months per year is not uncommon. This training should include areas that reach far beyond the scope of the company itself, such as personal health, first aid, construction skills, living skills, cooking, sewing, sanitation systems, and water purification. The training process will also help in the evaluation and selection of individuals who are natural leaders and who should be used as foremen and supervisors in the plant.

The book *Small Is Beautiful* by E. F. Schumacher (Perennial Library, 1975) is valuable reading, providing a clear perspective of how a developing country perceives the United States. The only image many workers have of the United States comes from television shows such as *Dallas, Knots Landing*, and Clint Eastwood's Dirty Harry movies. A better understanding of their view of the United States can only help in the development of good relationships.

All countries are not alike. Many of the basic assumptions about management styles and techniques are not transferable primarily because the management personnel sent to foreign operations are not up to par with their U.S. counterparts. They know what the home office wants and how to run the operations, but they lack familiarity with the details and may not have anyone whom they can telephone to help them out. So, they do the best they can.

In summary, the basic assumptions through which we develop a Supply Chain Management or production system for a particular country will rarely fit the U.S. model. We must look for more flexible methods in order to find solutions that will be more appropriate than those we have at home. We must be receptive to systems that can be adapted to these environments. Only by utilizing more appropriate systems will the host population, management, and production facility be able to maximize their benefits.

The key to working with Third World environments is simplicity—getting back to the basics. We need to set a goal, define the resources that are the most critical to the achievement of that goal, and then build a production planning and control data collection system around that goal. The data collection system will then monitor the success of the company in achieving its goal. It also transmits a message to the employees about the most important area of control for management. Often, as in the case of JIT, this data collection and control process does not require any type of computer at all.

The development of an international Supply Chain Management structure is focused on the integration; this can be challenging. Many elements of an international supply chain are managed quite differently than a domestic supply chain, and this chapter has attempted to demonstrate many of these differences. Because of these differences, the supply chain becomes even more challenging to construct. Distribution networks are managed differently, facilities are managed differently, and resources are managed differently. In spite of these differences, the effective management of an international supply chain can be performance responsive and cost effective.

SUMMARY

Supply Chain Management is the optimized operation of the supply chain. It requires someone who can optimize the resources while at the same time interacting with the forces that cause pressures against the supply chain. It requires someone who can develop a strategic plan for continuous optimization and improvement. It requires a supply chain manager.

So what is a supply chain manager? This individual is someone who can identify the critical resources that move through the supply chain; someone who can identify the forces that come into play and that affect the performance of these resources; and someone who can use this information to develop goals, objectives, and a strategy around which to optimize the flow of the supply chain. This sounds like a big task, and it is. But numerous tools are available to help you with this task, and as we move forward we will learn more about these tools.

REFERENCES

Burt, David, Donald Dobler, and Steven Starling. *World Class Supply Management*[sm]. 7th ed. New York: McGraw-Hill Irwin, 2003.

Plenert, Gerhard. *International Operations Management*. Copenhagen Business School Press, Copenhagen, Denmark, 2002. Reprinted in India by Ane Books, New Delhi, 2003.

Plenert, Gerhard. *Plant Operations Deskbook*. Homewood, IL: Business 1 Irwin, 1993.

Plenert, Gerhard. *The SCM Manager: Value Chain Management in an eCommerce World*. Los Angeles, CA: Blackhall Publishing, 2001.

Semler, Ricardo. *Maverick; The Success Story Behind the World's Most Unusual Workplace*. New York: Warner Books, 1993.

Chapter 3

What Are the Tools of Supply Chain Management (SCM)?

It isn't the technology that requires a change in process. It's the fact that a change in process itself is tough for organizations to deal with. If you want people to work more effectively together, you should first ask, "What's the process I'm trying to change?" not "What technology should I introduce?" Think first about how you want people to organize, then what technology is best to bring them together, as opposed to the other way around.

Ray Ozzie, CTO, Microsoft[1]

MEETING PPI, INC.

PPI, Inc. is a California-based high-tech plastics manufacturer that produces printed plastic that lights up. For example, signage and automotive dashboards have traditionally been clear plastic with backlighting behind it. In the PPI product, the lighting is built right into the plastic. It is actually part of the printed plastic, and it requires a minimal amount of low-voltage electricity. PPI's vision is to be able to put battery-powered signage in locations, such as in large department stores or on grocery store shelves, where "plug-ins" are inconvenient.

PPI's supply chain starts with its sourcing of colored inks and plastics and ends with the end customer that uses the product. The sourcing side of the supply chain has problems with product and schedule consistency. The arrival times of the product are often intermittent; the plastics quality is seldom consistent, and the colors are not always precisely the same from batch to batch.

Internally, PPI also has struggles that affect its supply chain. The product defect rate is over 14 percent. Customer on-time delivery is poor, and finished goods inventory is quite high. Often, PPI will produce a product that has not yet

---

[1]Barney, Doug, "Getting Close to Suppliers—The Human Factor," CSCO, August 2005, p. 30.

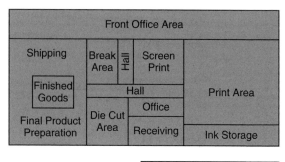

Chart 3.1 PPI Facilities Layout

been sold; this allows PPI to have larger batch runs of a product it feels will probably be sold in the future. As a result, a lot of money is tied up in finished goods inventory, a significant part of which will become obsolete.

The layout of the PPI operation is shown in Chart 3.1. Here we see several production processes, including the printing process (there are several printing presses and a couple of drying lines in this area), the die-cutting process (the plastic sheet may have several prints per sheet, and they need to be cut to size), and the final product preparation, which includes the trimming of fringe areas and may include some assembly.

The materials flow for PPI, presented in Chart 3.2, shows how the plastic, ink, and screens come together in the print room to create a printed product. The

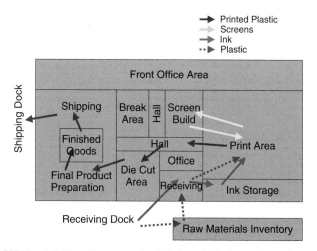

Chart 3.2 PPI Materials Flow. For a more detailed view of this figure, please visit our companion site at: http://books.elsevier.com/companions/0123705177

printing process requires numerous layers, some for the electronics and one for each of the colors being printed. This is a very precise process and requires a high level of expertise so that the lighting and the appropriate colors all come together as desired. The printed plastic is then taken to the die-cut area where the individual parts are cut to size. Then the pieces are taken to the final preparation area where electronic connections, testing, and trimming occur, depending on the part being produced.

Disruptions to the supply chain can occur via any of the suppliers, via the shipper, or internal to PPI's operations. But it is the poor quality and poor on-time delivery performance that has PPI worried. It fears the loss of several key customers if these issues cannot be resolved soon. What would you suggest? What options are available? Now it's your turn to get creative and search for ideas. We will be revisiting PPI later in the book to monitor its progress and changes. For now, let us see what tools are available to the SCM user to determine whether any would apply to PPI. Later we will learn that there are a lot of Lean tools that will also help PPI improve its processes.

SCM TOOLS

Before we address the specific tools that are available in an SCM environment, let us group them into categories. We will take our starting point from the last chapter where we listed the academic competency areas specific to an SCM manager. Using these same categories, we will start with the functional competencies:

Functional Competencies

1. *Supply Management.* Supply management relates specifically to managing vendors that produce the materials and to the shipping network that delivers the product. (The following explanations are extremely brief; entire books have been written on many of these subjects. Each tool requires a complete understanding in order to be optimally utilized). Tools for supply management include:

   a. *Requirement Generation.* Based on the production needs of our organization, we need to generate materials and shipping requirements. Our internal operations systems should have generated a complete list of all requirements, and we now need a system to break this list down by vendor source. Then we supply the customized list of requirements for each vendor.

b. *Strategic Sourcing.* The organization needs a sourcing plan that includes a methodology for identifying and selecting the most appropriate vendors. The selection process may include measures such as cost, quality, on-time delivery, and historical performance.

c. *Global Sourcing.* If the strategic sourcing plan suggests international sources, then a global sourcing plan is needed. This would require considerations such as tariffs, border-crossing delays, exchange rate fluctuations, and risk assessment.

d. *Cost and Price Analysis.* Numerous tools exist that would facilitate the analysis of cost and price performance for each vendor. These tools are critical in helping you achieve a strategic sourcing plan.

e. *Negotiations.* Negotiations is the art of getting the best deal while at the same time generating a win-win relationship with your vendors. This tool requires training and practice.

f. *Value Analysis and Engineering.* Developing a product configuration that optimizes the talents of both your internal resources and your vendor resources is an art. Far too much engineering is performed based on what is easy for the engineer rather than on what is easy to produce and what is the most cost-effective from the supplier. Value engineering requires an integrated supplier relationship so that developed product value can be engineered throughout the supply chain. Numerous tools exist that will facilitate an analysis of the optimal product design. These tools will focus on utilizing the core competencies of both the internal organization and the suppliers. These analysis tools are known as value analysis.

g. *Relationship Management.* Relationship management is also an art. Buyers need to be trained in how best to work with suppliers. In addition, tools exist that monitor the performance of suppliers. These evaluation tools are valuable for both the organization and the vendor. They help everyone stay on top of potential problems and help track performance history.

h. *Subcontract Administration.* Buyers need to have a tool that will facilitate the creation of the contract and then the monitoring of contractor performance. They need to be able to answer questions such as: Are the vendors adhering to the terms of the contract? What is the term (length) of the contract?

i. *Supplier Development.* Often the ideal supplier does not exist. So our organization finds itself in the position of settling for a less than desirable vendor. This is often true in the area of inventory or capacity information exchange and may also be true in the area of engineering capabilities. Supplier development is where the organization takes it upon itself to help the vendor increase its technological or administrative capabilities so that it can meet the organization's needs.

2. *Operations.* Operations is an internal-to-the-organization focus on those elements that affect the supply chain. There are tools that will help the organization to increase performance and to run more efficiently. Most of these tools are transferable to the remainder of the supply chain. However, if the organization does not know how to use and apply these tools internally, then it will not be capable of sharing any of this knowledge throughout the supply chain.

   a. *Systems Evaluation.* The systems evaluation tool helps us view the entire organization, and ultimately the entire supply chain, as an integrated system. Tools for charting and mapping the system, such as flowcharting, Spaghetti charting, and Value Stream Mapping, are designed to take a big-picture look at the overall flow of the system, as well as highlight specific step-by-step performance failures. These tools focus on the materials flow (Value Stream Mapping — a Lean tool), the people flow (Spaghetti charting — another Lean tool), and the information or money flow (flowcharting), thereby providing an analysis of each of the key Supply Chain Management resource flows that we discussed in Chapter 1.

   b. *Process Modeling.* Numerous excellent simulation tools (e.g., Extend) allow the user to create a model of each step within a production, service, or supply chain process. The model permits the specification of arrival rates, process times and their variability, flows, overlaps, and so on. The user can then run the simulation and watch what will happen during the process. It allows the monitoring of bottlenecks, surges, and flow discrepancies, and it calculates cycle times and inventory levels. This is an excellent tool for the design or the redesign of any operation or supply chain.

   c. *Productivity.* Productivity is measured as output divided by input. The measurement of productivity is valuable for internal and external benchmarking. Internal benchmarking is where we measure our performance over time to see if we are getting any better; external benchmarking is where we measure our performance against other companies within our industry. All of these measures can help us to better understand our competitive stance and identify opportunities for performance improvement.

   d. *Quality.* Quality has about as many definitions as there are people in the world, but the only definition that really matters is the one that the customer applies to your product. If the customer considers your product to be a quality product, then it is a quality product, regardless of what your internal definitions indicate or what your suppliers' definition is. Therefore, a methodology is needed that helps the organization understand the customers' definition of quality and then perform to that definition.

e. *Planning Systems.* A planning system includes two key elements; customer orders and forecast projects. These two elements generate the productive requirements for the organization from which all the demands on resources can be generated. This process is referred to as Aggregate Production Scheduling (APS). A good planning system will balance these requirements against available capacities in each resource area, often referred to as Rough Cut Capacity (RCC). Often this tool is only used internal to the organization, but it can be invaluable in planning the entire supply chain. Once the APS is in place, it is balanced against the RCC to create a Master Production Schedule (MPS), which is a list of all the finished goods required by the organization. The MPS is normally processed through an MRP (Material Requirements Planning) or MRP II (Manufacturing Resources Planning) system to generate component parts materials and labor requirements so that the necessary end items can be produced on schedule. These MRP reports are sent to the production floor and to the vendors.

f. *Scheduling Systems.* The scheduling system is used to monitor the day-to-day movement of materials and information through the production and delivery process. This tool tracks the performance of the schedule against the MRP plan that was generated by the planning system and identifies work disruptions and bottlenecks. The optimal tools for this process include Finite Capacity Scheduling (FCS) and/or Advanced Planning and Scheduling (APS). This subject is still fairly new, and most ERP systems do not contain FCS modules. However, the "Oliver Wight" definitional book on the subject is *Finite Capacity Scheduling.*

g. *Forecasting.* A forecasting system can be quite complex and requires interfacing with customers to identify a projection of their future requirements. It also requires a detailed look at historical performance. With this data, a projection can be made of the anticipated future demand for end items. This then becomes one of the two key elements of the planning system.

h. *Lean/Six Sigma.* Lean and Six Sigma are Change Management processes that "lean out" or remove all the waste from an existing process. Waste can take the form of excess inventories, excess travel times, non–value-added steps in the production process, and excessive wait times. Six Sigma specifically focuses on quality improvement through failure rate reduction. It attempts to eliminate the "waste" of producing bad parts. These tools originated with the Toyota Production System and have become key competitive tools throughout the rest of the world.

i. *JIT.* The Just-in-Time (JIT) production process is the Western name given to the Toyota Production System. JIT focuses on minimizing the flow time or cycle time of a process by reducing the delays in the process, primarily those caused by excessive inventory buildups. JIT combines scheduling philosophies with Lean methodologies to dramatically increase throughput within an organization.

j. *ERP.* Enterprise Resources Planning (ERP) takes the planning process one level higher to integrate other organizational elements (such as financial planning, accounting, human resources planning, and engineering) into the production planning process. An ERP system based on a supply chain — for example, SAP, Manugistics, and i2 — integrates all of an organization's systems and creates a database that will allow information sharing across organizations. Again, even though ERP is currently used primarily as an internal planning system, it is a tool with enormous potential in optimizing the overall supply chain. It can be used to integrate the ERP systems of the vendors and customers with those of your organization. An example of a web-based ERP integrator is World Chain.[2]

k. *Inventory Systems.* Inventory management is a basic tool required by every organization. However, there are numerous ways to manage inventory, some of which are not very optimal and which work best for specific types of organizations. It is important to make sure that each organization is utilizing the type of inventory planning and control system that fits it best.

l. *Measures/Motivation.* Appropriate measurement systems can mean the success or the failure of an organization. Measurement systems should never be established to satisfy an accounting need. This is because as soon as a measurement system is installed, the employees treat it as the focus of their efforts and then attempt to optimize these numbers. If these measures are not the ones that would achieve the company's goals, then they are motivating the wrong response from the employees. There are numerous cases of companies that run themselves into bankruptcy because they were motivating the wrong employee responses with their measurement system. The books, *The eManager* or *International Operations Management* (see References), tell numerous stories of these types of failures.

m. *Technology.* Technological advances are continuously improving the performance of operations management and control systems. For example, bar coding significantly reduced the data entry time on transactions

---

[2] See http://www.vitria.com/library/case_studies/vitria_casestudy_worldchain.pdf for more details.

at the check stand in your grocery store. The latest technology tool that is dramatically reducing workloads is RFID (Radio Frequency IDentification), which does not even require a scanner. Through a microchip attached to the product, when the product passes by a receiving unit its presence is immediately detected and the product is counted. Another technological advance is the wireless network that allows remote, handheld computer terminals. These can be used for scheduling, inventory control, supplier interfacing, and a multitude of other applications.

3. *Logistics.* Logistics is the movement of materials and information primarily between your organization and your customer or vendor. Logistics tools are mainly those tools that will facilitate and optimize this movement process.

   a. *DRP.* Distribution Requirements Planning (DRP) is the MRP of the logistics process. It generates plans for shipment and delivery. It interfaces with the ERP environment in much the say way as MRP or MRP II does, and it can be used as a subset of an ERP environment.

   b. *Routing.* A routing system takes all the generated trip requirements and designs a travel route that will optimize the shipment process based on criteria such as travel time, travel miles, and timing constraints.

   c. *Freight.* A freight system is the documentation and information system that generates and tracks bills of lading, shipping orders, receiving documents, and other documents needed to successfully complete the shipment.

   d. *Warehousing.* A warehousing system manages a warehouse and treats it as a holding area for the transfer goods. Most major retailers use warehouses to receive large quantities of a few items. Then they repackage them onto carriers that will make trips to a specific retail outlet, satisfying the specific needs of that retailer. In this way the warehouse is a redistribution center. Numerous warehouse management systems exist that can facilitate this inventory management process and generate the necessary documents.

   e. *Transportation.* A transportation management system is basically a vendor management system in which the vendor is the shipper. It monitors shipper performance issues such as number and seriousness of damaged goods, timeliness, reliability, and flexibility.

   f. *International Effects.* Crossing borders generates its own levels of complexity and paperwork. Each country is an entirely different process and requires a thorough understanding of legal, political, and information ramifications. Often, a staff of trained experts is needed to understand and manage border crossings. Having personal relations with customs officials frequently allows you to have a direct interface.

g. *Logistics Systems.* The logistics system is the integration of all the systems discussed in this section along with the financial and accounting systems. It is the ERP of the distribution and warehousing process.

h. *Integration.* Integration is a term that appears and reappears in any SCM discussion. In this case, it refers to the integration of the shipping organization with the sender and the receiver's ERP environments for the exchange of shipping schedules and shipping requirements.

4. *Information Technology.* The tools for optimized information utilization are constantly changing. The latest wave of improvements includes tools such as the Internet, which allows the interface with international suppliers and customers; wireless systems, which allow transportability; and RFID, which allows immediate and accurate identification without the use of scanning tools. The upcoming wave will include tools such as VoIP (Voice over Internet Protocol), which is basically a telephone communication system using the Internet at significantly cheaper Internet costs.

5. *Supplier Integration.* Here's that word "integration" again. SCM is all about integration up and down the supply chain, and the most challenging is the integration with the third tier, fourth tier, and beyond suppliers who do not understand why you are even talking to them. However, their inventory levels, capacities, performance, and quality can directly affect the organization's performance. Therefore, understanding their methodology and interfacing with these suppliers is important. For most organizations this is a very long-term objective. Most are still working on first-tier supplier interfaces. However, the long-term objective of supplier integrating should be part of the corporate SCM goal.

6. *Communications.* Communications, or rather the lack of it, is often the first hurdle that any organization must overcome. Most of the other tools will never be optimized if a relationship and communication (verbal and informational) methodology between organizations is not established.

Process Competencies

7. *Leadership.* Management is where we "push" direction on our employees; we detail every step of the process. In contrast, leadership is where the employees are guided by our example and are allowed to make many operating decisions on their own. Leadership is often classified as a "pull" management style. A good example is the sheepherder. You could try to drive the sheep with whips and a cane, or you could gain their trust and get them to follow your lead. The first method requires a lot more work than the second and is often less effective. (In the last chapter we briefly discussed this concept and mentioned that it is discussed in detail in *Maverick* and *The eManager.*)

a. *Leadership Skills.* A large number of skills and talents need to be learned in order for one to be a good leader. These tools include communication skills and employee relations skills.

b. *Collaboration.* Collaboration is where you create a working, goal-based relationship with the employees so that they become partners in the process rather than just tools.

c. *Strategy Development.* As we learned earlier, the organization sets goals, and from these goals it develops a strategy for achieving these goals. Without strategy development, the organization would suffer from a lack of direction.

d. *Goal Setting and Performance Management.* The goal setting we are talking about here does not refer to organization goals, but rather to individual employee goals. We set these goals with the employee, and we target them on the strategy area in which the employee is working. Then we set up measurement tools to help us manage the performance of the employee, and we use these as guideposts for performance reviews.

e. *Change Management.* The only constant in life is change. We can either fight the onslaught of change, or we can accept the fact that the change is going to occur and attempt to manage it to our benefit. Once we have accepted it, there are numerous tools for its management, notably TQM (Total Quality Management), Process Reengineering, Breakthrough Thinking, Concept Management, or even some of the tools mentioned earlier such as Lean or Six Sigma. For more details, consult several of the references listed at the end of this chapter or read a discussion of each of these in *eManager.*

f. *Project Management.* Project management is a tool that can be used in any type of business for a variety of reasons. Any time an organization takes on a new project like a business startup, a new change implementation like a computer system installation, a new and major product introduction or has a new building constructed, it is a valuable time for using project management such as Microsoft Project. With a project management tool you can monitor the planning stages of the project by seeing how long it is going to take, check on the allocation of resources for the project, calculate costs, and look for resource conflicts. During the running of the project, you can see if the project is on schedule, identify any variations in the critical path that monitors the total length of the project, and check budget overruns.

g. *Value Network Management.* Your value network includes all those supply chain resources that you interact with and that directly affect your value, or that receive or lose value from interacting with you. The management of all the relationships in this network is value network management. This structure can be quite complex because each relationship has its own collection of issues and there are numerous tools to manage relationship issues. Chapter 7 will discuss several of these tools during its discussion of Lean acceptance tools.

8. *Legal.* A good SCM manager should have a basic understanding of the legal ramifications of any transaction. International transactions possess a complexity of their own that requires an understanding of multiple countries and their relationships. In this arena the more someone knows, the fewer costly mistakes will be made.

9. *Ethics.* Ethics should be something everyone understands and observes, but it's not that simple. What is ethical in one country may be unethical in another. Even something as simple as a hand gesture could cause another to back off of a relationship. Offering someone a gift can be considered a required good-faith gesture in one country and a bribe in another. Or being on time may be mandatory in one culture but rude in another. And then, of course, there are the criminal aspects of unethical behavior.

10. *Finance.* The management of money in the United States is simplistic compared to what countries with high inflation rates or huge recessions face. In addition, the methodology of accruing funding can be quite complex. Tools such as Net Present Value and Cost/Benefit analysis can help you evaluate a financially valid course of action.

11. *Marketing.* Getting the product to the customer is critical in any culture if you are going to be successful. There are complex marketing systems and tools available to help accomplish this function.

Many of the tools discussed above, such as finance and marketing, are not the subject of this book and are therefore only touched on lightly. They are often the subject of entire courses of study at the university. But a good SCM manager has a rudimentary understanding of how these tools work so that he or she can integrate the tool and the appropriate staff into the overall SCM process.

An efficient supply chain is one that everyday, day in and day out, succeeds at selling to customers what we currently own and having those customers be extremely pleased that that's what they bought.

Paul Gaffney, executive vice president of supply chain, Staples[3]

---

[3]Barney, Doug, "How Staples Is Making It Easy to Do Business," CSCO, May 2005, p. 13.

REFERENCES

Burt, David, Donald Dobler, and Steven Starling, *World Class Supply Management*[sm], McGraw-Hill Irwin, Boston, 7th edition, 2003.

Nadler, Gerald, and Shozo Hibino, *Breakthrough Thinking; The Seven Principles of Creative Problem Solving*, Prima Publishing, Rocklin, CA, 1994.

Plenert, Gerhard. *The eManager: Value Chain Management in an eCommerce World*, Blackhall Publishing, Los Angeles, CA, 2001.

Plenert, Gerhard, *International Operations Management*, Copenhagen Business School Press, Copenhagen, Denmark, 2002, Reprinted in India by Ane Books, New Delhi, 2003.

Plenert, Gerhard, and Shozo Hibino, *Making Innovation Happen: Concept Management Through Integration*, St. Lucie Press, Del Ray Beach, FL, 1997.

Plenert, Gerhard, and Bill Kirchmier, *Finite Capacity Scheduling*, John Wiley & Sons, New York, 2000.

Semler, Ricardo, *Maverick; The Success Story Behind the World's Most Unusual Workplace*, Warner Books, New York, 1993.

Chapter 4

What Are the Measures of a Successful Supply Chain Management?

THE ROLE AND PURPOSE OF MEASURES

If it can't be measured,
    Then it won't be improved!

By way of explanation, how do you know something has improved if there is no way of saying how or what has improved? And if you can say what has improved, then how do you identify that improvement? This requires some form of quantification, or it is meaningless hearsay.

As mentioned in the last chapter, measures are critical to a successfully performing supply chain, enough so to warrant their own chapter. Measures are not a tool for data collection. They are not implemented because accounting wants another piece of information; they are only implemented when they add value to the process.

For example, Signetics Corporation manufactures electronics components. When a decline in sales forced them to identify one of their plants for closure, they selected the plant with the lowest quality performance, which happened to be in Provo, Utah. After the plant had been slated for closure, some of its managers asked me to come in and review (postmortem) why their quality was so poor. They wanted to learn from their mistakes so that they would not repeat them in the future.

After some lengthy discussions, it was easy for an outsider to identify the cause of the failure. They had implemented Six Sigma, TQM, and a variety of other quality initiatives. They had banners on the walls and extensive training programs. They held meetings and activities built around these quality initiatives. But their quality was still the poorest of all the plants, and they could not understand why until I asked them questions about their measurement system. I asked them what their performance measurements were for employee performance. They answered that it was "piece parts produced." These employees received a performance bonus based on the number of units produced, not on whether the units were any good. And the employees pumped out parts. Therefore, no matter how well publicized and trained they were on quality, the bottom line is that it did not help the paycheck and therefore the employees were not that interested in all the "quality stuff."

The only valid reason for a measurement system is motivation. No matter what you measure, the simple fact that you are measuring it will encourage employees to think that it is important to you, and they will therefore do their best to make those numbers look good. And employees can be very good at making numbers look good. So, if it is not important, or, as in the Signetics case, if the measurement detracts from the results you really want, then eliminate that measure and only implement measures that truly add value.

SOME EXAMPLES OF MEASURES

Having established the importance of measures, let us return to the example of Z Base introduced in Chapter 1. The problem that the customer was concerned about was that the processing flow time to process a part through the first article process had reached 141 days, and this was way too long for them. So would the "number of rejects" or the "detail and length of the discrepancy report" be valuable measures of performance for the first article managers? Obviously, it would not. The only measures of importance to the customer are "flow time" and "the accuracy of the analysis report." In the case of Z Base, accuracy was not the issue causing customer concern. In fact, the lab had a strong and respected reputation for accurate analysis reports. Therefore, the goal would be to come up with a measure that motivates reduced flow times without sacrificing quality. In Z's case, a combination of these two measures would be the most valuable.

Chart 4.1 gives examples of the types of process improvements that are typically experienced through supply chain improvements. These numbers are repeated again and again in journals, magazines, and conference presentations. In fact, most of these numbers are conservative, and I have successfully beaten many of these numbers in several cases. For example, at Z Base, at the end of the improvement process (the details will be given later in this book), we will see a 75 percent reduction in travel time, a 68 percent reduction in process flow time, and a 93 percent reduction in "jobs on hold."

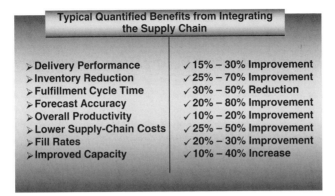

Typical Quantified Benefits from Integrating the Supply Chain	
➢ Delivery Performance	✓ 15% – 30% Improvement
➢ Inventory Reduction	✓ 25% – 70% Improvement
➢ Fulfillment Cycle Time	✓ 30% – 50% Reduction
➢ Forecast Accuracy	✓ 20% – 80% Improvement
➢ Overall Productivity	✓ 10% – 20% Improvement
➢ Lower Supply-Chain Costs	✓ 25% – 50% Improvement
➢ Fill Rates	✓ 20% – 30% Improvement
➢ Improved Capacity	✓ 10% – 40% Increase

Chart 4.1 Supply Chain Improvements

Digging a little deeper in our example, we can consider supply chain costs. In Chart 4.2, we see industry averages for the cost of the supply chain. For example, for the computer industry, we see that the difference between the industry average and the best of class is more than 7 percent of revenue. This goes directly to the bottom line. What company would not want an additional 7 percent net profit boost (which is more than many companies earn in total)?

Examining another important measure of supply chain performance, cycle time, we realize that there are several different types of cycle time. The most obvious one, the one that most people relate to, is the amount of time it takes to produce a product from start to finish. Initially, it took 141 flow days at Z

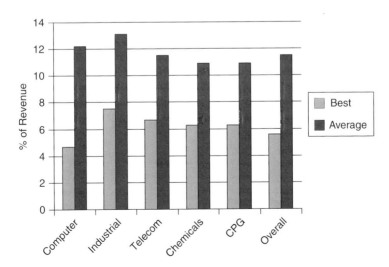

Chart 4.2 Total Supply Chain Management Costs. *Source*: PRTM Study

Base to process a first article part, and that was their critical cycle time measure. Or for PPI the cycle time was the 14 production days that PPI used to take to produce a dashboard panel. But cycle time is also the four production hours that Toyota takes to produce a car from start to finish. Supply chain examples of cycle time would include the amount of time it takes from the start of the supply chain through to the delivery of the finished product to the end customer (see Charts 1.2 or 2.2).

Any measure of cycle time/processing time is valuable as an indicator of supply chain performance. One specific and critically important example, which often is not even considered, is cash-to-cash cycle time (see Chart 4.3). Cash-to-cash cycle time is the amount of time it takes from the time you pay for the materials until the time you receive the cash payment from the customer. It is the amount of time your cash flow is tied up; it is the amount of time you have to finance the cost of having that cash tied up. And this can be quite an expensive investment for a company. Let us again look at the computer industry in Chart 4.3 as an example of what this means. Industry average cash-to-cash cycle time is 106 days. In an industry as volatile and dynamic as the computer industry, this could be suicide. Computer equipment can become obsolete very rapidly. When compared to the best of class average, we see it down to 21 days. The difference is 85 days. If we consider a $1,000 computer, with an inventory holding cost of 7 percent, this would be an increase in cost per computer of $16.30. Just for the sake of analysis, we can go even further and look at the best of the best of class, Dell Computers. Here we find an interesting situation. Dell has a cash-to-cash cycle time of minus seven days. Dell receives payment from the customer over the Internet prior to the time when it purchases the materials from the vendor. Its cash flow days advantage is 113 days when compared to

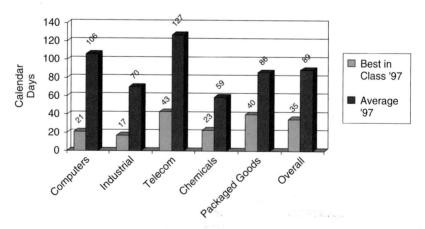

Chart 4.3   Cash-to-Cash Cycle Times. *Source*: PRTM Study

the industry average, which equates to a $21.67 financing cost advantage per $1,000 unit. Dell receives the additional benefit of running its operation using its customers' cash flow. In addition, Dell does not have to build up any inventory of finished goods that are just standing on hold, waiting for orders to be placed the way the other computer vendors do. This equates to a significant cost and cash flow advantage over most of Dell's competitors in the industry.

THE ROLE AND PURPOSE OF CONTROL SYSTEMS

At PPI (see Chapter 3) the measurement system and the employee reward systems were based on units produced, just as they were at Signetics. And that directly related to PPI's over 14 percent defect rate. It generated what it measured, and so its solution was to add control systems, such as Statistical Process Control (SPC), which, in and of itself, is a very good system when applied as a performance enhancement tool used to measure process performance "as it happens." But as a control system, which was "after the fact," it had no effect on quality output. All it did was confirm that indeed the defect rate was over 14 percent. It identified a varying number of areas where errors occurred, but it did little to aid in identifying solutions.

Inappropriately applied control systems are the enemy of an efficient supply chain environment.

Control Systems

- Add steps to the process.
- Increase the opportunities for failure since there are now more steps in the process.
- Increase the overall cycle time.
- Misdirect employees on what is important in achieving overall goals.
- Waste resources (time, floor space, etc.).
- Waste capacity.
- And most importantly, move the error to somewhere else in the process rather than fix or eliminate the error.

For the Labs at Z Base, as you will see later in the Lean discussion, one of the first activities conducted by the lab was to flowchart the entire first article process. In doing so, they were able to identify a large number of intersections in the communications flow. About one-third of these were the results of failures in the process. Their main customer, the DLA, had initiated a data collection and control process that increased the first article processing time by 4 to 10 hours per part. All of these extra steps were information flow failures and created control systems that had a significant impact on the overall process flow time, which had reached 141 days per part. By focusing on improved communications, they were able to eliminate many of the unnecessary communications and check points and after just six months were able to reduce flow time to 85 days. Other activities followed that reduced the flow time even more, and we will consider these activities later during our discussion of Lean. But for this discussion it is interesting to see the large impact that improving communications was able to have on the number of controls and how it was able to generate a significant impact on flow time.

AN INDUSTRIAL EXAMPLE — MANAGING YOUR SUPPLY CHAIN USING EVENT MANAGEMENT[1]

Toward the end of the twentieth century, large manufacturing companies began focusing on their core competencies. They therefore started doing the things they do best, which required them to subcontract many of their fabricated parts to suppliers. The result was the creation of increasingly elaborate supply chains to support their end product. This transition introduced a new way of doing business, one that caused more sophisticated Supply Chain Management requirements than ever before. Companies that previously focused on managing only their internal processes were now forced to manage global supply chains.

A leading aerospace manufacturing company began its transformation into the supply chain world through the use of event management. It felt that it could enhance supplier connectivity by implementing an event management communication tool that required suppliers to provide status to them on major milestones in the manufacturing process. The company hoped that it would gain a competitive advantage and realize lower costs.

As shown in Chart 4.4, in the old way of operating, field representatives and buyers are tasked with ensuring timely inputs from the supply chain and reporting this information to the various programs and material management. This is done verbally, through visibility reports, presentations, and so on. An internal database provides a means for collecting the data and interfacing to shortage reports. Because of the physical requirements of the process (i.e., traveling to and from the suppliers and calling suppliers), it takes an average of 7.32 minutes per part delivery to collect the required information. This process had survived in an environment of only 10,000 to 50,000 part number deliveries per year. However, a growth in business has generated over 160,000 part number deliveries to track.

---

[1] This section is taken from a case example developed for the University of San Diego, Supply Chain Management Institute, by Wink Williams and Harold Loth.

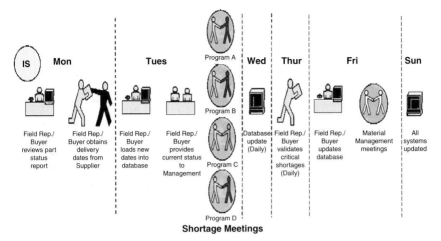

Chart 4.4 Before Event Management

Change was required. A new concept of operations was developed that would allow suppliers to provide milestone status through an event management tool. As shown in Chart 4.5, the new process would reduce the amount of field representative/buyer attention and would allow them to focus solely on exceptions — those parts with problems or those parts not supporting the need date of the assembly line. Aside from scheduled meetings with the programs and management during the week, other tasks would be completed in a continuous process and would not be subject to particular timetables.

The project was created and originally dubbed "supplier connectivity." Since supplier connectivity has so many other connotations, the name was revised

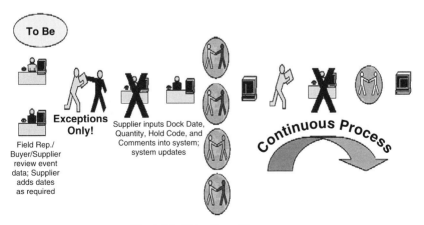

Chart 4.5 Using Event Management

early on to "supplier connectivity — event management." To ensure completion of the project and to demonstrate top-management buy-in, the task was added to the company's Annual Operating Plan (AOP). A team was assembled consisting of two co-project managers, a technical manager, a process manager, field representatives, buyers, and software representatives. Most importantly, the team had a sponsor at the director level, whose support throughout the program was exceptional.

Two software suppliers were chosen to pilot their event management tools over a three-month period. Since the project team was located in southern California, 16 part suppliers (8 for each software tool) were chosen from the area. This was done to provide better assistance for any issues or problems that might arise during the pilot. These were local suppliers that provided machined parts to 15 different programs from the company's different manufacturing sites around the United States.

The main objectives of the pilot were to:

- Pilot both software tools and associated processes.
- Gather supplier acceptance and performance data.
- Finalize internal process and concept of operations.
- Measure success.
- Obtain sufficient data and knowledge to support down-select process.

The team had its software, concept of operations, and objectives, and was ready to begin the pilot.

Two separate kickoff meetings were held to start the pilot, with each software supplier conducting training that was assisted by company personnel. It was hoped that the part supplier could also benefit from use of the software, but this was not considered a major factor in the success of the project.

The suppliers were asked to communicate the status of their parts through the event management tool by providing planned and actual dates for the following events on all part numbers on which they had open purchase orders with the company:

- P.O. receipt
- Raw material ordered
- Tooling available
- Raw material available
- Fabrication start
- Postprocessing start
- Inspection start
- On dock date

The suppliers received their first set of data the following Monday after the kickoff sessions.

Communication is always important, and while the team and suppliers were communicating well, the event management communication was failing miserably. Early on in the pilot, two problems became evident:

1. Both software tools were not user friendly. This resulted in major revisions to both.
2. Including all parts and all events would not be feasible in production. The pilot needed to ask for fewer data elements if any success was to be gained.

The issues were catastrophic enough to halt the pilot so that these problems could be addressed. The corrections to the software were significant and took weeks before being rolled back out to the part suppliers. The software suppliers were extremely supportive.

The pilot resumed with the revised software and continued for four to eight weeks. The team dubbed this the "Lite" version because it entailed the following events and data:

- Fabrication start (critical shortages and first time make parts only)
- Postprocessing start (critical shortages and first time make parts only)
- Inspection start (critical shortages and first time make parts only)
- On dock date (all parts)
- Ship quantity (all parts)
- Internal/external comments (as required)
- Hold codes (as required — A number of hold codes were determined to help with the communication of supplier holding factors.)

Amy Azzam notes, "Event management gets away from screaming on the phone at your supplier and gets down to managing by exception and trying to minimize the number of exceptions."[2]

After the pilot ended, it took about 30 days to gather sufficient data that would allow reaching meaningful conclusions. This information would aid the event management process to transition into production. As shown in Chart 4.6, the pilot time studies proved that it takes less time to obtain and communicate the status of parts in the supply chain using an event management tool. It proved we could conservatively save over 25 percent of the time field representatives were spending on statusing parts and allow them to focus more on relieving the holding factors and working technical issues. If they were tracking 160,000 part deliveries during the year, this would equate to a savings of almost 5,000 man-hours in a year. After a learning curve in production, the savings would be even greater.

---

[2] Azzam, Amy M., "Looking Down the Road," *APICS — The Performance Advantage,* March 2003.

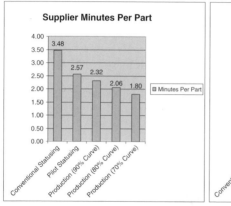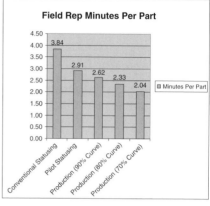

Chart 4.6   Pilot Time Study Results

The pilot also validated that more parts could be used because of the increased visibility and communication with the supply chain (see Chart 4.7). For instance, in today's environment the company would only be able to gather the status of 22 percent of the parts that were within 45 manufacturing days (Mdays) of the assembly need date. Through use of the event management process they will be able to gather status for 98 percent of the parts in that window.

Many lessons were learned from the pilot, including:

- The system must be simple, quick to use, and error-proof to ensure part supplier support.
- The connectivity system is only as good as the effort a supplier puts into it.
- Programming the process is much more complicated than was previously thought.
- An ideal system is web-based to avoid software issues on supplier computers.
- The system must be easily adaptable to constantly changing demands.
- Event management is also adaptable to major subcontract parts.

As Peter Stiles tells us, "The most frequent issue we have observed with commercial software is that software designers tend to develop fixed event models. They do this by defining the commonly observed milestones and events in the supply chain and assume that these satisfy the majority of the monitoring requirements."[3]

Their biggest challenge in implementing event management during the pilot was to make inflexible tools adaptable to a dynamic supply chain. But once that hurdle is overcome, the benefits and applications of event management are limitless.

---

[3]Stiles, Peter, "Demystifying Supply Chain Management," www.ascet.com.

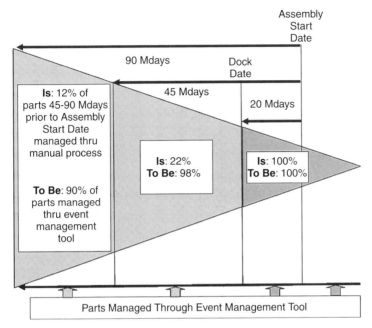

Chart 4.7 Parts Managed Through Event Management Tool

WHAT IS THE BEST MEASURE FOR YOUR ORGANIZATION?

Numerous effective measures of supply chain performance exist, but the best focus on (1) cycle time, which offers inventory reductions and capacity increases, (2) on-time performance to customer expectations, and (3) quality, which is the foundational building block of a satisfied customer base.

Other measures can be seen in Chart 4.1. But the most important criterion for an effective measurement system in any supply chain environment is that it focus on motivating the correct response from the employee base. When we consider Lean management principles in the next section, we will find another collection of measures that are valuable in optimizing a supply chain. But the measure that will fit your organization the best depends on:

The goals of the organization
The expectations of the customer
The response that employees or suppliers will have to the measure
The accessibility and reliability of the measure

You start by looking at these criteria for a measurement system, and then you attempt to identify as few measures as possible that will drive everyone's response toward optimizing that measure. You should never base your measurement system on tradition. An appropriate and effective measure may be challenging to identify, but it will be surprising how directly it can affect overall organization performance.

SUMMARY

In an attempt to use information technology (IT) to enable the global Supply Chain Management of a micro-motor manufacturing company headquartered in Hong Kong, the KE Group was commended by financial analysts as one of the few local companies that was unaffected by the Asian economic crisis. The reported, measurable results of this implementation included a 43.3 percent growth in net profit with only an 8 percent increase in sales.[4]

Without meaningful measures you will achieve your goal: no meaningful results. And with incorrect measures, you will receive incorrect results. The selection and proper implementation of a measurement system is critical to successful Supply Chain Management.

REFERENCES

Plenert, Gerhard, *The eManager: Value Chain Management in an eCommerce World*, Blackhall Publishing, Los Angeles, CA, 2001.

Plenert, Gerhard, *International Operations Management*, Copenhagen Business School Press, Copenhagen, Denmark, 2002, Reprinted in India by Ane Books, New Delhi, 2003.

[4]Taken from a 2005 IRMA presentation in San Diego titled "IT Enabled Global Supply Chain Management: A Case Study" by Narasimhaiah Gorla, Administrative Staff College of India, Harish Verma, Wayne State University, and Tam Wai Chou, Hong Kong Polytechnic Institute, Hong Kong.

Chapter 5

What Does It Take to Create a World-Class Supply Chain Environment?

We like to have a highly efficient supply chain behind the scenes, where nobody knows you're there. Supply chain is not glamorous, but if the supply chain does not work, the company does not work.

Ellen Martin, Vice President of Supply Chain Systems, VF Corp.[1]

WORLD CLASS

VF Corporation, the world's largest apparel company, stresses that "thriving in the apparel supply chain requires the right combination of technology, strategy, and core competencies." By focusing its efforts on supply chain optimization, it was able in 2004 to achieve a 16 percent increase in sales along with a 19 percent increase in net income. VF credits this achievement to a number of organizational changes, not the least of which is a new, standardized IT platform that crosses diverse division lines. This standardization allowed the company to stay on top of supply chain movements throughout its organization. The goal of the IT platform was to create an infrastructure that would improve VF's responsiveness. This is complicated by the need to optimize the supply chain over international borders. The internationally integrated IT environment helped VF to access and utilize data that was underutilized.[2]

---

[1] Terry, Lisa, "VF Corp. Stitches Together a Brand New Supply Chain," CSCO, May 2005, p. 28.
[2] Ibid., pp. 26–33.

As good as you may be at designing and marketing your brand, if you cannot get products to consumers, it doesn't matter.

Ellen Martin, Vice President of Supply Chain Systems, VF Corp.[3]

Part of the problem with being world class is that the target is always moving: what is defined as being world class today will no longer be world class five years from now. For example, bar coding was considered to be world class 10 years ago; today being world class requires RFID (Radio Frequency IDentification) labels.

The first four chapters of this book gave the readers a foundation of tools so that they could define and develop a model for World-Class Supply Chain Management within their industry. Chapter 1 helped define what supply chains are all about and gave several examples. Chapter 2 focused on the management of a supply chain and identified tools such as models and step charts that would help the manager identify what World-Class status requires. It also reviewed the need to identify and manage improvement "gaps" so that the reader's organization could become world class. Chapter 3 discussed some of the tools of Supply Chain Management, and Chapter 4 stressed the importance of selecting an appropriate measurement system.

Numerous additional tools, notably books and articles, are cited in the References sections at the end of most chapters. The reader is urged to consult these references for a deeper understanding of concepts introduced in that particular chapter.

Having established a basic foundation of what a World-Class Supply Chain Management system entails, we now know the answer to the question of this chapter; What does it take to create a World-Class supply chain environment? With that understanding we are now ready to examine the second major topic of this book, Lean management. After that we will see how the two systems synergistically integrate to create an optimal environment that is greater than the sum of its parts.

[3] Ibid., p. 27.

Part II

Developing a Lean Environment

Chapter 6

What Is Lean?

DEFINING LEAN

Numerous articles stress the importance of Lean in the Supply Chain Management world. For example, in *Supply Chain Systems* we find "Manufacturing Shifts from Push to Pull,"[1] or in *Quality Digest* we find "Using Lean and Six Sigma in Project Management."[2] From these articles we learn about the importance of implementing Lean methodologies to:

- Eliminate waste.
- Reduce cycle and flow time.
- Increase capacity.
- Reduce inventories.
- Increase customer satisfaction.
- Eliminate bottlenecks.
- Improve communications.

So what is this mysterious tool called "Lean"?

Lean is the Westernization of a Japanese concept that has carried several names. It has variously been known as the Toyota Production System, JIT (Just in Time), Pull Manufacturing, TQM (Total Quality Management), and other names. Each of these names incorporates some aspect of Lean, and vice versa. What we know as "Lean" today is not really any of these any more. One possible

---

[1] Navas, Deb, "Manufacturing Shifts from Push to Pull," *Supply Chain Systems: Solutions for Supply Chain Managers*, June 2005, pp. 18–22.

[2] James, Derrell S., "Using Lean and Six Sigma in Project Management," *Quality Digest*, August 2005.

definition of Lean, taken from MainStream Management, a Lean consulting company, is as follows.

> Lean is a systematic approach that focuses the entire enterprise on continuously improving quality, cost, delivery, and safety by seeking to eliminate waste, create flow, and increase the velocity of the system's ability to meet customer demand.

What we call Lean today is a collection of tools and methodologies, very few of which are actually required in any specific Lean process. When working on a specific Lean project, part of what a Lean facilitator is required to do is to design and assemble the correct mix of tools to optimally facilitate the desired result. For example, if the goal is to improve the flow time for the Z Base labs (see Chapter 1), we assemble one set of tools but we use an entirely different set of tools if we are trying to improve quality for PPI (see Chapter 3).

Lean has developed into its own entity, and along with that it has developed its own award process, the Shingo Prize for Excellence in Manufacturing (see Chart 6.1). The Shingo Award program has become the international standard for what Lean should look like. Therefore, as we begin to define Lean, it would be appropriate to start with the Shingo model.

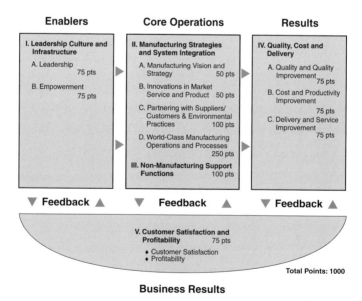

Chart 6.1 Shingo Prize Model

The Shingo model evaluates Lean performance in the following categories:

- Enablers

  I. Leadership, Culture, and Infrastructure—Implementing World-Class strategies and practices requires an aligned management infrastructure and organizational culture.

     a. Leadership—Here they are looking for a vision, mission, values, strategies, and goals that are used in the planning process. Organizations also want demonstrated knowledge of management systems and business results.
     b. Empowerment—The focus here is on employee training and on team participation. The measures, the reward system, and the safety programs are also critical.

- Core Operations

  II. Manufacturing Strategies and System Integration—The focus is on the core manufacturing strategy, practices, and organizational techniques. Organizations are looking for World-Class results.

     a. Manufacturing Vision and Strategy—Are the corporate visions brought down to the manufacturing level?
     b. Innovations in Market Service and Product—Here Organizations look for innovative cost reductions in logistics, sales, service, and so on, using quality and benchmarking tools.
     c. Partnering with Suppliers/Customers and Environmental Practices—Here they are looking for an effort to form integrated relationships with suppliers and customers.
     d. World-Class Manufacturing Operations and Processes—They are looking for the application of many of the Lean tools that will be discussed in Chapter 8.

  III. Nonmanufacturing Support Functions—Here they are evaluating the degree of integration between manufacturing and the nonmanufacturing functions of the organization, and the extent to which Lean improvement tools have been applied in nonmanufacturing settings.

- Results

  IV. Quality, Cost, and Delivery—Here they evaluate the outputs of the core business systems

     a. Quality and Quality Improvement—Here they look for zero defects reaching the customer. Are the measures in place to assure zero defects?

    b. Cost and Productivity Improvement—Are the measures in place that will certify a reduction in cost and an increase in productivity?

    c. Delivery and Service Improvement—Are the products on time and in the correct quantities? Are customer expectations being met?

- Feedback/Business Results

  V. Customer Satisfaction and Profitability—Here they evaluate the outcomes of quality, cost, and delivery on customer satisfaction and business results.

    a. Customer Satisfaction—Here they look for evidence of customer satisfaction.

    b. Profitability—Here they look for documentation that supports the business financial attainment.[3]

Using these criteria for evaluation, we employ a point system to evaluate the applicants on their Lean capabilities, and if their performance meets the standard, they are awarded the Shingo Award for Lean Excellence.

Lean is also about team building, integration, and ownership. Someone commonly referred to as the Lean facilitator is tasked with organizing the appropriate teams and then giving them the appropriate guidance and training in the selected tools so that the Lean effort can progress with the greatest efficiency. The team is the one that makes the decisions about any changes in process, and they have ownership of these changes. The role of the facilitator is to keep the team on task so that they develop and implement these changes in the minimal amount of time.

CHANGE

The one thing that is consistent in life is change. You can either manage the changes or you can let them manage you. Lean focuses on continuous improvement or managed change. We find that there are organizations that:

- Resist change. This is a small number; these are often dysfunctional organizations that may never get it.
- Lead change. This is also a small number; these are early adaptive and innovative organizations.

---

[3]Utah State University, College of Business, *Shingo Prize—Business Prize—Application Guidelines 2005*, p. 7.

- Walk a balancing act between the opposing forces to see which is going to win. This is where the majority of companies have positioned themselves. These organizations need some other dynamic for creating a change-adaptive culture. They need something like Lean to organize them and push them through the change process.

With the success of Lean within early adaptive companies comes the desire for fence-sitting companies to realize the benefits of Lean. Knowing that Lean works, these companies look for change management opportunities and tools that can help their cultures adapt so that they can succeed in transforming themselves to Lean. The Lean process looks for a change transformation process that results in sustainable change. For example, one model that MainStream Management uses is an adaptation of the CAP (Change Acceleration Process) Model (see Chart 6.2). This model was adapted from the one used by GE, which was originally developed by Noel Tichy and which is similar to Kotters Change Model. The model indicates several stages of change and the change management process. The first section is about selling the Lean change process to the organization. The second section focuses on sustaining the Lean change process so that the process continues even after the facilitator discontinues his or her oversight activities.

In the selling phase of the CAP change model, we first see the need to create a need for Lean within the organization. This is accomplished by identifying a need for change. What are the organization's large problem areas or strong growth needs? Without the proper change management driver, problems may never get resolved, or, worse yet, they may not get resolved in the best possible

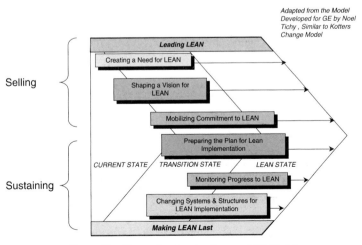

Chart 6.2 Change Acceleration Process CAP Model

way. We need to identify opportunities where the Lean change process can be effective.

Shaping the vision for Lean requires that we look first at the goals of the organization and then for ways to help the organization optimize those goals. This requires a Lean study of both growth opportunities and error correction opportunities. It also requires a look at the gap analysis similar to the one that we performed in our Supply Chain Management step chart in Chapter 2.

Mobilizing the commitment to Lean requires team identification and team-building efforts, which we will discuss in the next chapter. It means identifying and setting aside the resources that will be required for this effort. It means getting management commitment to facilitate the Lean effort.

Preparing a plan requires timelines and schedules; it requires a plan of attack with specific steps; it requires the agreement and support of management all the way to the top so that there are no delays or disruptions to the change management process.

Monitoring the Lean process requires checkpoints and measures, which were discussed in Chapter 4. It is about checklists and action items to make sure that all the concerns of the team are resolved and that action is taken on every activity.

Change systems and structures for Lean implementation require ownership and commitment from top management down to the workers on the floor. The teams need to own the change process, and they need to be excited about it so that they will maintain it even after the facilitator leaves. This is about putting structures and systems in place that continue to facilitate the Lean change management process by having all the necessary people properly trained in order to avoid future doubt or confusion about the process. And it is about making Lean a lasting cultural change within the organization.

Traditionally, the change management process has been top down, with top management owning and driving the change process. With Lean, all employees become owners of the change process. It is the working ranks that determine what changes need to be made, and the management role becomes one of being the provider of resources and tools so that the desired changes can rapidly take place. With Lean management, everyone becomes a thinker and a creator.

Some organizations try to drive Lean down through edicts. However, with Lean we learn that

- Lean is not something you do to people.
- Lean is a set of tools that you provide people with in order to meet the organization's objectives.
- Lean is best served when supported from the leadership and then is implemented by the workforce.

The common pitfalls found in implementing a Lean change process include the following.

- Organizations think of Lean as an event and not a new business paradigm.
- Organizations fail to seek expertise regarding cultural change and development.
- Organizations maintain a "business as usual" attitude while attempting broad transformations.
- Organizations tend to avoid dealing with active or passive resistance in their leadership groups.
- Organizations don't always "get the right people on the bus." The process owners need to be involved, not just staffers.

In order to achieve Lean leadership success, the organization needs to:

- Establish a clear vision and direction.
- Create top down support (dealing with detractors).
- Engage in bottom up implementation.
- Manage complex change.
- Run interference—eliminate or reduce barriers.
- Continually train and add momentum.

Another change model that can be used is the one designed by John Kotter.[4] This model can be used in place of the CAP model and has also been found to be a very effective tool. It contains an eight-stage process for implementing major change and can be seen in the following table.

The Eight-Stage Process of Creating Major Change

1. Establishing a Sense of Urgency
   - Examining the market and competitive realities
   - Identifying and discussing crises, potential crises, or major opportunities
2. Creating the Guiding Coalition
   - Putting together a group with enough power to lead the change
   - Getting the group to work together like a team
3. Developing a Vision and a Strategy
   - Creating a vision to help direct the change effort
   - Developing strategies for achieving that vision
4. Communicating the Change Vision
   - Using every vehicle possible to constantly communicate the new vision and strategies
   - Having the guiding coalition role model the behavior expected of employees
5. Empowering Broad-Based Action
   - Getting rid of obstacles
   - Changing systems or structures that undermine the change vision
   - Encouraging risk taking and nontraditional ideas, activities, and actions

---

[4]Kotter, John P., *Leading Change*, Harvard Business School Press, Cambridge, MA, 1966, p. 21.

6. Generating Short-term Wins
   - Planning for visible improvements in performance, or "wins"
   - Creating those wins
   - Visibly recognizing and rewarding people who made the wins possible
7. Consolidating Gains and Producing More Change
   - Using increased credibility to change all systems, structures, and policies that don't fit together and don't fit the transformation vision
   - Hiring, promoting, and developing people who can implement the change vision
   - Reinvigorating the process with new projects, themes, and change agents
8. Anchoring New Approaches in the Culture
   - Creating better performance through customer- and productivity-oriented behavior, more and better leadership, and more effective management
   - Articulating the connections between new behaviors and organizational success
   - Developing means to ensure leadership development and succession

Before a Lean transformation can achieve significant change, an acknowledgment and commitment must come from the organization's leadership. There needs to be leadership acceptance throughout the organization that the current process that they are now running either does not, or will not, meet the needs of customers and therefore will not ensure the continued survival of the organization. Once this acknowledgment is made, then we can get the organization committed to change. With that commitment to change, the Lean process is the tool that will facilitate the change process.

THE FACILITATOR

At some point it becomes important to define the characteristics of a facilitator. The facilitator is someone who is highly trained and experienced in the Lean process. The facilitator is also an agent of positive change, a results-oriented generalist, flexible and adaptable, as opposed to the narrow generalist. One of the facilitator's most valuable contributions to a team's growth and development is helping the team members become aware of the team's own processes, enabling them to discuss their own communication, problem-solving, decision-making, and conflict resolution practices. The facilitator helps the team learn how to work more effectively to fulfill their charter, roles, and responsibilities—not doing it for them, but by helping them to do it and to take ownership in it. The facilitator must not allow the team to run from the responsibility of taking control of the change process.

Not just anyone can be an effective mentor and facilitator. It is an art developed and mastered through practice, not by formal education. The facilitator's most important characteristics are willingness, real experience, desire, and motivation to help others learn. The criterion for selecting a facilitator is to select individuals who have been performing this function naturally all their lives. Many people have a natural tendency to help others grow. We continue to develop these characteristics and these interpersonal competencies by practicing:

- Empathy
- Acceptance
- Authenticity
- Active listening
- Artful intervention

LEAN TOOLS

As mentioned earlier, Lean change management is not a specific methodology. It is more about adaptation, goal fulfillment, and sustainment. Lean tools and concepts will focus the organization on changing the system so that it is capable of adapting and flowing to changing customer needs. But because *change is hard* we find that the technical implementation of Lean alone will not create the acceptance required to sustain the change. Chart 6.3 shows that the acceptance process represents 80 percent of the effort in a Lean implementation and that the technical tools account for only 20 percent of the effort. We also see that sustainability cannot be achieved with only one or the other of these two elements. Both are required.

The following chapter will discuss a few of the acceptance tools that are designed to motivate cultural change. There are far too many of these tools to discuss them all in detail; a preliminary list of these tools could include

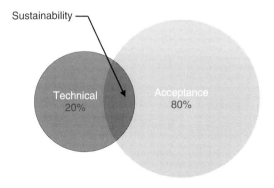

Sustainability = Technical • Acceptance

Chart 6.3 Technical and Acceptance Tools

1. Change Acceleration Process (CAP) Model (already presented in this chapter)
2. Kotter Change Model (already presented in this chapter)
3. Breakthrough Thinking
4. Concept Management
5. Scan (discussed later in this chapter)
6. Team Effectiveness Surveys
7. Change Readiness Surveys
8. Myers Briggs
9. Empowerment
10. Team Development
11. Johari Window
12. Ladder of Inference
13. PAPT (Passive/Aggressive – People/Task)
14. Situational Leadership
15. Value Systems
16. Learning Curves

Chapter 8 will discuss a few of the technical tools that are designed to analyze the existing process and to design methodologies for systems changes. Again, there are far too many of these tools to discuss them all in detail, but a preliminary list of these tools could include

1. Value Stream Mapping
2. Systems Flow Chart
3. Spaghetti Chart
4. Future State Value Stream Map
5. TAKT Time
6. Lean Action Item List or Lean Newspaper
7. Lean Events
8. 5S
9. Cell Design
10. JIT (Just-in-Time)
11. Poka-Yoke
12. PQ Analysis (Product/Quantity)
13. Six Sigma
14. SPC (Statistical Process Control)
15. TPM (Total Productive Maintenance)
16. Visual Workplace
17. Wastes
18. *Kaizen*
19. Design for Manufacturing
20. SMED (Single Minute Exchange of Die)

21. TQM (Total Quality Management)
22. TQC (Total Quality Control)
23. Business Process Improvement (BPI)
24. Kanban
25. Jidoka
26. Standard Work
27. Brainstorming

With these tools available to the Lean process, we can look further to see how the Lean process should proceed.

HOW THE LEAN PROCESS WORKS

At this point the reader should understand that the Lean process consists of three stages: the acceptance stage, the technical stage, and the sustainment stage. We start with the acceptance stage where we try to get the organization to recognize the need for change.

ACCEPTANCE STAGE

The first thing we need in the Lean process is some kind of trained facilitator who is highly experienced in the Lean process and its available tools. This facilitator will initially talk to the CEO or the board of directors of the organization in order to get some guidance on where they want him or her to focus their efforts. Since Lean is disruptive, there has to be a compelling reason to adopt this process. This compelling need must come from the organization's position in its respective industry and its need to be able to adapt to changes that might affect its growth and survival. The facilitator needs to come away from the meeting with the CEO with a clear, measurable objective for the Lean activity.

Let's walk through the Z Base example that we highlighted in the first chapter. We will use this case as our example of how to perform a Lean activity in a service environment. Later we will also look at PPI to see how we would conduct a Lean effort in a manufacturing environment. But the processes are nearly identical; it is only the technical tools we use that are different.

At Z Base, the process started with a meeting between the Lean facilitator and directors who are over the lab area. The Base General had given a clear directive to management. The directive was that the flow time of 141 days for the first article process was unacceptable. The maximum time was to be 120 days, and the preferred flow time would be about 90 days. In addition, the facilitator was given a maximum of one year to accomplish this objective. With this guidance, the facilitator now knew what his marching orders entailed. The next step was for the facilitator to understand the process and to get some type of meaningful commitment from management to support the Lean process. In Z's case, the support was already in place. Management wanted this process optimized every bit as much as the Base General, and they were 100 percent supportive of any of the facilitator's efforts. They were eager to see progress.

Having identified a direction, possibly even a measurable mission for the Lean effort, the facilitator will next talk to the people who are closest to the issues being evaluated. Often these conversations are on a one-on-one basis and attempt to get each employee's perspective on what needs to be accomplished. This process utilizes one of the acceptance tools and is referred to as the scan.

For Z, the facilitator went to the lab area and interviewed all the first article program managers (review the discussion in the first part of Chapter 1 if any of these terms are confusing). He also interviewed all the members of the quality verification lab (QVC), all the team leads, all the engineers in the electronics labs, all their management, and a few individuals who had recently left the lab area for work elsewhere on the base. The facilitator focused on these questions:

- *How does the first article process work?*
- *What does the flow look like through the first article process?*
- *What are the inputs into the processing of a first article? What are the outputs?*
- *What disruptions to the workflow are occurring?*
- *Who are the suppliers of the inputs? Who are the customers?*
- *What are the work backlogs in each area?*
- *What do you see as the key problems that are causing the first article flow times to hit an average of 141 days?*

The information from this scan was for the facilitator's eyes only, and the purpose of the scan was to identify the key areas of concern as well as the key players in the process. The actual focus of the Lean effort had to be determined by the steering team, not the facilitator. However, by using the information gained in the scan, the facilitator was now ready to create the steering team that would be focused specifically on the mission of the Lean effort. The facilitator now knew all areas of the organization, all customers, all suppliers, and any other stakeholders that need to be invited on to the team.

Looking back at Chart 1.1, which is now repeated as Chart 6.4, we see numerous stakeholders in the first article process. This chart was developed by the Lean facilitator for his own purposes to help him understand the process; it was not to be used by the Lean team. They would later need to develop their

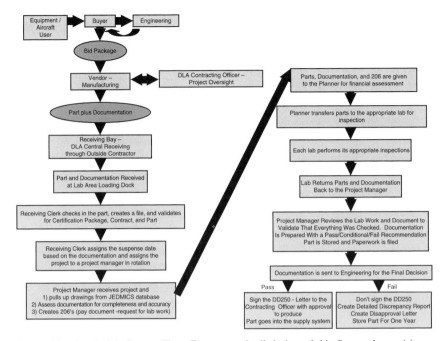

Chart 6.4 First Article Process Flow. For a more detailed view of this figure, please visit our companion site at: http://books.elsevier.com/companions/0123705177

own flowchart of the process, but this effort turned out to be quite a bit more complex than the facilitator's version. The stakeholders included:

First article
Contracting
Engineering
DLA
Supply Chain Management

Lead managers from each of these organizations were identified, and they were invited to be part of the first article Lean steering team. All of the managers readily accepted the invitation because of their direct involvement or direct needs when related to this process. In all, the steering team included 14 individuals, some of whom had to travel across the United States in order to participate in the process.

Once the steering team has been identified and invited, some of the acceptance tools discussed in the next chapter are needed. These tools are used to evaluate the change readiness and the team dynamics of the steering team. All this is done before the steering team meets, so that the facilitator can be prepared for the team dynamics that he or she will be encountering.

In the case of Z Base, three tools were used:

- *A change readiness survey to see how willing and open each of the steering team members were to changes in the first article process*
- *A team effectiveness survey to see how well each team member would be able to work together*
- *A personality survey (in this case the Myers Briggs indicators were used) to determine the personality dynamics that the facilitator would be encountering with the members of the team*

Now we are ready to get the steering team together in the same room. We start with a training session, teaching them the whys and hows of Lean. Then we show them what their role will be in the Lean process. If we look at Chart 6.5, again borrowed from MainStream Management training materials, we see the steering team on top, which becomes the lead and the driving force behind all the Lean efforts throughout the organization. The facilitator is not the leader of the Lean effort. The facilitator should subordinate himself or herself to the steering team and will take direction from the steering team on what needs to be done, when it needs to be completed, and how it should be done. The process owners are the steering team, and they need to own the changes to the process. However, the facilitator needs to give the steering team direction in the form of training about the Lean tools. And the facilitator needs to share findings, problems, and successes with the steering team.

Once the steering team is in place and trained, they are now tasked with looking closely at the process or system under study. They discuss the issues of this structure, in an attempt not to find solutions, but to identify specific areas that should be addressed by Lean activities. These activities are targeted with specific charters and are referred to as "events."

Chart 6.5 also shows how the steering team identifies Lean leaders who will be the champions of the Lean process in their respective areas. These individuals will identify and create Resource Support Teams (RST) that can collect information and access information to support the lean effort. The RST, in conjunction with the steering team, will then identify the team members that are necessary to make each event as effective as possible.

At Z, the steering team was extremely receptive to the training and the entire change process. The Lean leaders were quickly identified, and their access to resources would be utilized throughout the Lean process. Over time the steering team came up with the following specific events that needed to be addressed:

- *Value Stream Mapping Event. This is where the technical analysis tools are applied.*
- *Communications and Customer Relations Event. This focuses on the communications breakdowns among the labs, the suppliers, and the customers.*

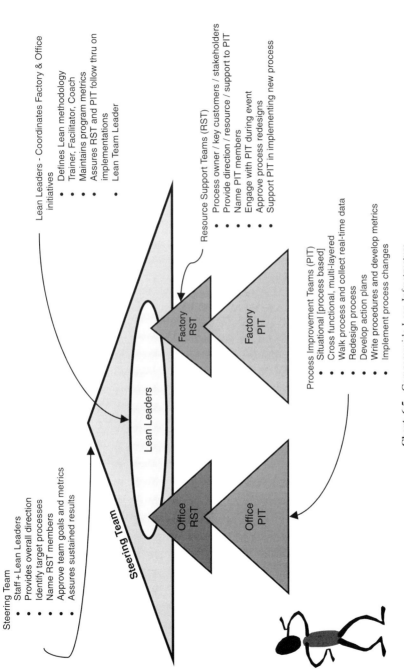

Steering Team
- Staff + Lean Leaders
- Provides overall direction
- Identify target processes
- Name RST members
- Approve team goals and metrics
- Assures sustained results

Lean Leaders - Coordinates Factory & Office initiatives
- Defines Lean methodology
- Trainer, Facilitator, Coach
- Maintains program metrics
- Assures RST and PIT follow thru on implementations
- Lean Team Leader

Resource Support Teams (RST)
- Process owner / key customers / stakeholders
- Provide direction / resource / support to PIT
- Name PIT members
- Engage with PIT during event
- Approve process redesigns
- Support PIT in implementing new process

Process Improvement Teams (PIT)
- Situational [process based]
- Cross functional, multi-layered
- Walk process and collect real-time data
- Redesign process
- Develop action plans
- Write procedures and develop metrics
- Implement process changes

Steering Team

Lean Leaders

Office RST

Factory RST

Factory PIT

Office PIT

Chart 6.5 Companywide Lean Infrastructure

- *Staffing and Training Event. This focuses on analyzing whether the correct type of people and the correct number of people were employed within the lab, and whether they were trained properly.*
- *Facilities Event. This looks at the building layout, the movement of people, and the movement of parts throughout the lab.*
- *Supply Chain Management Event. This looks at the movement of information and parts throughout the structure of the first article process.*
- *Systems Event. This looks at the information systems that existed and at how well they interfaced with the customers and vendors. It identified internal systems requirements.*
- *6S Event (often referred to as 5S). This looks at the organization and cleanliness of the work areas (you will see this event again in Chapter 8).*

The steering team at Z met together every two weeks for about one hour. They were updated on the events that had already occurred or were in process, and they facilitated the planning of future events. They became a critical tool in identifying resources that needed to be tapped so that the Lean activities did not stall out.

Once the target events have been defined, the Lean facilitator, with the help of the steering team and the RST, goes through the process of identifying the key players needed on each of the Process Improvement Teams (PIT; see Chart 6.5). The facilitator then performs an acceptance analysis on each member of the team. Then he or she schedules the team event, and on the first day of the event he or she goes through the training required by the team members so that they will have all the tools necessary for the performance of their Lean event. The facilitator needs to have identified which correct tools are available and which will focus the Lean effort. Training should only cover tools that are viable for this process.

TECHNICAL STAGE

The technical stage begins with the first event, which is almost always some type of mapping event where the team tries to thoroughly understand the process or system under study. This is almost invariably a Value Stream Mapping (VSM) event, where the current "value stream" is mapped out in detail. More information on this event can be found in Chapter 8. In industrial environments like a factory, the VSM is performed on the materials flow of the organization. There are also other tools, such as Spaghetti charting which focuses on people movement, or systems flowcharting, which focuses more specifically on the information flow of the organization. The objective of all these maps and charts is to study the process in as much detail as possible so that bottlenecks, systems holes, and other opportunities for improvement can be identified.

For Z Base, a VSM of the first article process was created as well as a Spaghetti chart of the people flow and a systems flow chart of the information flow. The entire team traveled to the location of each key supplier and customer so that their process could be fully understood by the entire team. All of the team members learned a lot about how they interface with vendors and customers; they learned things that they had not realized in the past. After completing this process, it was obvious that the constraining resource behind the effective timely performance of the first article assessment was information flow and that communications was the area that needed to be addressed first.

After the technical assessment, the findings are presented to the steering team, and based on these findings they determine what events should be scheduled next. Then it again becomes the facilitator's task to organize, evaluate, and train the next event team so that they can move the Lean process forward. Each event creates an action item list that is referred to as a Lean newspaper; this action item list is then moved forward until each action item is resolved.

SUSTAINMENT STAGE

It is at the sustainment stage that the Lean effort takes on a life of its own. At this point everyone has been trained at all levels of the organization, and they have taken ownership of their piece of the process. The steering team no longer needs the facilitator. The steering team meets regularly and requests reports from, and gives direction to, each of the event PIT team leads. PIT teams are organized as new areas for improvement are identified, and obsolete PIT teams are disbanded as they achieve their desired goals. Lean becomes a way of life for the organization as a whole.

SUMMARY

This chapter sought to give the reader a quick overview of what Lean is all about and how it works; it is not intended to certify the reader as some kind of Lean black belt. There is a lot more to this process than can be discussed even if this entire book were to be dedicated only to the details. Even the training that a facilitator should go through could be a book all by itself. There are, however, numerous other supportive materials on the subject of Lean that would give the reader more in depth understanding. Some suggested books for further reading include:

- *Lean Thinking* by James Womack
- *The Goal* by Eliyahu M. Goldratt

- *Real Numbers* by Jean Cunningham
- *7 Habits of Highly Effective Managers* by Stephen Covey
- *Good to Great* by Jim Collins
- *Breakthrough Thinking* by Gerald Nadler and Shozo Hibino
- *Maverick* by Ricardo Semler
- *Built to Last* by Jim Collins and Jerry Porras
- *The Game of Work* by Charles Coonradt
- *Balanced Scorecard* by Robert Kaplan and David Norton
- *Scenario Planning* by Mats Lindgren and Hans Bandhold
- *The eManager* by Gerhard Plenert
- *Concept Management* by Gerhard Plenert and Shozo Hibino
- *The Toyota Way* by Jeffrey Liker
- *The Fifth Discipline, the Art & Practice of a Learning Organization* by Peter M. Senge

A second layer of books for the reader who just can't get enough includes:

- *Learning to See* by Mike Rother, and John Shook
- *One Piece Flow* by Kenichi Sekine
- *Process Consultation* by Schein, Edgar
- *Kaizen for Quick Changeover* by Kenichi Sekine
- *Standard Work* by Productivity Press
- *Kanban made Simple* by John MGross and Kenneth McInnis
- *5S* by Hiroyuki Hirano
- *Performance by Design* by David Felten
- *Productive Workplaces* by Marvin R. Weisbord
- *Mining Group Gold* by Thomas A. Kayser
- *The Toyota Production System* by Taiichi Ohno
- *Organizational Culture and Leadership* by Edgar Schein
- *The Perfect Engine* by Anand Sharma and Patricia Moody
- *The Machine that Changed the World* by James Womack
- *Lean Manufacturing for the Small Shop* by Conner Gary
- *Who's Counting* by Jerrold M. Solomon
- *Leadership and the New Science, Learning about Organization from an Orderly Universe* by Margaret J. Wheatley
- *Organizational Dynamism* by Wayne R. Pace
- *When Giants Learn to Dance* by Rosabeth Moss Kanter
- *Leading Change* by John Kotter
- *Performance Management* by Robert Bacal

Once the readers have a thorough understanding of this material, they will also have a clearer understanding of the power of Lean.

Chapter 7

What Are the Acceptance Tools of Lean Management?

WHAT IS AN ACCEPTANCE TOOL?

As mentioned in previous chapters, the hardest part of change is the acceptance of the change. This is true for both Supply Chain Management and Lean. Within the Lean process we find numerous tools that have been adapted and that help facilitate the change process. You would rarely use all of these tools in any specific Lean implementation, but not using any of them will most likely result in a change process that is owned by the facilitator and is never really accepted by members of the organization.

Acceptance tools are tools that a facilitator can utilize to get the team members to buy into the change process and to take ownership of the process. To achieve this acceptance, the facilitator would start with a model for change, something like the CAP model discussed in the last chapter. Using this model, the facilitator would work through the change steps necessary to make the organization receptive to the changes occurring. Other models include Breakthrough Thinking or Concept Management, both of which have their origins in the Toyota production process (see the references at the end of the chapter).

The next step in the acceptance process is for the facilitator to gain credibility in the process. This requires that the facilitator get a cursory understanding of the process that he or she is working on. To accomplish this understanding, the facilitator needs to perform a scan of the existing operation, attempting to develop a basic understanding of the process. This process was also discussed in more detail in the previous chapter.

At this point, the facilitator should be ready for team development, starting with the establishment of the steering team. From the scan the facilitator should now have a feeling for what types of individuals are needed on the steering team. He or she should then go to the individuals who gave him the charter for this project and get their suggestions on specific names for the steering team. The facilitator would then interview each of these individuals and get his or her approval to join on the team. With their approval in place, the team building and change readiness assessment can begin.

The facilitator needs to understand the relationship within the various functional aspects of an organization, as well as between the various levels of the organization. This could, and often should, include interviews and surveys with customers and suppliers so that their perceptions of the current process can be recorded. This information is also valuable for a "before and after" evaluation of how effective the Lean process really was. Numerous proprietary survey tools exist that would facilitate this process. One can select a tool that allows for a comparison of the preparedness levels between each of the elements being surveyed.

As we saw in the previous chapter, Z Base used a change readiness survey and a team effectiveness survey. Using S Base as an example, their change readiness assessment included questions about the process under consideration from various perspectives (taken from the MainStream Management change readiness survey):

For Management (If management is doing the survey, they would answer the questions about how they perceive themselves. If staff is answering the question, they would answer based on how they perceive management to be.)

- *Give personal time for Lean.*
- *Drive policy changes to support Lean.*
- *Communicate everything about Lean.*
- *Be honest about negative issues associated with Lean.*
- *Make a long-term commitment to Lean.*
- *Stick it out in tough times getting to Lean.*
- *Provide training to employees to work in Lean.*
- *Ask employees for their ideas on Lean.*
- *Provide time, money, and people for Lean.*
- *Try out ideas generated by employees.*

For Implementation Team (IT) members (If management is doing the survey, they would answer the questions about how they perceive the staff doing the work. If staff is answering the question, they would answer based on how they perceive themselves to be.)

- *Try new way of doing work.*
- *Work with management to develop Lean ideas.*
- *Provide honest feedback.*
- *Improve on work methods.*

- *Participate on committees or implementation teams.*
- *Cooperate with each other during Lean implementation.*
- *Be willing to refine ideas getting to Lean.*
- *Deal with confusion while trying out Lean ideas.*
- *Take risks trying out new ideas.*
- *Learn new skills.*

Policies and Procedures

- *Allow employees and managers to do work in new and innovative Lean ways.*
- *Implement recommendations painlessly.*
- *Allow employees to move to where the work is.*
- *Reward team and individual accomplishments.*
- *Motivate people to change to Lean.*
- *Allow employee time to participate in Lean activities.*
- *Have communication channels inform about Lean changes.*
- *Encourage employee feedback.*
- *Monitor change to Lean.*
- *Recognize new ideas at Headquarters.*

Similarly, at Z Base, the survey for team effectiveness included the following categories (taken from the MainStream Management teaming effectiveness survey):

Goals and Objectives

1. *Be clear on team's objectives.*
2. *Have all pull in same direction.*
3. *Do what is needed for company's success.*
4. *Have numerical goals and chart progress.*
5. *Meet our objectives in the 90 percent range.*

Roles and Responsibilities

6. *Clear expectations.*
7. *Comfort level with role.*
8. *Understanding of my role by my management.*
9. *Awareness of each other's roles.*
10. *Knowledge of how our roles fit in the big picture.*

Enthusiasm and Motivation

11. *Work is fun and rewarding.*
12. *Team is optimistic.*

13. *Self-satisfaction is derived from achievements.*
14. *Caring is prevalent in our team.*
15. *Challenges are to be enjoyed.*

Trust and Openness

16. *Trust is a part of the team.*
17. *Sensitive matters are kept confidential.*
18. *Team members assist each other.*
19. *There is no fear of reprisals upon bringing up concerns.*
20. *Respect is gained.*

Leadership and Direction

21. *Encourage decision making.*
22. *Make input into decision making.*
23. *Share leadership.*
24. *Lead by example.*
25. *Accept decisions.*

Information and Communication

26. *Information is readily shared.*
27. *There are no surprises—effective communication.*
28. *Information is readily at hand.*
29. *Performance data is available.*
30. *Proactive communication vs. grapevine method.*

For Z Base, these surveys were invaluable and generated the following information.

- *Staff perceived management to be disconnected and uninterested in their process.*
- *Staff felt that management did not care about their ideas.*
- *Staff had confidence in their direct line supervisors but not in anyone above that level.*
- *Staff felt that the reward system did not motivate them to facilitate changes.*
- *Management felt that staff was resistant to change, showing the attitude that they already felt they knew how to do things in the best way possible.*
- *Management felt that staff would be unwilling to take time from their workload to facilitate the change process.*

All this information was invaluable in designing the training and in building the team.

At this point, the facilitator should have a good sense of the team-building and change motivation issues that he or she will confront. If the challenges seem significant, the facilitator may want to look deeper into the personalities of the team members that he or she will face. A good tool for this evaluation is the Myers Briggs Assessment. It was developed in the 1950s and has proven to be an excellent tool in helping people understand themselves. It ranks everyone by the following.

- How we energize ourselves (in the range from E to I)
  - Extravert (E)
    - Attention that seems to flow out to objects and people in the environment
    - Desire to act on the environment
    - Action taking
    - Impulsive, frank
    - Communicates easily
    - Sociable
  - Introvert (I)
    - Attention to the inner world of concepts and ideas
    - Reliance on enduring concepts vs. transitory external events
    - Thoughtful contemplative detachment
    - Enjoyment of solitude and privacy
- What We Pay Attention to (in the range from S to N)
  - Sensing (S)
    - Focus on here and now—immediate situation
    - Enjoyment of the present moment
    - Realistic attitude
    - Acute powers of observation
    - Memory for details
    - Practical
  - Intuition (N)
    - Ability to tie seemingly unrelated events together
    - Creative discovery
    - Perception beyond the here and now
    - May overlook current facts
    - Theoretical, abstract
    - Future oriented

- How We Make Decisions (in the range from T to F)

  - Thinking (T)

    - Tough minded
    - Able to make logical connections
    - Principles of cause and effect
    - Tendency to be impersonal
    - Analytical, objective
    - Concern for justice
    - Desire of a connection from the past to the present to the future

  - Feeling (F)

    - Tender minded
    - Ability to weigh the relative merits of the issues
    - Application of personal and group values subjectively
    - Attendance to what matters to others
    - Concern for the human as opposed to the technical aspects of the problem

- How We Are Oriented to the World (in the range from P to J)

  - Perceptive (P)

    - Open to incoming information
    - Curious and interested
    - Spontaneous and curious
    - Adaptable
    - Open to new events and changes
    - Willing to take in more information before making a decision

  - Judging (J)

    - Seeks closure
    - Organizes events
    - Plans operations
    - Shuts off perceptions as soon as enough has been observed for a decision to be made
    - Is organized
    - Is purposeful
    - Is decisive

This analysis can be invaluable in team creation because what you need on your team is a balance. Too many of any one personality type can disrupt the decision-making process. For example, in Chart 7.1 we can see all the different categories in which individuals can be placed. If, for example, we had a lot of I's and few or no E's, we would have very quiet discussions in our teams.

ISTJ	ISFJ	INFJ	INTJ
Analytical MANAGERS of FACTS / DETAIL	Sympathetic MANAGERS of FACTS / DETAIL	People Oriented INNOVATORS	Logical, critical, decisive INNOVATORS
ISTP	**ISFP**	**INFP**	**INTP**
Practical ANALYZER	Observant, loyal HELPER	Imaginative, independent HELPER	Inquisitive ANALYZER
ESTP	**ESFP**	**ENFP**	**ENTP**
REALISTIC ADAPTERS material world	REALISTIC ADAPTERS human relations	Warm, enthusiastic PLANNERS of CHANGE	Analytical PLANNERS of CHANGE
ESTJ	**ESFJ**	**ENFJ**	**ENTJ**
Fact-minded practical ORGANIZER	Practical HARMONIZER	Imaginative HARMONIZER	Intuitive, innovative ORGANIZER

Chart 7.1 Myers Briggs Type Indicator

Digging a little deeper, we can learn conditional information about a Myers Briggs Assessment. For example, people with a specific management style have the following characteristics:

SJ Management Style

Leadership style	Traditionalist, stabilizer, consolidator
Work style	Works from a sense of loyalty, responsibility and industry
Learning style	Learns in a step-by-step way with preparation for current and future utility
Acknowledged for contributing	Timely output
Values	ORDER

SP Management Style

Leadership style	Troubleshooter, negotiator, firefighter
Work style	Works via action with cleverness and timeliness
Learning style	Learns through active involvement to meet current needs
Acknowledged for contributing	Expeditious handling of the out of the ordinary and unexpected
Values	FREEDOM

NF Management Style

Leadership style	Catalyst, spokesperson, energizer
Work style	Works by interacting with people about values and inspirations
Learning style	Learns self-awareness through personalized and imaginative ways
Acknowledged for contributing	Something personal or a special vision of possibilities
Values	HARMONY

NT Management Style

Leadership style	Visionary, architect of systems, builder
Work style	Works on ideas with ingenuity and logic
Learning style	Learns by an impersonal and analytical process for personal mastery
Acknowledged for contributing	Strategies and analyses
Values	COMPETENCE

Or exploring further, we find the following personality characteristics:

IS	THOUGHTFUL REALIST
	Leads through attention to what needs doing
	Individual focus: practical considerations
	Organizational focus: continuity
	"Let's keep it!"
IN	THOUGHTFUL INNOVATOR
	Leads through ideas to what needs doing
	Individual focus: intangible thoughts and ideas
	Organizational focus: vision
	"Let's think about it differently!"
ES	ACTION-ORIENTED REALIST
	Leads through action, doing
	Individual focus: practical action
	Organizational focus: results
	"Let's do it!"
EN	ACTION-ORIENTED INNOVATOR
	Leads through enthusiasm
	Individual focus: systems and relationships
	Organizational focus: change
	"Let's change it!"
NF	Warm
	Trusting
	Spiritual
	Idealistic
	Unselfish
	Romantic

	Affirming
	Caretaker
	Empathic
	Sympathetic
	Compassionate
	Wanting harmony
	Great communicator
	Likes to please people
	Promoting growth, well-being
	Relates current experience to past experiences
SJ	Firm
	Stable
	Efficient
	Realistic
	Decisive
	Punctual
	Dependable
	Orderly, neat
	Seeks closure
	Good planner
	Goal oriented
	Executive type
	Organized person
	Providing security
	Always has a view
	Good at sorting/weeding out
NT	Creative
	Original
	Rational
	Powerful
	Visionary
	Objective
	98% right
	Firm-minded
	Under control
	Seeking judgment
	Superior intellect
	Able to find flaws
	Able to reprimand
	Calm, not emotional
	Precise, not repetitive
	Eminently responsible
SP	Eclectic
	Carefree
	Practical
	Spontaneous
	Problem-solver
	Good negotiator
	Hands-on person

Flexible, adaptable
Proficient, capable
Able to do many things at once
Curious, welcomes new ideas
Able to deal with chaos
Fun-loving, enjoys life
Superior ability to discriminate among options, sees shades of gray

In the end, Myers Briggs Assessments help the facilitator and team members by

- Helping individuals to know themselves
- Giving a tool to "be with" others
- Giving a baseline from which to develop adaptive behaviors
- Helping learn how to better communicate by understanding and by talking others' "language"
- Developing better facilitation methods
- Developing more effective exercises
- Appreciating the differences in others
- Teaching us the value of type diversity
- Learning to accept others for who they are
- Leveraging each person's type by identifying his or her role in a team environment
- Conducting more effective meetings
- Helping understand how previously annoying behavior can be seen as amusing, interesting, and as a strength

The web sites for the Myers Briggs Assessments are http://www
.humanmetrics.com/cgi-win/jungtype.htm   or   http://www.myersbriggs.org/
my_mbti_personality_type/, which introduces you to the Myers Briggs
test. These lead you to the web site http://www.humanmetrics.com/
cgi-win/JTypes1.htm where you can actually take the test and get your score.
In addition, MainStream Management, the source of a lot of the Myers Briggs
information, can give the reader even more depth on the usefulness of this tool.

Myers Briggs is just one of many personality analysis tools that are available.
However, since I have found this tool to be one of the most useful, I have spent
more time on it than I will on many of the other tools.

*Z Base used the Myers Briggs Indicators to check on the balance of the
team and to validate anticipated team performance (see Chart 7.2). They
learned that the steering team (ST) was reasonably balanced with IS, IN, and
EN team members, but it had more thinkers than doers. However, for the
Implementation Team (IT), a group that would become the core team for all
the events, they discovered a serious problem. The team was heavily skewed
toward introverts, especially ISTJs. This was a strong indicator that the team*

ISTJ	ISFJ	INFJ	INTJ
IT - 7	ST - 2 IT - 1	ST - 1 IT - 1	ST- 2 IT - 3
ISTP	ISFP	INFP	INTP
			ST - 2
ESTP	ESFP	ENFP	ENTP
ESTJ	ESFJ	ENFJ	ENTJ
		ST - 1 IT - 2	ST - 2

ST = Steering Team

IT = Implementation Team

Chart 7.2 Myers Briggs for Z Base

may get bogged down in data collection and may tend to go toward "paralysis by analysis." The facilitator would have to take a strong lead in keeping the team moving along.

In the end, however, after the two Z Base teams got the vision of Lean, they both moved along at lightning speed.

The steps for the acceptance process are as follows.

1. Get approval for the project and set a target objective.
2. Select a change model with which to proceed through the change process:

   - CAP Model
   - Breakthrough Thinking
   - Concept Management

3. Perform the scan.
4. Organize the steering team.
5. Perform a cultural assessment of the steering team and of the organization that is being transformed.

   - Perform some type of team-building assessment.
   - Perform some type of change readiness assessment.
   - Perform some type of personality assessment of the team members to see how well they will work together.

     - Myers Briggs

6. Meet with the steering team and start the technical assessment process (which is continued in the next chapter).

7. There are other acceptance tools that are listed in this chapter and which are used during the ongoing technical phase, the event phase, and the sustainment phases of the lean process. These tools are focused on maintaining stability in the process and are often used for relationship issues, for problem solving, or for adding new team members.

SOME SUCCESS STORIES

For PPI we see a need for a quality improvement process to occur. However, PPI needs to experience a cultural change before it will be ready to experience a quality transformation. As we have already seen, the measurement system is a major roadblock in achieving a focus on the importance of quality. Initially, the process required the training of managers so that they would recognize the opportunities and the need for changes in the process. This step occurred over a period of several months. Then, as management became convinced of the need for change, the rest of the workforce was also brought into the process through declaration of a "quality week." During this week, no bad parts could be made. The week started with a day of training on quality identification, JIT, and Lean principles. Then the employees were instructed that the goal for the week was not quantity but quality only. The employees were allowed to change anything, but they were not allowed to produce bad parts. Management initially feared they would lose one week's productivity but still made the commitment to give it a try. Within a day of transformations, the production lines were again up and running, but this time without bad parts. The transformation was immediate and stunning. The capacity gained by not having as many reruns on parts made up for the lost production time within less than one week. The results can be seen in Chart 7.3, which shows the dramatic reduction in errors and in finished goods inventory.

Another example of the types of improvements that can be achieved by Lean can be found in Organization W, which was struggling with forecast delays, product delivery delays, and schedule inconsistencies. The facilitator was tasked with the following:

- Mission: Reduce waste in the Forecasting Process to allow timely and correct parts requirements entry the first time (sustained workloads).
- Process Boundaries

  - Process begins: Identification of future requirements (sustained products)
  - Process ends: Delivery of parts/assets to supply point

- Mission Goals

  1. Address forecasting shortfalls.
  2. Develop and communicate changes in demand, condemnation rates, spikes, and so on.

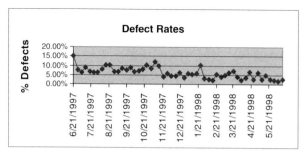

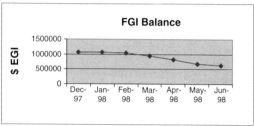

Chart 7.3 PPI Transformation

3. Provide clear performance expectations for program managers, item managers, equipment specialists, supply supportability specialists and planners.

Teams were formed, and the team members identified the following responsibilities of members.

- Analyze parts availability vs. shopfloor requirements to support end item repairs.
- Submit material forecasts to source of supply; identify changes in demand.
- Use proactive team to address parts supportability.
- Have subject matter experts at the working level communicate effectively across directorates to support production.
- Find a way to avoid future production shortages or inventory overages.

Team meetings were not to become:

- Another reactive meeting
- Another management finger-pointing session where they were not involved.

Through this process the teams discovered:

- There are two forecasting subprocesses:
  - New products
  - Sustained workload (changes to existing products)

- The team must focus on:
  - Sustained workload

The team created an action item list which determined that

- There was a need for more resources to resolve New Product Forecasting.
- There was a need to create Material Review Teams (MRT) to review supportability issues on a weekly basis.
- Business Process Improvement needs to take place in forecasting new workloads.
- Move/ship end items and parts to point-of-use and develop visual inventory systems.
  - Provide Two-Bin, Line Side Markets, Kanban, Vending Machines, Lektrievers.
  - Determine proper inventory buffers (special levels) for routed parts leaving cell to back shops (i.e., welding, machining, plating, etc.).
- Load all stock data into central database; users need to be educated as to why this needs to be top priority.
  - APIs need to be audited.
- Use and train on portal system in conjunction with legacy systems to review real-time demand, make adjustments on weekly/monthly basis vs. quarterly.
- Create career progression for current positions and co-locate staff in Lean cell.
- Train and authorize correct staff to process transactions in order to capture usage/demand outside of supply system.
- Utilize Supportability Specialist (SS) in proper role.
  - Jobs need to be visible in portal system—for review of trends.
- Have contracting organization review new systems in process.
- Transfer management of consumables to DLA.

The team created an improvement action list, which included the following next steps:

- Continue monitoring the major functional areas to ensure correct and timely Forecasts of Material Requirements for the Suppliers (DLA).
- Have customer organizations communicate changes in requirements, funding capacity in a timely manner.
- Continue implementing material at point-of-use (POU) systems.
- Work to eliminate emergency orders and to reduce backorders.
- Maintain Lean concept by visual indicators (metrics) that show that the process is being sustained after implementation.

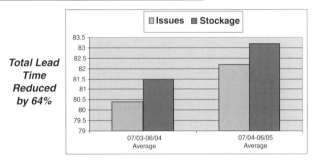

Forecasting			
FUNCTION	BASE LINE	IMPROVED TO	REDUCTION PER CENT
Value Added	1,140 Min.	1,140	
Non-Value Added Touch Time	1,108 Min.	707	38%
Total Lead Time	66,051 Min.	24,148	64%
Handoffs	15	8	47%
Walking Distance	89,495 Ft.	20,584	77%

Chart 7.4   Organization W Transformation

The results of this Lean effort can be seen in Chart 7.4 where we find an immediate improvement in timely deliveries and stock performance. We also see a reduction in lead time, touch time, and travel time.

REVIEWING A FEW EXAMPLES OF ACCEPTANCE TOOLS

It is difficult to discuss each of these acceptance tools in detail in the space available. However, they at least need to be introduced so that the reader knows what is available, and then if desired the reader can research any of them in more detail.

1. Change Acceleration Process (CAP) Model—See Chapter 6.
2. Kotter Change Model—See Chapter 6.
3. Breakthrough Thinking—This change model utilizes "purpose expansions" rather than "root cause analysis" and has become quite popular in Japan, especially among the users of the Toyota production system. The following discusses the concept briefly.

    To solve difficult problems and find creative solutions, our present thinking paradigm and process must change. Gerald Nadler and Shozo

Hibino published *Breakthrough Thinking* (BT) in 1990 and *Creative Solution Finding* in 1993. In these two books, they defined Japan's developed paradigm shift in thinking and called this new thinking paradigm "Breakthrough Thinking." From a historical viewpoint, our thinking paradigms have been continuously shifting over time. Our conventional thinking paradigm (Descartes Thinking) is out of date in this rapidly changing world and needs to shift again to a new thinking paradigm. In the twenty-first century, we have to be Multithinkers able to use three thinking paradigms; God Thinking, Conventional (Descartes) Thinking, and Breakthrough Thinking (BT).

God Thinking focuses on making decisions based on God's will. Some decisions require no analysis. Behavior is firmly dictated by God's will, our values systems, and our life philosophies. For example, morality or ethical issues are decided and are not open for discussion. Conventional Thinking starts with an analysis process that focuses on fact or truth finding. When we make a decision, our behavior is based on the facts or on scientific truth. We need the facts in order to make our decisions. Breakthrough Thinking starts with the ideal or ultimate objective. When we make a decision, we base our behavior on this objective.

The three thinking paradigms are completely different, and each has a different approach. We have to select and utilize each of these paradigms on a case-by-case basis. Someone who uses and interchanges these thinking paradigms is referred to as a Multithinker.

Since there is no future that continues along the same lines as our past and present (because of the drastic changes going on in the world), we cannot find futuristic solutions based on past and present facts. Our thinking base should be changed away from facts and should refocus on the substance, essence, or ideal.

To identify the substance of things is not easy. We have to transform ourselves from having a conventional machine view to a systems-oriented view. The traditional perspective of conventional thinking is to view things as a reductionistic machine, breaking everything down into elemental parts and neglecting the "whole" organic view.

The epistemology of Breakthrough Thinking is that "everything is a system," which focuses BT on a "holonic view." If we define everything as a system, then everything is a "Chinese box," which means that a bigger box (system) includes a series of smaller boxes (systems). A small box (system) contains still smaller boxes (systems) and so on. Each box (system) has its purpose(s). If you repeatedly ask, "What is the purpose?" and then "What is the purpose of that purpose?" and then "What is the purpose of that purpose of that purpose?" ad infinitum, you can reach the biggest box, which is "wholeness." You can view everything from the perspective of this wholeness. BT calls this search the "Purpose Expansion."

Breakthrough Thinking consists of a thinking paradigm and thinking process. The thinking paradigm of Breakthrough Thinking is the opposite of the paradigm of conventional thinking. Its main points are expressed as seven principles.

(1) *Uniqueness Principle*—Always assume that the problem, opportunity, or issue is different. Do not copy a solution or use a technique from elsewhere just because the situation may appear to be similar. In using this principle, we have to think about the locus or solution space of the problem. This locus is defined using three points:

> Who are the major stakeholders? Whose viewpoint is most important?
> What is the location?
> When (What is the timing)?

(2) *Purposes Principle*—Explore and expand purposes in order to understand what really needs to be accomplished and to identify the substance of things. You can tackle any problem, opportunity, or issue by expanding purposes, providing you change your epistemology to a systems view. Understanding the context of purposes provides the following strategic advantages:

a. *Pursue the substance of things.* We can identify the most essential focus purpose or the greater purpose, often referred to as the substance (core element) of things by expanding purposes.

b. *Work on the right problem or purpose.* Focusing on right purposes helps strip away nonessential aspects to avoid working on just the visible problem or symptom.

c. *Improve the ability to redefine.* Redefining is usually very difficult. Once you have redefined, you can have different viewpoints, each of which enables you to solve problems from different directions.

d. *Eliminate purpose/function(s).* From Systems Theory we learn that a bigger purpose may eliminate a smaller purpose. By focusing on the bigger purpose, you can eliminate unnecessary work/systems/parts, which means that you can get more effective solutions.

e. *Have more options, be more creative.* If you have a purpose hierarchy, you have a lot of alternative solutions.

f. *Take a Holonic view.* Take a "big picture" perspective.

(3) *Solution-After-Next (SAN) Principle*—Think and design futuristic solutions for the focus purpose and then work backwards. Consider

the solution you would recommend if in three years you had to start all over. Make changes today based on what might be the solution of the future. Learn from the futuristic ideal solution for the focus purpose and do not try to learn from the past and present situation.

(4) *Systems Principle*—Everything we seek to create and restructure is a system. Think of solutions and ideas as a system. When you see that everything is a system, you have to consider the eight elements of a system in order to identify the solution.

> Purpose—mission, aim, need
> Input—people, things, information
> Output—people, things, information
> Operating steps—process and conversion tasks
> Environment—physical and organizational
> Human enablers—people, responsibilities, skills, to help in the operating steps
> Physical enablers—equipment, facilities, materials to use in the operating steps
> Information enablers—knowledge, instructions

(5) *Needed Information Collection Principle*—Collect only the information that is necessary to continue the solution finding process. Know your purposes for collecting data and/or information. Study the solutions, not the problems.

(6) *People Design Principle*—Give everyone who will be affected by the solution or idea the opportunity to participate throughout the process of its development. A solution will work only if people know about it and help to develop and improve it.

(7) *Betterment Timeline Principle*—Install changes with built-in seeds of future change. Know when to fix it before it breaks. Know when to change it.

The Breakthrough Thinking (BT) process is an approach of reasoning toward a Situation Specific Solution and a Design Approach. It is an iterative, simultaneous process of mental responses based on the Purpose–Target–Results Approach (PTR Approach). PTR's three phases are

> *Purpose*—Identifying the right solution by finding focus purposes, values, and measures
> *Target*—Targeting the solution of tomorrow—ideal SAN vision and target solution
> *Result*—Getting and maintaining results toward implementation and systematization

For a more detailed discussion, see *Breakthrough Thinking*.

4. Concept Management—This is another change model from Japan, and it integrates Total Quality Management and World-Class Management principles into a change management process.

Concept Management (CM), as just noted, is a Japanese movement that integrates Breakthrough Thinking (BT), World-Class Management (WCM), and Total Quality Management (TQM). BT is the technique utilized to develop ideas. It moves away from the slowness and costliness of traditional root cause analysis commonly used in the United States and Eurpoe. WCM offers the formal structure around which the ideas are turned into goals and a measurement/motivation system. TQM is the process for team-based idea/change implementation. CM is an idea generation and implementation process used by companies such as Toyota and Sony that breaks us out of the traditional analytical thinking common to companies such as the Ford Motor Company, which uses the TOPS program, or the Russian TRIZ program. Instead, CM focuses on forming a purpose hierarchy through a series of steps.

Concept Management uses the term *concept* to mean innovative, purpose-driven, change creation and *management* to mean leadership. Therefore, Concept Management is "innovative, change-oriented, purpose-driven (goal focused), creative leadership." This leadership occurs through the integration of ideas, primarily the ideas expressed in two leading-edge philosophies: Breakthrough Thinking and World-Class Management.

World-Class Management has a broad application, and numerous publications discuss the subject in detail (see Plenert's *World Class Manager* and *Making Innovation Happen: Concept Management Through Integration*). However, in order to get a clear understanding of how World-Class eManagers manage change, the focus should be on:

(1) *People*. Employees and stakeholders are the source of change opportunities. They need to be motivated properly through an appropriate measurement system in order to drive change.
(2) *Customers*. Customers are the reason for change. In order to be competitive, we need to give our customers a clear reason why they should not buy from anyone else but us.
(3) *Performance*. Performance requires focus on a goal, whether financial or quality or other. Then we need to measure, monitor, and offer feedback information about our performance.
(4) *Competitors*. Competition creates fear, but it also creates opportunity. Competitors need to be analyzed and understood in order to be defeated.

(5) *Future.* The future is coming whether we're ready for it or not. If we're not ready for it, it will pass us by, along with our customers and competitors.

(6) *Integration.* Through integration everyone and everything work together. Managers are not merely bosses, but are leaders and facilitators by example. They work side by side with the employee.

World-Class Management is not a system or a procedure, it is a culture. It is a continually molding process of change and improvement. It is a competitive strategy for success.

In the United States, TQM has fallen into disfavor because of its analytical approach to change. The analysis process is deemed too slow to be competitive. But that is primarily because TQM utilizes root cause analysis. With Breakthrough Thinking we can revisit our use of TQM.

TQM has two major aspects: philosophical and operational. From the philosophical aspect we get guidelines, and from the operational we get techniques. Traditionally, the philosophy of TQM could be stated as "Make Sure You're Doing the Right Things Before Your Worry about Doing Things Right." Total Quality Management focuses on careful, thoughtful analysis. However, the analysis should be creative, innovative, and innoveering. It wants to make sure that we are implementing positive, goal-focused changes before we move a muscle.

TQM is an enterprisewide change model, and for this reason some people define it as making the "entire organization responsible for product or service quality." To some, TQM is a behavior-based philosophy of motivation and measurement. It does, in fact, require a cultural shift for all members of an organization in that it uses an entire philosophy about how businesses should be run. TQM is filled with ideas and attitudes:

Attitude of desiring and searching out change
Think culture—move from copying to innovating
Focus on the goal
Measurement/motivation planning
Top to bottom corporate strategy
Companywide involvement
Clear definition and implementation of quality
Education, training, and cross-training
Integration and coordination
Small, step-by-step improvements

TQM implementation starts with a coordinating team, often referred to as a quality council. This team is composed of high-level corporate leaders from all the functional areas, usually at the vice president level.

It is appointed by the CEO and operates under his or her direction. The CEO actively directs the endeavors of the team and is often an active team member. This quality council is then responsible for organizing, chartering, and measuring the performance of the other TQM teams within the organization. It oversees the installation, training, performance, and measurement of the other teams. This team seeks to keep all teams focused on the corporate goal and vision.

Concept Management works in a series of stages.

(1) *Concept Creation.* The development and creation of new ideas through the use of Breakthrough Thinking's innovative methods of creativity.

(2) *Concept Focus.* The development of a target, which includes keeping your organization focused on core values and a core competency. Then, utilizing the creativity generated by Concept Creation, a set of targets are established using World-Class Management and a road map is developed helping us to achieve the targets.

(3) *Concept Engineering.* This is the engineering of the ideas, converting the fuzzy concepts into usable, consumer-oriented ideas. TQM through the use of a focused, chartered team and through a managed SPS process helps us to manage the concept from idea to product.

(4) *Concept In.* This is the process of creating a market for the new concept. We transform the concept into a product, service, or system, using World-Class Management techniques. We may utilize Breakthrough Thinking to help us develop a meaningful and effective market strategy.

(5) *Concept Management.* Both the management of the new concepts and a change in the management approach (management style) are effected by the new concept. Concept Management is the integration of the first four stages of the Concept Management process (Creation, Focus, Engineering, and In).

For more details on the Concept Management process, please read *Making Innovation Happen: Concept Management Through Integration* (see References).

5. Scan. see Chapter 6.
6. Team Effectiveness Surveys. See earlier in this chapter.
7. Change Readiness Surveys. See earlier in this chapter.
8. Myers Briggs. See a detailed discussion earlier in this chapter.
9. Empowerment. This is the stage where employees become the major decision makers in the organization and management becomes the facilitators. Empowerment can be defined as an organizationwide commitment to establish a much greater degree of teamwork among all employees

and distributing more of the responsibility for decisions throughout the organization.

The basic steps of empowerment are:

a. The conditions for effective empowerment must be in place. This requires having an informed staff that is ready for change. They need to know why and how changes will be made, and they need to be properly rewarded for their participation in the change process.
b. Trust needs to be established between all organizational silos and between all organizational levels. Trust must be earned as well as given. This requires everyone to be predictable. This predictability is needed between all stakeholders demonstrating reliability and mutuality (really caring about each other).
c. Goals need to be established between all levels of the organization. They need to align between levels, and they need to be measurable with a timeline.
d. An acceptable methodology needs to be developed for motivation. Measures and how they motivate employees have been discussed several times already in this book.
e. People should be assisted in working through the change process, as discussed in the last chapter. Fear of change and risk of failure can be reduced through training and trust.

Most management books offer a cursory discussion of how empowerment works. For an extreme case of the use of empowerment, read the book *Maverick* listed at the end of this chapter.

10. Team Development—Proper team development is an art. This chapter has discussed team selection and team assessment, whereas previous chapters have dealt with team goal setting, measures, and motivation. The one piece that is still needed is proper training. A team needs to have the tools with which to perform to expectations or they will not be effective. So the first thing that should occur after the team has been organized and has established their goals is for the team to know what tools and options are available for them to achieve their goals. The next chapter will discuss several of these tools from a Lean perspective. However, there are also task-specific tools that need to be understood. For example, in a review of the materials management IT systems, an understanding of inventory scheduling and control features may be critical to the success of the team. With the correct tools, and with proper team management, the team will rapidly move toward success.

Once a team is formed, there are stages of team development, which, if understood, will help the facilitator manage the progress of the team. All teams go through four stages of development when they are newly formed, and again if there are significant changes in the structure of the team, such as new members being added or deleted. These stages are Forming, Storming, Norming, and Performing.[1]

Forming—Birth   This phase is like giving birth. The fact that six or seven people have gathered together does not guarantee effectiveness. Teams, like individuals, need to grow up and to move through development stages, from formation to maturity. Several practitioners and researchers have proposed any number of clearly definable stages or phases of group life. Teams do not experience these stages exactly as they are identified, but the general descriptions are helpful. The stages are normal and are to be grown through just as individuals move from adolescence to adulthood. As teams struggle with these growing pains and become more effective as a team, they will even find their personal lives richer, fuller, and more satisfying.

During the early formative and dependent stages, it is not surprising that individuals are concerned about membership, about belonging to the group and being included. They have just as strong a need to be liked and accepted and usually avoid conflict at all costs. Personal needs and wants are characterized by the following:

- There is conformance to the established company line.
- Feelings are hidden and suppressed.
- There is little listening and caring for others.
- Personal inadequacies and weakness are kept hidden.
- Objectives and action plans are poorly prepared and communicated.
- Hidden agendas remain hidden.
- Cliques and alliances begin forming.
- Feedback and disclosure are at a minimum.
- There is a strong need for approval.
- Mistakes are often used as evidence.
- Real feelings are shared outside the meeting.

Storming—Control   Once team members get the lay of the land, they begin to feel comfortable. Then they usually want to figure out who is in control and how much influence they will have on the team. Look for the following characteristics:

- People do not work in a unified way.
- The cliques grow and wield influence.

---

[1] Taken from information supplied by Scott Larkin of MainStream Management, a Lean consulting firm.

- Conflict intensifies and is generally resolved through voting.
- There are a lot of win/lose interactions.
- Infighting exists.
- Personal strengths and weaknesses become better known.
- Commitment is debated.
- Self-centeredness becomes evident.
- Team identity is low.
- Self-disclosure is still cautious.
- Close-mindedness is evident.
- People are defensive.
- Ground rules are ignored.

This is a critical time for teams, and some teams may even self-destruct. If there is order without freedom, team members will rebel against rigidity or formality. If there is freedom without order, the chaos will produce confusion and frustration. Member freedom within an orderly process, a structure to which the team has agreed, offers the most desirable result.

Norming—Effectiveness   To arrive at this point is a real struggle. It provides the team with the vehicle for becoming an effective team, and it allows them to dig in and truly be productive with their time. This stage is characterized by the following:

- There is an attitude of change.
- Real constructive cooperation begins.
- People are more open-minded.
- Better listening is evident.
- Cliques dissolve.
- Leadership becomes more shared.
- Previously dormant people contribute.
- There is a willingness to experiment and to explore all sides of an issue.
- Conflict is viewed as needed.
- Methodological processes begin developing.
- Operating methods are reviewed.
- Problem-solving skills are developed and utilized.

Performing—Maturity   As the team continues to constructively explore and struggle, developing orderly processes and methods, tasks are accomplished much quicker and more easily. The work team begins functioning as mature, interdependent members. Leadership becomes less of an issue; anyone can take the lead role when appropriate. The team will appear to be less structured because the members themselves understand and monitor the discipline. This level of maturity can be recognized by the following:

- Close relationships.
- Resourcefulness and economy.
- High spirits and morale.
- Informality and respect.
- Happy and rewarding.
- Encouragement of outside help.
- Mistakes still made but eagerly examined.
- Cohesiveness.
- Common spirit.
- High goal attainment.
- Intense loyalty.
- Open relationships with other teams.
- Flexibility, adaptability.
- Individual needs recognized and met.
- Continual review and feedback.
- New members welcomed and included.

The mature team, like the mature individual, reflects on itself and organizes its own continuous growth and development.

These stages are not tied to time. Some groups never achieve maturity, and others get so bogged down at stages that it is difficult to move on. Even mature groups may have to recycle to work out some new issue or problem, or they may simply lose their willingness to work together.

11. JoHari Window—The JoHari Window is a tool for gaining insight into how we see ourselves and how others see us. It is invaluable when we are trying to investigate the openness of team members, for it helps us understand their willingness to communicate. To accomplish this understanding, the JoHari Window uses "disclosure" (or telling) and "feedback" (or asking) to determine our individual openness. As with the Myers Briggs Assessment, in the JoHari window we take a survey and then plot the results of this survey on a graph. The graph divides us into four segments, as seen in Chart 7.5.

The JoHari Window is a conceptual model for describing, evaluating, and predicting aspects of interpersonal communication. The windowpanes show us how we present and receive information about others and ourselves. The model allows us to see movement from one pane to another as trust ebbs and flows and as actors exchange feedback. The size and shape of the panes change over time.

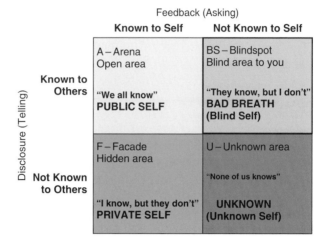

Chart 7.5   JoHari Window

The literature on human behavior is filled with similar two-dimensional models, including the Blake Grid and Kilman Conflict model. But I have found that the JoHari Window offers the most significant insights into Lean acceptance and understanding.

Using the JoHari segments, we identify each of these segments as:

- A—arena. This represents the part of yourself that is known by you yourself and by others. This windowpane represents free and open exchange of information between others and you. This is public behavior information that is available to everyone. The pane increases in size as the level of trust increases between others and you. As more information, particularly personally relevant information, is shared, this trust increases. This represents a manager with a capacity for open relationships. In this window the glass is two-way. There is open exchange of facts, feelings, and opinions between the people communicating through this pane.

- BS—blind spot. This represents what others know about you but what you do not realize about yourself. As you work with others, you communicate all kinds of information of which you may be unaware but which others pick up. This occurs through the use of verbal cues, mannerisms, the way you say things, or the style in which you relate to others. The extent to which you are insensitive to much of your own behavior and what it may communicate to others can be surprising and disconcerting. For example, we see it in a manager's tendency to press too hard in trying to speed up relevant discussion at a meeting to the detriment of what others may feel is needed, like open discussions. Many of us know and realize that others find things we do or say difficult or puzzling. "Blind spotting" demands considerable self-awareness and self-control. When you look in the mirror, you see yourself as you would like to see yourself. You may not like certain personal traits that are in the blind spots, but you are unable to address these areas and change them because you are unaware of them.

- F—façade. This represents what you know about yourself but what is hidden from others. For one reason or another you keep information hidden; you fear risking too much. One reason for "my façade" could be that I do not feel supported at home or in my work situation. Perhaps you want to protect yourself from being criticized. You may keep certain kinds of information secret to support and protect others. Your reasons may be selfish in that you wish to control the situation and nondisclosure could be tactically helpful. Another reason may be in the interest of tact or diplomacy, deflecting potential resentment. "Privacy" may protect you and others. The private self is controlled.
- U—unknown. This is that part of you that is unknown by others as well by yourself. What affects you may be below the surface of awareness of both parties. For example, early childhood experiences may give rise to aversions learned through experience. We may have unrecognized resources and traits.[2]

The goal of a good communicator is to enlarge the arena window as much as possible in a balanced fashion. To do so, we attempt to reduce the "unknown" regions. We attempt to reduce what we don't know about ourselves and what others don't know about us. The result is shown in Chart 7.6.

We increase disclosure because we increase trust. We are more willing to give out information about ourselves. We share more of what we think and how we feel. We share, but we do not become the "chatter box" that rambles incessantly. What we share is meaningful disclosure. We become more open and honest in answering questions and in sharing information as needed. We share our thoughts and feelings while still making others feel important.

---

[2]Many of the comments in this section are the result of the work of Chris Jarvis who cites the following references: Luft, J., and Ingham, H., "The JoHari Window: A Graphic Model for Interpersonal Relations," University of California, Western Training Lab, 1955. Berne, E., *The Games People Play*, Grove Press, New York, 1964. Goffman, I., *The Presentation of Self in Everyday Life*, Penguin, New York, 1999. Shannon, C., and Weaver, W., *The Mathematical Theory of Communication*, Illinois University Press, 1968.

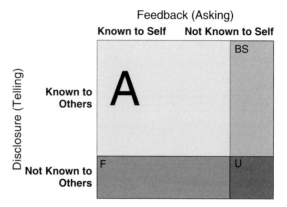

Chart 7.6   JoHari Window Increased Openness

We increase feedback by being willing to listen. Asking meaningful questions triggers this. We must be truly interested in how others perceive us. We want to know their honest opinions about the actions that we take. This helps us improve our relationship and decreases the size of the blind box.

As we take the test, we will find ourselves in one of four types of configurations (see Chart 7.7).

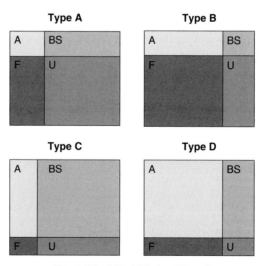

Chart 7.7   JoHari Window "Types"

Type A is like the children who are just learning about life and about how to express themselves. The arena is very small, and the unknown is by far the largest.

In type B we have a huge façade and a midsized unknown. This is a person who knows how to ask questions and how to listen, but is not very good at opening up and disclosing his or her own feelings.

In type C we have a huge blind spot and a small façade. This is "Chatty Charlie," always talking and mostly about himself. He always supplies far more information than anyone is interested in. This individual is a poor listener and is fearful of what may be disclosed in any feedback process.

Type D is well rounded and a good communicator. This person has a balanced ability to tell and ask.

It would not be good to be too extreme in our sharing and asking. In certain areas of intimacy and privacy, we can learn "more than we really want to know." In addition, some areas of our lives remain undiscovered. There will always be some unknown territory.

The JoHari principle includes an adaptation of the "ladder of inference" (see the next acceptance tool topic). In the ladder of inference, we see the well-balanced individual who is capable of moving up and down the ladder, as more or less information is required. As we move up and down the ladder by telling and asking, we expand our arena and develop a higher level of understanding and capability.

In order to be a good facilitator, you would need to be a strong type D personality.

Appendix 7-A contains one version of the JoHari test. There are many other versions as well, and these can be found on the Internet if desired.

12. Ladder of Inference—The ladder of inference is a tool designed to help its user get a better grasp of the information that is being exchanged. It helps process information, including thoughts and ideas, and it assists us in arriving at meaningful conclusions so that we take the most appropriate actions. The tool helps us avoid jumping to early conclusions that are often inaccurate. We strive to gather as much information as possible before formulating our conclusions. The ladder of inference promotes the use of asking questions and sharing information in open conversations in order to make sure that we are on the right track toward an appropriate conclusion. (See Chart 7.8.)

The ladder of inference is a reasoning process that allows individuals to perceive events that surround them throughout their entire life. The interactions that occur during our lifetime affect the conclusions that we draw in our current and future encounters. The encounters are considered

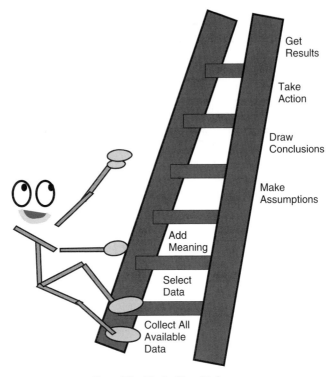

Get
Results

Take
Action

Draw
Conclusions

Make
Assumptions

Add
Meaning

Select
Data

Collect All
Available
Data

Chart 7.8   The Ladder of Inference

to be filters through which we see the world. These encounters result in the opinions or beliefs that we form about what we see and hear, and then they affect our reactions. In the ladder of inference we are cycling new data through our filters, thereby allowing us to formulate the most objective conclusions possible. The process of interacting with new data and formulating conclusions may be very rapid and may only take a matter of seconds. Therefore, the objective is to gather as much data as possible and to defer judgment for as long as possible.

For the ladder of inference to be the most effective, we must become the masters of two activities: asking and telling. Through asking we try to create an openness that allows others to express their opinions without fear of retaliation so as to bring as much information as possible to the surface. In telling we state our viewpoint in a tactful manner, which avoids conflict but still allows the listener to fully understand what we are saying. We climb the ladder using "telling," and we come back down the ladder by "asking" in an attempt to maximize the strength of our conclusions.

The first step of the ladder is to *Collect All Available Data* (see Chart 7.8). We try to gather as much data as possible so as to facilitate the decision-making process. At this step we ask questions such as who, what, where, when, why, how, and how much. We attempt to look at all sides of an issue, drawing from our own experiences as well as the experiences of others. We want to lay as thorough a foundation as possible.

The second step is to *Select Data*. Not all data is relevant to the topic under consideration. We need to be selective about the data and also open minded to the fact that others may see data as relevant when you do not see it as such. We need to consider all perspectives. We need to be sure that we have collected data that is clear and relevant and that allows a complete picture of the topic under consideration. If not, go back and collect more data.

The third step is to *Add Meaning*. Each person who views the data will add his or her own perspective and meaning to the information based on personal feelings, passions, biases, and experiences. It may become necessary to validate the information in order to achieve uniformity of interpretation. We need to carefully listen to viewpoints different from our own. By selecting the wrong information, we are increasing the difficulty of developing a clear understanding of the information. We need to be careful not to add meaning to incomplete information and therefore achieving invalid conclusions. One way to make sure this does not happen is to consider this issue from every stakeholder's perspective.

The fourth step is to *Make Assumptions*. We always make assumptions anyway, but the concern here is to make sure we are making the correct assumptions. We need to validate our assumption process. We need to be aware of feelings and biases creeping in on the assumptions. We may need to defer judgment if we have any concerns about any of our assumptions that may not be based on concrete facts.

The fifth step is to *Draw Conclusions*. Conclusions come from judgments based on the facts and on a clear thought process. We want to arrive at meaningful conclusions by carefully performing each step up to this point. We evaluate our conclusions by validating them against the other stakeholders to see if they see the facts and the assumptions in the same way that we do. If they are not all on the same page, then there is most likely something wrong with one of the earlier steps in the ladder. This becomes a critical process in team interaction. You want the team members to be in sync with each other, and this cannot happen if any of the previous rungs of the ladder are not processed correctly.

The sixth step is to *Take Action*. At this point the action to be taken should be obvious, and everyone (team members and stakeholders) should be unified in their opinions about what that action is. If the foundation

for control. Too many Relaters will help us get along, but we will never accomplish anything. And too many Entertainers will make the project fun but extremely unproductive.

Take the test in Appendix 7-C where you first test yourself and then you take the test looking at how you see others. This information should be collected for your entire team where each person looks at themselves and the other team members. With this information the facilitator can see if the team is skewed or if it is well balanced.

14. Situational Leadership—Situational leadership is a tool that attempts to help the facilitator, the boss, or anyone else influence someone to complete a task successfully. There is a follower and a leader, and these roles may be reversed depending on the task. We start with an understanding of the needs of the follower. Does the follower want to complete the task? Does the follower know how to complete the task?

The leader's responsibility is to offer moral support in the form of reassurance. In addition, the leader offers direction by facilitation skills training and by making the necessary resources available to complete the task.

The situational leadership follower grid is shown on Chart 7.11. Here we see four quadrants, each representing a different role. For D1 we have the enthusiastic beginner who has a high level of commitment but a low level of competency. We classify this individual as the enthusiastic beginner who is very eager and has a high desire to achieve. This individual is dedicated but has little or no experience relevant to the job. The D1 individual has almost no job knowledge and does not understand what needs to be accomplished.

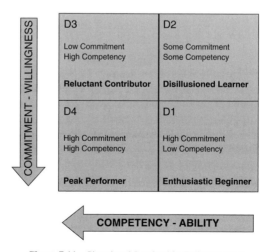

Chart 7.11   Situational Leadership Follower Grid

For the D2 individual we have the disillusioned learner. This is some-one who is moderately eager and has an average desire to achieve. This individual is somewhat dedicated. Unfortunately, he or she also has few experiences relevant to the job and so has only minimal job knowledge and an incomplete knowledge of what needs to be accomplished.

For D3 we have the reluctant contributor, who is someone who is not eager at all. This individual has a low desire to achieve and is not dedicated to the job or the organization. This individual has job experience and a great deal of job knowledge. This individual understands that task and what needs to be accomplished but is not driven to make a difference in the job.

In D4 we find the peak performer who is a very eager person and has a high desire to achieve. This individual is also very dedicated. This individual is highly experienced in relevant job-related issues and has a great deal of job knowledge. This individual thoroughly understands what needs to be accomplished and has a high desire to do the job.

The situational leadership leader grid is shown in Chart 7.12. Here we also see four quadrants, each with its classification of the individual. For S1 we have the directing/telling type of personality where the leader sets all the goals and solves all the problems. The leader controls the who, what, when, where, how, why, and how much of all decisions. This is a one-directional top down communication where the leader supervises all and evaluates everyone and everything.

The S2 type of leader is the coaching/selling type of leader where again the leader sets all the goals but in this case the leader consults with

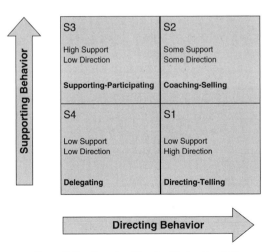

Chart 7.12 Situational Leadership Leader Grid

the follower. There is two-way communication, but the leader makes all the final decisions.

In the S3 leader we find a leader who is supporting and participating. This leader provides assurance and support and offers the necessary resources to assure peak performance. This leader actively listens. This leader is a follower and makes final decisions jointly with the employees.

The S4 type leader is the delegator who follows defined problems and sets the way for participative problem solving. This is the maverick-type leader who accepts the employees' decisions and offers them the resources to implement their decisions. This leader does minimal monitoring of the employees' progress.

The purpose of the situational leadership questionnaire is to discover your leadership style in a variety of situations. It tests your ability to recognize situations, and it evaluates your leadership effectiveness. It also helps the facilitators to determine what types of management they are dealing with. It helps them to determine a strategy for moving the project forward.[3] Go to Appendix 7-D to find one sample of the questionnaire.

Once you have completed the evaluation in the appendix, you can challenge yourself in your leadership abilities by considering the following questions:

a. **Do I See Myself as Others See Me?** Circle the highest percentage in the box labeled Self-Perception. The highest percentage tells you what you think your primary leadership style is. If you have a tie between two of the options, then you have two primary styles. Circle the highest percentage under your boss's perception, associates' perception, and team members' perception. If the highest percentage of your boss's, associates', and team members' perceptions fall into the same quadrant as your highest percentage falls, you have an accurate perception of your leadership style. Research shows that a difference of more than 13 percent between others' perceptions and yours would mean that you do not see yourself accurately. For example, if a manager's perception shows that 55 percent of the answers fall in the S3 quadrant, and the team members' perception shows 40 percent in S3, that manager would not have an accurate perception of his or her leadership style. Do you see yourself accurately?

b. **Am I Flexible?** You will be seen as moderately flexible if your team members perceive that you use at least two styles, and as very flexible if you use three styles. To determine whether you use more than one

---

[3] Major pieces of this section are taken from the work of Tim Hutzel of MainStream Management.

style, examine the differences between the percentages. If the differences between the two or three highest percentages are less than 13 percent, you use more than one style. For example, if team members' perceptions were S1 = 10%, S2 = 45%, S3 = 40%, and S4 = 5%, his or her team would see this manager as flexible with only two of the four styles: Styles 2 and 3. Using another example, S1 = 5%, S2 = 35%, S3 = 34%, and S4 = 26%, this manager is flexible enough to use three styles: Styles 2, 3, and 4. Statistics show that from their team members' perspective, 50 percent of managers only have one style, 30 percent of managers use two styles, and 19 percent use three styles. Only 1 percent of managers have flexibility in all four styles. Look at the percentage data from your boss, your associates, and your team members and make a similar assessment. Are you perceived as a flexible manager?

c. **Do I Manage People Differently?** To understand whether or not your team members perceive that you use different styles in different situations, examine the quadrants in the boxes from the leader grid. Identify your primary style under self-perception by circling the number that is the highest in quadrant S1, S2, S3, or S4. If you have a tie, circle both. Complete this step for each person who rated your leadership style. If at least two team members or two associates circle two different primary styles, you are perceived as managing people differently. Do you manage people differently?

d. **Do I Diagnose Well?** To completely understand how you might improve your effectiveness as a manager, it is helpful to examine the appropriateness of the styles others predict you would use in each of the 20 situations. Effectiveness scores should have been computed for each respondent. Notice the symbols printed next to the style choices on the raw score sheets. A *b* is an excellent answer. An *nb* indicates a good selection. Poor or fair responses are left blank. Multiplying the excellent answers by 4, the good answers by 3, and the poor or fair answers by 1, and adding the numbers together computes the effectiveness scores. An average score by team members is $48 +/- 3$. If your team members' effectiveness scores for your leadership style average above 51, you are seen as diagnosing their needs and using the appropriate leadership style. Do you diagnose well?

At this point, the leader and the facilitator have a valuable tool about the management style and the effectiveness of each leader. With this information, an effective lean implementation strategy is facilitated.

15. Values System—The Values System is an individual survey tool that focuses on helping you understand where you rank in your personal

relationship development. It can also be used as an effective communications tool.

Personality profiles utilizing the Values System survey focus on improving understanding and communications between individuals.[4] One of the key elements of a productive change culture is the ability of the individuals within that culture to understand the inherent diversity that exists within their organization. Another element is to understand that diversity can be used to strengthen the organization and to ensure that checks and balances are in place to prevent groupthink and isolation. Improving understanding of diversity and developing improved communications based on an understanding of diversity are at the heart of creating an effective team of diverse individuals, and therefore an effective organization.

Although various profiling tools have traditionally been used in Human Resource departments as a way of identifying desired characteristics relative to filling job classifications and as a tool for filtering out undesired candidates, the use of this tool is more focused on creating understanding and improving the ability of individuals to effectively communicate their thoughts and ideas to others whose way of processing information or analyzing information differs from their own.

Values training stems from work developed by Dr. Clare Graves's "Level of Existence," in which he identified and classified various core values of individuals. Dr. Graves believed that individuals' value systems are based on responses to their environment and that as they grow and experience life, their values systems develop and change. Dr. Graves's work focused on hiring practices and on matching the right individuals to the right job. The Center for Values Research (CVR), a company out of Texas, refined Dr. Graves's work for the purpose of focusing organizations on understanding the various values systems of individuals within the organization and utilizing that knowledge to create an improved working environment. The core purpose of CVR's work is to help organizations create and maintain a "union-free" environment, by eliminating the need for third-party intervention within an organization. Although values training is effective in both of these areas, it is also a highly effective tool for understanding barriers to communication and helping individuals to improve their ability to effectively communicate.

Although each of us as individuals has within us varying levels of the core values, most of us have a dominant and a backup value system that forms the focus of our response to information and situations. The

---

[4]Major pieces of this section are taken from the work of Tom Cluley of MainStream Management, a Lean consulting firm focused on optimizing the acceptance phase of the Lean effort.

dominant system is our actualized system. It is the system that reflects who we want to be and how we feel we should react. The backup system is more of a natural system, reflecting our developed, reactive self. When we are under extreme pressure, we tend to fall back on this backup system to resolve conflict.

The survey, which can be found in Appendix 7-B, scores your responses and reactions to specific situations. After completing the survey, you end up with scores in each of the following areas:[5]

- *Reactive.* This is where you respond without forethought or planning. All healthy individuals are born with a reactive value system. It is this survival-based system that causes us to respond to active stimuli in our environment. When we touch a stove, we pull back. When we are cold, we seek shelter. The reactive value system, though important in our development, becomes buried within our subconscious as we encounter more complex stimuli, and as such it is not a focus of our understanding of adults. It can best be characterized by the statement "Life is."

- *Tribal (category e in the survey).* This is the individual who is cliquish and responds with the group rather than individually. Individuals with dominant tribal values or security-based systems tend to be comfortable in small, tightly knit groups where they feel secure. They trust members of their group and tend to distrust outsiders. Tribal individuals are inherently resistant to and distrusting of change, and when confronted with change they tend to seek approval of their informal leaders, or authority figures, rather than the formal leaders of the organization (unless those individuals happen to be one and the same). They will respond to leaders whom they perceive to be benevolently autocratic, someone who tells them kindly and firmly what to do. Tribal individuals like to know what is expected of them, and they tend to like repetitive tasks. They often look at work as something they do, and not as a thing that defines who they are. As a result, they tend to like some level of physical or manual activity in their work. They learn best through step-by-step hands-on training, and they respond best to regular reinforcement of their performance rather than scheduled reviews. These individuals will support change if they, or their informal leaders, perceive that change will strengthen and protect the tribe. This individual is best characterized by the statement, "Life is assurance."

---

[5]This is a modification of some of Clare Graves's work.

- *Egocentric (b)*. This individual is paranoid and insecure about his or her position. This feeling comes out in authoritarian behavior, and this behavior is how this type of individual shows power. Individuals with egocentric values systems see life as a challenge with them pitted against the world. Egocentrics or self-oriented individuals express themselves impulsively without concern about the impact on others. They tend to be distrusting and confrontational, and they like to see themselves as heroes, taking on and overcoming challenges. These individuals are inherently distrusting of change and look at how the change will affect them, rather than how it will affect the organization. Egocentric individuals do not tend to make good team members, and as leaders they are often autocratic, insisting on obedience. While egocentric individuals have problems in group settings, they can make excellent single contributors and can sometimes be relied on to overcome significant challenge in achieving an objective. If they perceive a change to be good for them, they will push for the change. If a leader is able to obtain the respect of an egocentric individual, that individual will be extremely loyal and will go to great lengths to prove his or her worth to that leader. As with tribal individuals, egocentric individuals learn best with hands-on training and respond best to continuous feedback. This classification is best characterized by the statement, "Life is a fight."

- *Conformist (c)*. This individual follows the rules and wants everyone else to follow them as well. Individuals with conformist or systems-oriented value systems are rules-based individuals. They believe that life can be best served if everyone follows the rules. These individuals believe in honor and commitment. They favor structure in their lives and in their work environment. They learn from structured documentation, and they prefer structured, formal reviews. They are loyal and hard-working people who need to know clearly what is expected of them. Conformists do not mind change if that change is planned, standardized, and documented, and if the change leads to improving structure and conformance. They are best characterized by the statement, "Life is duty."

- *Competitive (f)*. Life's a game and we're each out to win. This individual tends to be manipulative and entrepreneurial, and often this category is referred to as the "manipulative category." Individuals with manipulative values systems see life as a challenge that they are out to win. They are materialistic, success-oriented, competitive, adventurous, and status-conscious individuals. They are risk takers and do not mind bending or at times outright ignoring the rules to achieve their objectives. Therefore, they like the power to make decisions and the authority to wheel and deal. They prefer to work as independents where they have control over their success or failure. To them change is a tool used to win. They like to set goals or to have goals set for them, but then they want to be given the freedom to be inventive and resourceful in meeting their objectives. Manipulative individuals tend to be creative in solving problems, but they do not have any problem letting others clean up the mess left in their wake. They work well with management by objectives. These individuals see that "Life is a game."

- *Sociocentric (a)*. This is the union member who wants to influence and work within a group. Individuals with sociocentric values systems are interested in a cooperative and nurturing environment. They have strong feelings about social responsibility. They like working with people rather than things, and they want everyone to get along and be comfortable in their environment. These individuals tend to avoid confrontation, and they reject hostility. They do not mind change as long as they perceive change as something that will improve the environment and create more harmony. They perceive performance reviews as an informal encounter with peers who share their needs, feelings, and goals. For them "Life is equality."

- *Existentialist (d)*. These are ethical individuals who tend to do what they think is right in spite of the rules or the group. They are higher level thinkers. They tend to be leaders rather than managers who prefer to influence rather than control. Behavior has to make logical sense. Individuals with existentialist or reality-oriented values systems are goal-oriented problem solvers. These individuals tend to value personal freedom, independence, and autonomy. They form their own system of ethics and rules of conduct, and they remain very consistent within their definition of right and wrong. Although these self-motivated individuals tend to make good leaders, they often fall short as managers because they tend to be big picture thinkers and they avoid getting trapped in the details that are sometimes at the heart of success or failure. They prefer work that requires creativity and complex problem-solving skills. These individuals tend to be able to adjust to their environment, accepting a wide range of diversity and ambiguity in people, and thus they work well with varying values systems in order to create consensus. They like to create their own goals and plans of action for a diversity of tasks. They see their supervision as a resource and expect the employees to share information as needed. They tend to make good change agents. They see "life as acceptance and change."

This survey tool is used to define what you "want to be" more than "what you are." As you classify yourself, you will find that each of these categories has a clearly defined and unique value system.

These brief overviews, through in no way intended to be comprehensive, help set the stage for an understanding of why individuals respond differently to situations and ideas. The first thing we need to do in order to improve our understanding of this level of diversity and improve our effective communications is to be able to recognize these values systems within individuals with whom we interface during the course of our daily interactions. We then need to be able to change the way we communicate with these individuals so that we can (1) properly reflect our ideas in a manner that they can relate to and (2) understand their point of view, filtering their communications in order to identify those elements that we can relate to.

Victor Frankel, a survivor of Auschwitz and father of a school of psychology, attributed his survival to his ability to understand the nature of power. Frankel defined power as our ability as human beings to alter our response to stimuli in a manner that will achieve the greatest opportunity for a desired outcome. The opportunity to exercise power exists in that brief period in time during which we can choose not to respond based on instinct, but control and thereby alter our response. Our natural tendency is to react and respond to the world based on our individual values systems and what is important to us. If we can learn to assess the situation and communicate in a manner that addresses the values systems of those around us, we will have a much greater chance of gaining consensus, and thereby achieving our desired outcome. Although some may see this as manipulation, in truth, it is the foundation of effective communications.

Shape Electronics was a subsidiary organization of the Wiremold Corporation. Although Shape had been utilizing Lean and conducting *Kaizen* events for the prior seven years, their progress was limited, and they were not achieving the level of sustained improvement exhibited in other Wiremold organizations. As a result, the president of the company requested some "Lean" help. Tom Cluley was asked to work with them to get their "Lean" going.

On the first day, after checking in with the president, Tom sat in on a production meeting. During the meeting the operations manager and the engineering manager disagreed over a product prototype that was pending shipment. The operations manager challenged engineering to have his people get the documentation completed on the product prototype that was scheduled to ship the next day. Operations told engineering that if they could not get the product shipped, they would lose the large order that was pending on the approval of the prototype. The operations manager even went so far as to state that he did not think engineering could get the job done, and laid out a personal challenge to prove him wrong. The values systems of these two managers was so different that they continually were in conflict with each other.

As it turned out, several of the company's key staff members had diverse personalities and differing values systems. The president himself was a combination sociocentric and competitive individual, and as such had always tried to smooth over differences among his staff. Tom ended up working with his staff for about two months before ever setting foot on the production floor. His explanation to the staff was that until the leadership learned how to work as a team and send a uniform message to the workforce, it would be impossible to expect the workforce to work together using Lean tools to solve problems. When Tom's team did get around to conducting Lean activities on the floor, it was with a unified staff and a clear and consistent message.

If an idea is sound, it can be presented in such a manner as to engage the support of individuals of any value system. In contrast, whenever an idea has trouble being accepted by someone of a particular value system, it probably has some level of self-motivated interest at one of the other levels and therefore is not the best overall solution.

A simple survey tool (shown in Appendix 7-B) can identify where an individual stands relative to work-related values systems. Simply identifying an individual's value system is not very useful. It is our ability to take advantage of that moment in time between when we first want to express ourselves and, based on what we know of that individual's values and what is important to them, how we then alter our communications, that dictates how effective we will be in producing consensus and achieving our desired outcome.

By understanding values systems, we can improve our understanding of group dynamics and become more effective communicators, both within our team and between levels of an organization.

16. Learning Curves—The learning curve suggests that employees are not fully efficient at a new process immediately after a change in the process occurs. Some amount of lead time is always required before full efficiency can take place. Chart 7.13 shows us how change occurs. Change is a process that is integrated over a period of time by building transition bridges between the phases of the change.

The chart shows that we are currently operating at a certain level of proficiency (Stage A) considered appropriate for current operating practices. Then a change is introduced into the status quo (Point X). The change causes performance to go down (Stage B). This is where

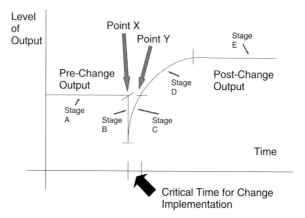

Chart 7.13   Learning Curve

many managers lose interest in the improvement process. They declare that they expected output to increase rather than decrease, and many times their immediate reaction is to pull the plug on the change process. This is completely the wrong reaction. Rather, they need to give the change process a chance to work its way through the learning curve (Stages C and D). During Stage C, the employee is simply trying to get back on track and to get familiar with the new process. Part of this reduced performance can be caused by training or by the disruptions caused by facilities remodeling. Whatever the cause, initial performance will decline, and management needs to realize and accept it as part of the change process.

As we work our way through Stage C, we finally recover to the initial level of performance (Point Y). Then, as we enter Stage D we see that the change will actually increase the output of the process. The learning curve continues through Stage D on into Stage E where the process returns to a new, higher stabilized level of performance for the new methodology.

The change curve is not always as quick as we would like. The "Critical Time for Change Implementation" in Chart 7.13 can be quite slow. For example, if a facilities remodel takes more than a year, the change process at this point may also take more than one year.

There are no hidden secrets to how the change curve works. The key here is for management to realize that change initially causes output to drop. And by anticipating this drop, they can better plan and predict the effects on overall long-term performance.

WRAP-UP

The acceptance tools discussed in this chapter are just a few of the many tools available. Those included in the chapter are the ones I have used and found effective in the Lean management acceptance process. Try them on a team and see if they are useful for your SCM Lean optimization efforts.

REFERENCES

Beck, Edward, and Christopher Cowan. *Spiral Dynamics: Mastering Values, Leadership and Change*, Blackwell Publishing Ltd., Malden, Ma., 1996.

Nadler, Gerald, and Shozo Hibino, *Breakthrough Thinking; The Seven Principles of Creative Problem Solving*, Prima Publishing, Rocklin, CA, 1994.

Plenert, Gerhard. *The eManager: Value Chain Management in an eCommerce World*, Blackhall Publishing, Los Angeles, CA, 2001.

Plenert, Gerhard, *International Operations Management*, Copenhagen Business School Press, Copenhagen, Denmark, 2002, Reprinted in India by Ane Books, New Delhi, 2003.

Plenert, Gerhard, and Shozo Hibino, *Making Innovation Happen: Concept Management Through Integration*, St. Lucie Press, Del Ray Beach, FL, 1997.

Plenert, Gerhard, and Bill Kirchmier, *Finite Capacity Scheduling*, John Wiley & Sons, New York, 2000.

Semler, Ricardo, *Maverick; The Success Story Behind the World's Most Unusual Workplace*, Warner Books, New York, 1993.

Appendix 7-A

The JoHari Window Assessment Test[6]

Directions: Using a five-point scale, you assess yourself and other coworkers on interpersonal communication styles and the use of 24 behaviors important for respectful and trust-building human relations. Read each behavior and determine how much it is like you. Or, if you are rating someone else, then how much is this behavior like that other person (from your perspective). Select a numerical value from the scale and enter the number in the appropriate space to the right.

Step 1: Total the scores you gave yourself for the odd-numbered questions (all questions with (T) in front of them). This total represents your evaluation of your willingness to express yourself. Record the score on the **TRUST** axis in Chart 7A.1. Next, total the scores you gave yourself for the even-numbered questions (all the questions with (R) in front of them). This is your willingness to listen to others. Record this score on the **RESPECT** axis. Then find the point where the two scores intersect and shade in the enclosed area.

Step 2: You are now ready to analyze the scores you gave your coworker. Similar to Step 1, total the scores you gave your coworker for all

---

[6]This test was taken from the MainStream Management Consultant database, and they got it from TAMCO, Training and Management Consultants, Inc., which in turn picked up the test from: Luft, Joseph, *Group Process: An Introduction to Group Dynamics*, Mayfield Publishing Co., Mountain View, CA., 1984; Manning, G., Curtis, K., and McMillan, S., *The Human Side of Work: Building Community in the Workplace*, South-Western Publishing, Nashville, TN., 1995. From *Total Quality in Managing Human Resources* by Joseph A. Petrick and Diana S. Furr, St. Lucie Press, NY, 1995.

profile, and the Picture Window profile. As indicated in Chart 7A.3, each category exhibits different degrees of respect and trust. The four profiles differ in three important respects: (1) skills used in listening and expressing, (2) effects on the individual, and (3) the effects on the relationship. The optimal interpersonal self-disclosure profile is the Picture Window because it enlarges the areas known to self and others, thereby allowing more of the performance potential of an individual to be recognized and invested in the organization.

JoHari Window Test

Scale Value	Meaning
5	Extremely characteristic; always does this
4	Quite characteristic; usually does this
3	Somewhat characteristic; occasionally does this
2	Quite uncharacteristic; seldom does this
1	Extremely uncharacteristic; never does this

Human Relations Behavior	**Self**	**Coworkers(s)**
(T) 1. States opinions in an uncensored manner	_____	_____ _____ _____ _____
(R) 2. Invites ideas from others; does not dominate discussion	_____	_____ _____ _____ _____
(T) 3. Admits to confusion or lack of knowledge when uncertain	_____	_____ _____ _____ _____
(R) 4. Shows interest in what others have to say through body posture and facial expressions	_____	_____ _____ _____ _____
(T) 5. Expresses self openly and candidly	_____	_____ _____ _____ _____
(R) 6. Gives support to others who are struggling to express themselves	_____	_____ _____ _____ _____

(*Continued*)

(T) 7. Admits to being wrong, rather than attempting to cover up or place blame	_____	_____	_____	_____	_____
(R) 8. Keeps private conversations private; does not reveal confidences	_____	_____	_____	_____	_____
(T) 9. Tells others what they need to know, even if it is unpleasant	_____	_____	_____	_____	_____
(R) 10. Listens to others without being defensive	_____	_____	_____	_____	_____
(T) 11. Is honest with his or her feelings	_____	_____	_____	_____	_____
(R) 12. Shows respect for the feelings of others	_____	_____	_____	_____	_____
(T) 13. Shares concerns, hopes, and goals with others	_____	_____	_____	_____	_____
(R) 14. Does not act as if others are wasting their time	_____	_____	_____	_____	_____
(T) 15. Shares thoughts, no matter how "far out" they may seem	_____	_____	_____	_____	_____
(R) 16. Does not fake attention or merely pretend to listen	_____	_____	_____	_____	_____
(T) 17. Speaks truthfully, refused to lie	_____	_____	_____	_____	_____
(R) 18. Does not act hurt, angry, or mistreated when others disagree	_____	_____	_____	_____	_____
(T) 19. Is sincere; does not pretend	_____	_____	_____	_____	_____
(R) 20. Values suggestions from others	_____	_____	_____	_____	_____
(T) 21. Uses language and terms others can understand	_____	_____	_____	_____	_____

(*Continued*)

(R) 22. Tries to prevent interruptions, such as telephone calls and people walking in during important discussions	_____	_____	_____	_____	_____
(T) 23. Tells others when they are wrong or need to change	_____	_____	_____	_____	_____
(R) 24. Encourages others to express themselves	_____	_____	_____	_____	_____

Appendix 7-B

The Values Systems Survey[7]

Given a total of 12 points for each statement, assign points to each response based on how much you agree with the response.

1. To me, company loyalty means . . .

supporting the goals of the company as long as they don't go against one's principles.		**d**
sticking with the company through good years and bad, and making sacrifices as necessary to keep the company strong.		**c**
giving up my freedom and being an apple-polisher.		**b**
being on the job as much as I can and doing what I'm told.		**e**
commitment to a company that is concerned with the needs of its employees.		**a**
supporting the organization that lets me succeed.		**f**
Total points for this question –		12

[7]This test was taken from the MainStream Management Consultant database, and they got it from the work of Clare Graves.

2. The kind of boss I like is one who . . .

tells me exactly what to do and how to do it, and encourages me by doing it with me.	e
is tough but allows me to be tough too.	b
calls the shots and isn't always changing his mind, and sees to it that everyone follows the rules.	c
doesn't ask questions as long as the job gets done.	f
gets us working together in close harmony by being more a friendly person than a boss.	a
gives me access to information I need and lets me do my job in my own way.	d

3. Money is important to me because . . .

it enables me to enjoy many friendships and to support worthwhile causes.	a
it provides freedom and the opportunity to be myself; having money is not as important as what I do with it.	d
it allows me to buy the things I need, such as a sharp car and clothes, and makes me feel like somebody.	b
it allows me to save for a rainy day, to aid the less fortunate, and to have a decent standard of living.	c
it pays for groceries, the rent, and other things I need to keep going.	e
it is a measure of my career success in my company and my community.	f

4. In my opinion, the profit a company makes . . .

is its primary reason for existing and is the most important measure of success.	f
goes to the people who already have a lot of money.	b
keeps the company strong so the employees can continue to have good jobs.	c
is important, but there isn't much I can do about it.	e
is not as important as its products and services and the way it treats its people.	a
will be greater in the long run when the needs of the employees and the company are both considered.	d

5. My work . . .

I prefer work of my own choosing that offers continuing challenge and requires imagination and initiative, even if the pay isn't high.		**d**
I don't like any kind of work that ties me down, but I'll do it if I have to in order to get some money; then I'll quit and do what I want until I have to get another job.		**b**
The kind of work I usually do is ok as long as it's a steady job and I have a good boss.		**e**
I have worked hard for what I have and I think I deserve some good breaks. I believe others should be loyal to the organization if they want to get ahead.		**c**
I am responsible for my own success and always on the lookout for new opportunities which will lead to a more responsible position and greater financial reward.		**f**
I believe that doing what I like to do, such as working with people toward a common goal, is more important than getting caught up in a materialistic rat race.		**a**

6. Job freedom, for me means . . .

the opportunity to work where I want and have a steady job.		**c**
the opportunity to do interesting and challenging work, to be able to express myself openly, and freedom to change jobs if I want to.		**d**
having enough independence so I won't be pushed around by higher-ups in the company.		**b**
the opportunity to be friends with anyone without worrying about where they fit into the company.		**a**
not having to worry about my job, sickness, paying bills, and other problems.		**e**
the opportunity to stand on my own two feet and to pursue success without too much interference from supervision or anything else.		**f**

7. I believe that big companies . . .

and their employees should be dedicated to the goal of maximizing profits because both "win" when this goal is achieved.		**f**
are doing their duty when they provide steady jobs and pay enough to allow employees to maintain a decent standard of living.		**c**

make fat profits at the expense of most workers.		**b**
are probably necessary in our world, but they must be more concerned with better balance between organizational and individual needs.		**d**
should take good care of employees by giving them good pay, hours, and working conditions.		**e**
should support causes of social and economic justice, provide a pleasant work climate, share profits, and be selective in choosing products and customers.		**a**

8. In my opinion company rules are . . .

useful only if they promote social and economic justice.		**a**
necessary to keep employees from doing wrong things and protect us from people who want to break the rules.		**e**
best when they are few, and effective if they succeed in putting the burden of responsibility on the employees.		**d**
made by top management for the top management, and rules don't give the employee a chance.		**b**
necessary as guidelines, but it is sometimes necessary to look for loopholes in order to get the job done.		**f**
necessary to preserve order in the company, and employees who violate the rules should be told how important it is to follow the rules.		**c**

Total All Points Assigned to Each Letter						
Total Should Equal 96 Points	**d**	**a**	**f**	**c**	**b**	**e**

Appendix 7-C

The PA-PT Survey[8]

Circle one word from each pair, responding to the statement:
(if doing the survey for someone else) "If I were to choose, I would say the person is . . . ", or
(if doing the survey for yourself) "I am . . . "
Pick the answer that applies at least 51% of the time or more.
Mark at least one of each pair of items.

A	**B**
More animated	More passive
More "take charge"	More "get along"
More assertive	More hesitant
More challenging	More accepting
More active	More thoughtful
More confronting	More supporting
More talkative	More quiet
More bold	More retiring
More intense	More relaxed
More forceful	More subtle

Total Number of A's Circled = _____

Total the circled statements in Column A and put the score on the **Total** line. Then circle the matching number on the horizontal line on the graph of Chart 7C.1.
Perform the same process for the items below.

---

[8]This test was taken from the MainStream Management Consulting database.

C	D
More flamboyant	More proper
More spontaneous	More disciplined
More responsive	More self-controlled
More impulsive	More methodical
More close	More distant
More feeling	More thinking
More people oriented	More task oriented
More outgoing	More reserved
More dramatic	More matter or fact
More warm	More cool

Total Number of D's Circled = _____

Total the circled statements in column D and put the score on the **Total** line. Then circle the matching number on the vertical line on the graph of Chart 7C.1.

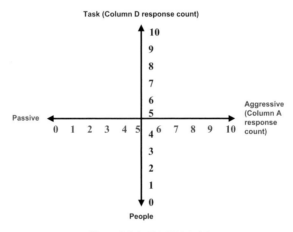

Chart 7C.1 PA-PT Model

The Situational Leadership Survey[9]

Select and circle your answer for each question.

1. **A new employee has been asked to write a report to buy new equipment for the division. She needs to learn more about this equipment in order to make a sound decision about options and costs. She feels this assignment will stretch her already full schedule. This manager would:**

   a. Tell her when the report is needed, and what should be in the report. Outline the steps the employee should take to become knowledgeable about the new equipment. Set weekly meetings with her to track progress.

   b. Ask her to produce the report, and discuss its importance. Ask her for a deadline for completion. Give her the resources she thinks she needs. Periodically check with her to track progress.

   c. Tell her when the report is needed, and discuss its importance. Explain what the report should include. Outline the steps the employee should take to learn more about the equipment. Listen to her concerns and use her ideas when possible. Plan weekly meetings to track progress.

   d. Ask her to produce the report, and discuss its importance. Explore the barriers the employee feels must be removed and the strategies for removing them. Ask her to set a deadline for completion and periodically check with her to track progress.

[9]This test was taken from the MainStream Management Consultant database.

2. **This manager's task force has been working hard to complete its divisionwide report. A new member has joined the group. He must present cost figures at the end of next week, but he knows nothing about the report requirements and format. He is excited about learning more about his role in the group. This manager would:**

   a. Tell him exactly what is needed, and specify the format and requirements. Introduce him to the other members of the task force. Check with him frequently during the week to monitor his progress and to specify corrections.

   b. Ask him if there is anything he or she can do to help. Introduce him to the other task force members. Explore with him what he thinks he needs to get "up to speed" with the report. Check with him frequently during the week to see how he is doing.

   c. Specify the report format and information needed, and solicit his ideas. Introduce him to each task force member. Check with him frequently during the week to see how the report is progressing and to help with modifications.

   d. Welcome him and introduce him to the members of the task force who can help him. Check with him during the week to see how he is doing.

3. **This manager has recently noticed a performance problem with an employee. He seems to show a "don't care" attitude. Only his manager's constant prodding has brought about task completion. The manager suspects this employee may not have enough expertise to complete the high priority task that has been given him. This manager would:**

   a. Specify the steps this employee needs to take and the desired outcome. Clarify timelines and paperwork requirements. Frequently check to see if the task is progressing as it should.

   b. Specify the steps this employee needs to take and the desired outcome. Ask for his ideas and incorporate as appropriate. Ask him to share his feelings about this task assignment. Frequently check to see the task is progressing as it should.

   c. Involve the employee in problem solving for this task. Offer help and encourage him to use his ideas to complete the project. Ask him to share his feelings about the assignment. Frequently check to see that the project is progressing as it should.

   d. Let the employee know how important this task is. Ask him to outline his plan and to send the manager a copy. Frequently check to see if the task is progressing as it should.

4. **The composition of this manager's work group has changed because of company restructuring. Performance levels have dropped. Deadlines**

are being missed, and the manager's boss is concerned. Group members want to improve their performance but need more knowledge and skill. This manager would:

a. Ask the group members to develop their own plan for improving performance. Be available to help them, if asked. Ask them what training they think they need to improve their performance, and give them the resources they need. Continue to track performance.

b. Discuss a plan to solve this problem. Ask the group members for their input and include their ideas in the plan, if possible. Explain the rationale for the plan. Track performance to see how it is carried out.

c. Outline the specific steps the group should follow to solve this problem. Be specific about the time requirements and skills they need to learn. Continue to track performance.

d. Help them determine a plan, and encourage them to be creative. Support their plan and continue to track performance.

5. **Because of budget cuts, it is necessary to consolidate. A highly experienced department member has been asked to take charge of the consolidation. This person has worked in all areas of the manager's department. In the past, she has usually been eager to help. While this manager feels she is able to perform the assignment, the employee seems indifferent to the task. This manager would:**

a. Reassure her. Outline the steps she should take to handle this project. Ask her for ideas and incorporate them when possible, but make sure she follows the manager's general approach. Frequently check to see how things are going.

b. Reassure her. Ask her to handle the project as she sees fit. Be patient, but be available to help. Frequently check to see what is being done.

c. Reassure her. Ask her to determine the best way to approach the project. Help her to develop options, and encourage her to use her own ideas. Frequently check to see how she is doing.

d. Reassure her. Outline an overall plan and specify the steps she should follow. Frequently check to see how the steps are being implemented.

6. **For the second time in a month, an employee's weekly progress reports have been incomplete and late. In the past year he has submitted accurately completed reports on time. This is the first time this manager has spoken to him about this problem. This manager would:**

a. Tell him to improve the completeness of his paperwork. Go over the areas that are incomplete. Make sure he knows what is expected and how to fill out each report section. Continue to track his performance.

    b. Ask him to turn in his paperwork on time and accurately, without pushing him. Continue to track his performance.

    c. Discuss time and completion standards with him. Listen to his concerns, but make sure he knows what is expected. Go over each report section, and answer any question he may have. Use his ideas, if possible. Continue to track his performance.

    d. Ask him why the paperwork is incomplete. Listen to his concerns, and do what can be done to help him understand the importance of timeliness and completeness. Continue to track his performance.

7. **A senior employee has been asked to take on a new project. In the past, his performance has been outstanding. The project he has been given is important to the future of this manager's work group. He is excited about the new assignment but doesn't know where to begin because he lacks project information. The manager's relationship with him is good. This manager would:**

    a. Explain why this employee has the skills to do the job. Ask him what problems he anticipates and help him explore alternative solutions. Frequently stay in touch to support him.

    b. Specify how this employee should handle the project. Define the activities necessary to complete the job. Regularly check to see how things are going.

    c. Ask the employee for a plan for completing the projects in two weeks. Ask him to send a copy for approval. Give him enough time to get started, without pushing him. Frequently offer support.

    d. Outline how the project should be handled, and solicit the employee's ideas and suggestions. Use his ideas when possible, but make sure the manager's general outline is followed. Regularly check to see how things are going.

8. **A staff member is feeling insecure about a job that has been assigned to him. He is highly competent, and this manager knows that this employee has the skills to successfully complete the task. The deadline for completion is near. This manager would:**

    a. Let the employee know of his or her concern about the impending deadline. Help him explore alternative action steps, and encourage him to use his own ideas. Frequently check with him to lend support.

    b. Discuss his or her concerns about the impending deadline. Outline an action plan for the employee to follow, and get his reactions to the plan. Modify the plan if possible but make sure the employee follows the general outline. Frequently check with him to see how things are going.

    c. Specify the reasons for on-time completion of the assignment. Outline the steps the employee should follow. Ask that the steps be followed. Frequently check to see how he is progressing.

    d. Ask the employee if there are any problems, but let him resolve the issue himself. Remind him of the impending deadline, without pushing him. Ask for an update in three days.

9. **The staff has asked this manager to consider a change in their work schedule. Their changes make good sense, and the manager is well aware of the need for change. Members are very competent and work well together. This manager would:**

    a. Help them explore alternative scheduling possibilities. Be available to facilitate their group discussion. Support the plan they develop. Check to see how they implement their plan.

    b. Design the work schedule and explain the rationale behind the design. Listen to their reactions, ask for their ideas and use their recommendations when possible.

    c. Allow the staff to set a work schedule on their own. Let them implement their plan after the manager has approved it. Check with them at a later date to assess their progress.

    d. Design the work schedule and explain how it will work. Answer any questions they may have. Check to see that the schedule is followed.

10. **Due to an organizational change, this manager has been assigned six new people whose performance has been declining over the past three months. They do not seem to have the task knowledge or skill to do their new jobs, and their attitudes have worsened because of the change. In a group meeting, this manager would:**

    a. Make them aware of their three-month performance trend. Ask them to decide what to do about it and set a deadline for implementing their solution. Monitor their progress.

    b. Make them aware of their three-month performance trend. Specify the action steps they should follow. Give them constructive feedback on how to improve their performance. Continue to monitor their performance.

    c. Make them aware of their three-month performance trend. Outline the steps they should follow. Explain why the steps are important, and seek their feedback. Use their ideas when possible, but make sure they follow the general approach. Continue to monitor performance.

    d. Make them aware of their three-month performance trend. Ask them why their performance is declining. Listen to their concerns and ideas. Help them create their own plan for improving performance. Track their performance.

11. **A department member has had a fine performance record over the past 22 months. This employee is excited by the challenges of the upcoming year. Budgets and unit goals have not changed much from last year. In a meeting with him to discuss goals and an action plan for next year, this manager would:**

    a. Ask this employee to submit an outline of his goals and an action plan for the next year for the manager's approval. Tell the employee to expect a call if there are any questions.

    b. Prepare a list of goals and an action plan for the employee to accomplish next year. Send it to him and meet with him to see if he has any questions.

    c. Prepare a list of goals and an action plan for the employee to accomplish next year. Meet with him to discuss his reactions and suggestions. Modify the plan while listening to his ideas, but make the final decisions.

    d. Ask this employee to submit an outline of his goals and an action plan for next year. Review the goals and plan with him. Listen to his ideas and help him explore alternatives. Let him make the final decisions on his goals and plan.

12. **This manager's unit has had an excellent performance over the past two years. However, they have recently experienced three major setbacks due to factors beyond their control. Their performance and morale have drastically dropped, and this manager's boss is concerned. In a group meeting, this manager would:**

    a. Discuss the recent setbacks. Give them the specific steps they should follow to improve their performance. Continue to track performance.

    b. Ask them how they feel about the recent setbacks. Listen to their concerns, and encourage them and help them explore their ideas for improving performance. Continue to track performance.

    c. Discuss the recent setbacks. Clarify the steps they should follow to improve performance. Listen to their ideas and incorporate them, if possible. Emphasize results. Encourage them to keep trying. Continue to track performance.

    d. Discuss the recent setbacks, without pressuring them. Ask them to set a deadline to improve performance and support each other along the way. Continue to track performance.

13. **This manager was recently assigned a new employee who will perform an important job in the unit. Even though this employee is inexperienced, she is enthusiastic and feels she has the confidence to do the job. This manager would:**

a. Allow her time to determine what the job requires and how to do it. Let her know why the job is important. Ask her to be in touch if she needs help. Track her progress.

b. Specify the desired results and timelines. Clearly define the steps the employee should take to achieve results. Show her how to do the job. Track her progress.

c. Discuss the desired results and timelines. Clearly define the steps she can take to achieve the results. Explain why these steps are necessary and get her ideas. Use her ideas if possible, but make sure the manager's general plan is followed. Track her performance.

d. Ask her how she plans to tackle this job. Help her explore the problems she anticipates by generating possible alternative solutions. Encourage her to carry out the plan. Be available to listen to her concerns. Track her performance.

14. **This manager's boss has requested a 7 percent increase in the units output. This manager knows this can be done, but it will require his or her active involvement. To free the manager's time, the task of developing a new cost control system must be reassigned. The person chosen has had considerable experience with cost control systems, but is slightly unsure of doing this task on her own. This manager would:**

a. Assign her the task and listens to her concerns. Express confidence in her skills to handle this assignment. Help her explore alternatives if she thinks it would be helpful. Encourage and support her by providing needed resources. Track her progress.

b. Assign her the task and listen to her concerns. Discuss the steps she should follow to complete the task. Ask for her ideas and suggestions. After incorporating her ideas, if possible, make sure she follows the manager's general approach. Track her progress.

c. Assign her the task. Listen to her concerns, but let her resolve the issue. Give her the time to adjust, and avoid asking for results right away. Track her progress.

d. Assign her the task. Listen to her concerns, and minimize her feelings of insecurity by telling her specifically how to handle the task. Outline the steps to be taken. Closely monitor her progress.

15. **This manager's boss has asked to have someone assigned to serve on a companywide task force. This task force will make recommendations for restructuring the company's compensation plan. This manager has chosen a highly productive employee, who knows how**

her coworkers feel about the existing compensation plan. She has successfully led another unit task force. She wants the assignment. This manager would:

   a. Give this employee the assignment, but tell her how she would represent her coworkers' point of view. Specify that she give the manager a progress report within two days of each task force meeting.
   b. Ask this employee to accept the assignment. Help her develop the point of view she will take on the task force. Periodically check with her.
   c. Give the employee the assignment. Discuss what she should do to ensure her coworkers' perspective is considered by the task force. Ask her for ideas and make sure she follows the manager's general approach. Ask her for a report after every task force meeting.
   d. Give this employee the assignment. Ask for updates as things progress. Periodically check with her.

16. **Due to a family illness, this manager has been forced to miss two meetings of a committee he or she directs. Upon attending the next meeting, the manager finds the committee is operating well and making progress toward completing its goals. All group members come prepared, participate, and seem to be enthusiastic about their progress. The manager is unsure of what his or her role should be. This manager would:**

   a. Thank the committee members for their work so far. Let the group continue to work as it has during the last two meetings.
   b. Thank the committee members for their work so far. Set the agenda for the next meeting. Begin to direct the group's activities.
   c. Thank the committee members for their work so far. Make the members feel important and involved. Try to solicit alternatives and suggestions.
   d. Thank the committee members for their work so far. Set the agenda for the next meeting, but make sure to solicit their ideas and suggestions.

17. **The manager's staff is very competent and works well on their own. Their enthusiasm is high because of a recent success. Their performance as a group is outstanding. Now, this manager must set unit goals for next year. In a group meeting, this manager would:**

   a. Praise them for last year's results. Involve the group in problem solving and goal setting for the next year. Encourage them to be creative and help them explore alternatives. Track the implementation of their plan.

b. Praise them for last year's results. Challenge them by setting the goals for next year. Outline the action steps necessary to accomplish these goals. Track implementation of the plan.

c. Praise them for last year's results. Ask them to set the goals for next year and to define their action plan to accomplish these goals. Be available to contribute when asked. Track the implementation of their plan.

d. Praise them for last year's results. Set the goals for next year and outline the action steps necessary to accomplish these goals. Solicit the group's ideas and suggestions and incorporate them if possible. Track the implementation of their plan.

18. **This manager and his or her boss know that the manager's department needs a new set of work procedures to improve long-term performance. Department members are eager to make some changes but, because of their specialized functions, they lack the knowledge and skills for understanding the "big picture." This manager would:**

a. Outline the new procedures. Organize and direct the implementation. Involve the group in a discussion of alternatives. Use their suggestions when possible, but see that they follow the general outline. Track their use of the new procedures.

b. Outline and demonstrate the new procedures. Closely direct the group in their initial use of the new procedures. Track their use.

c. Involve the group in a discussion of what the new procedures should be. Encourage their initiative and creativity in developing the new procedures. Help them explore possible alternatives. Support their use of the new procedures. Closely track results.

d. Ask the group to formulate and implement a set of new procedures. Answer any informational concerns, but give them the responsibility for the task. Closely track the use of the new procedures.

19. **This manager was recently appointed head of the division. Since taking over, there has been a drop in performance. There have been changes in technology, and this manager's staff has not mastered the new skills and techniques. Worst of all, they do not seem to be motivated to learn these skills. In a group meeting, this manager would:**

a. Discuss the staff's drop in performance. Ask for their solutions for improving performance. Express faith in their strategies. Emphasize their past efforts, but track performance as they carry out their strategies.

b. Outline the necessary corrective actions they should take. Explore alternatives and incorporate their ideas. Modify the plan if appropriate, but see that they implement it. Track their performance.

c. Tell them about the drop in performance. Ask them to analyze the problem, and draft a set of action steps for approval. Set a deadline for the plan. Track its implementation.

d. Outline and direct the necessary corrective actions they should take. Define roles, responsibilities, and standards. Frequently check to see if their performance is improving.

20. The manager has noticed that an inexperienced employee is not properly completing certain tasks. She has submitted inaccurate and incomplete reports. She is not enthusiastic about this task and often thinks paperwork is a waste of time. This manager would:

a. Let the employee know that she is submitting inaccurate and incomplete reports. Discuss the steps she should take and clarify why these steps are important. Ask for her suggestions, but make sure she follows the manager's general outline. Monitor her performance.

b. Let the employee know that she is submitting inaccurate and incomplete reports. Ask her to set and meet her own paperwork deadlines. Give her more time to do the job properly. Monitor her performance.

c. Let the employee know that she is submitting inaccurate and incomplete reports. Ask her what she plans to do about it. Help her develop a plan for solving her problems. Monitor her performance.

d. Let the employee know that she is submitting inaccurate and incomplete reports. Specify the steps she should take with appropriate deadlines. Show her how to complete the reports. Monitor her performance.

Scoring the questionnaire:

1. Circle the corresponding letter from your answers on the questionnaire. Compute the total number of marks for each column.

	S1	S2	S3	S4
1	A▲	C#	D	B
2	A#	C▲	B	D
3	A▲	B#	C	D
4	C#	B▲	D	A
5	D	A▲	C#	B
6	A	C	D#	B▲
7	B#	D▲	A	C
8	C	B	A#	D▲
9	D	B	A▲	C#
10	B	C#	D▲	A
11	B	C	D▲	A#
12	A	C	B#	D▲
13	B#	C▲	D	A
14	D	B	A#	C▲
15	A	C	B▲	D#
16	B	D	C▲	A#
17	B	D	A▲	C#
18	B#	A▲	C	D
19	D▲	B#	A	C
20	D▲	A#	C	B
TOTALS				

2. Count the number of #'s, ▲'s and blanks (neither # or ▲).

	#	times	4	=	
	▲	times	3	=	
	Blanks	times	1	=	

Style Effectiveness Score _____

3. Multiply and total all numbers. Put the total in the style effectiveness score box.
4. Multiply each column total by 5 and print the number in the appropriate S1, S2, S3, or S4 box below (matching the column heading).

S3	S2
_____% Support	_____% Coach
S4	S1
_____% Delegate	_____% Direct

Chapter 8

What Are the Technical Tools of Lean Management?

WHAT IS A TECHNICAL TOOL?

In the last chapter we looked at the tools that would help us develop teams and team leaders. We also learned about tools for addressing the charter with which we have been tasked. In this chapter we take that team to the next level and give them the tools for identifying and attacking the issues. We start by looking at the areas of flow within our organization, much the same as we did in Supply Chain Management. The three key areas of flow are:

- Materials movement
- People movement
- Information movement

At this point, the facilitator would need to identify which tools would be the most appropriate in analyzing each of these flows and would teach the team how to use each of these tools. Once again, there are numerous tools available. However, I will demonstrate those tools that have been the most successful for me personally.

At Z Base, the team quickly realized that each person on the team understood only a small part of the whole process. In fact, the entire team together did not understand all the interrelationships and interactions that were involved in the complete first article process. The team went through the process of sharing their knowledge with each other. Then they went on "field trips" to locations throughout the base to learn about the movement of materials and information in areas that were beyond their direct control. The information gathered from these fact-finding activities helped the team develop maps of each of the three movements.

A good foundational tool developed by Toyota and used in the Lean activities to assist teams in understanding the overall process is the Value Stream Mapping (VSM) exercise. But before we discuss this tool we need to understand what a value stream is. We start by defining value as the amount that a customer is willing to pay for a product or service. It is the amount required to fulfill a customer need or desire. Components of value include items such as:

- Durability
- Quality
- Utility
- Price
- Capacity
- Functionality
- Timeliness
- Aesthetics
- Availability

The value stream incorporates all the events and activities in a product or a process's supply chain that would affect those items to which the customer gives "value." Which brings us to the point where we need to differentiate between value-added and non–value-added activities.

- Value-added activity: anything that directly increases the value of the product or service being performed.
- Non–value-added activity: any support activity that does not directly add value to the product or service. Activities that add cost or time to the process, such as control systems, are non-value added.

For example, drilling a hole is value added. But positioning the item to be drilled, changing the drill bit, cleaning the workstation, moving the item to inventory, and so on, are all non–value-added steps. In a service environment, value added is the performing of the service. Non–value added includes all the support functions that occur and that prepare the environment to perform the service. In Value Stream Mapping (VSM) we try to differentiate between value added and non–value-added activities.

MAPPING THE PROCESS

Value Stream Mapping is a waste identification tool that is used to identify Lean improvement opportunities based on the non–value-added processes that get identified. It does not focus on working harder; it focuses on working smarter.

VSM creates a visual description of the value stream by looking at the entire system, including all inputs, the process, and all outputs. VSM shows the linkages that exist throughout the system and challenges the current state of all activities. It identifies the sources of non–value-added waste that is identified in the value stream.

In the end, VSM becomes the foundation for developing an improvement plan by presenting a complete picture of the processes involved. Using this information, VSM can then be used to establish a vision of what the desired future state condition should look like. This future state becomes the vision for the improvement plan, and from this we develop a collection of improvement actions, often referred to as "events."[1]

The VSM process has four phases:

- Preparation
- Current state map
- Future state map
- Improvement plan

PREPARATION

In the preparation phase, we focus on identifying the limits and ranges of the system under consideration. If we are dealing with a manufactured product, we identify the interactions involved in developing that product or the related product family. The product family is a group of products that go through a similar processing sequence and that use common equipment and resources. If we are dealing with a service, we look at the customer, the service performed, and the sources of materials or information that are required pieces of that service. We need to map out that product or process that has the largest impact on the business. The mapping process gets down to a level of detail that would make it difficult to map out any more than just one product or one product family at a time.

Product or process selection needs to be done carefully. If the VSM limits are set too narrow, we may miss some big opportunity improvements. If the limits are set too large, we spend a lot of time going way beyond anything that will help the process under consideration. We end up trying to solve world hunger. The product or service selected for mapping should be one that has established a history of problems, such as delivery problems, quality failures,

---

[1] As in previous chapters, major pieces of this section are taken from MainStream Management training materials.

and cost overruns. The VSM should focus on a product that has an urgent need for improvement.

Once the product or process has been selected, the team needs to bring in the resident "gurus" on that item. The team also needs a facilitator who is often referred to as the Value Stream Focal. This individual makes sure that the VSM process stays on track, and he or she reports the progress of the VSM team to the steering team. The facilitator is the lead in the VSM discussion and implementation efforts. This individual becomes the scheduler, negotiator, and arranger, making sure the VSM team has the resources they need in order to stay on track.

CURRENT STATE MAP

Before the actual mapping process can begin, the facilitator needs to make sure that the team has been properly formed to include all relevant stakeholders and product authorities. In a manufacturing environment, this would include experts from the customer and supplier locations as well as internal experts from production, engineering, maintenance, quality, scheduling, shipping and receiving, and transportation. The team should include at least one process expert for every step in the product's value stream.

With the team in place, the facilitator organizes training in the VSM tools that will be used for the mapping exercise. Then the team goes on to define "value" from the perspective of the customer. What is it that the customer wants, and what is the customer currently settling for? We need to look at the product "what, when, where, how, why, and how much" from the customer's perspective. This needs to be documented and displayed for the team to keep at the forefront of their VSM effort. This information should become the improvement goal of the VSM and later the Lean effort.

With the customer information documented, the team needs to review the key performance indicators that are in place and to challenge whether they are the correct performance indicators. These should include indicators such as demand, quality, cost, capacity, backlog, delivery, and bottlenecks. (For a more thorough discussion of Lean measures see Chapter 9.) The team needs to select and concentrate on just a few key measures. These measures need to focus on the customer while at the same time balancing between the needs of the other stakeholders and the members of the organization.

At this point in time, the team is in place and the goals have been established. Now the team is ready to observe the process and to gather data on the process. This requires a detailed walk through every step of the value stream. The team takes detailed notes on the flow of the materials, information, and people as they move through this flow. They have a basic set of data that they need to take for each step, which would include information like the following.

- How are we performing to the specific measures which were selected as a system measurement goal?
- What triggers the process to begin at this step?
- How do we define the completion of this step?
- What is the total flow time through this process?
- What is the amount of time where value is actually added to the product?
- How many people are involved in the process?
- What is the inventory level before and after this process? What is the backlog? Is this step a bottleneck?
- How much time is the equipment actually used? How much of this equipment time is value added? How does machine value-added time affect worker value-added time?
- What is the batch size?
- What are the changeover times?
- What is the yield?
- Are there any specific quality issues?
- Who supplies this step?
- Who is the customer of this step?

After the interview process, the team is now ready to create the Value Stream Map. A table is created for each step in the process, which has all the relevant information that will be needed to analyze the value stream. In Chart 8.1 this table is referred to as the Process Baseline Data.

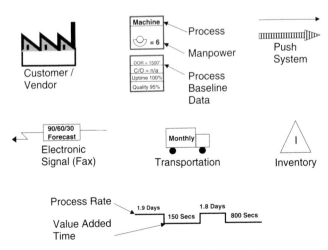

Chart 8.1 Some Value Stream Mapping Icons

In order to draw the map, some specific icons are used. Consistency is important throughout the organization so that everyone can look at someone else's Value Stream Map and immediately understand the message that is being projected. A basic set of icons that are used can be found in Chart 8.1.[2]

With these icons and the foundational data we are ready to map out the process that we are studying. An example of a very short process map is shown in Chart 8.2. Most maps will be much larger because the number of steps in a process can be quite extensive. Often we use butcher paper that is about 3 feet wide and as much as 20 feet long to graph out the complete value stream. We post the paper on a wall and tape the value stream icons and Process Baseline tables on the paper, and then draw the appropriate connecting lines.

Chart 8.2 is the VSM of a pump production process. In it we see vendors providing materials input into the system and customers receiving the material output from the system. We also see the customer's input into the information system that, after being processed by the internal production control

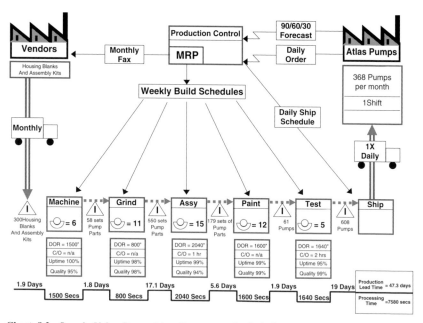

Chart 8.2 Sample Value Stream Map. For a more detailed view of this figure, please visit our companion site at: http://books.elsevier.com/companions/0123705177

---

[2]Most of the slides from this chapter are taken with permission from the MainStream Management Consultants training program; the author was graciously allowed to use this material in this book. These graphics help to make the concepts more understandable.

system (MRP), feeds the suppliers and the production process with production plans and schedules. In the production process itself, we see each of the production steps, starting with Machining and ending with Shipping. For each of these steps we see the number of employees assigned and some other relevant data that we deemed critical for measuring this production process. The VSM also shows us the total production lead time (47.3 days or 1,362,240 sec [47.3 days × 8 hr/day × 60 min/hr × 60 sec/min]) and the actual processing time (7,580 sec). This information will be used to identify the total value-added and non–value-added time. For this example the value-added time is 0.56 percent of the total time, and the non–value-added time is 99.44 percent of the total time. In this case there is tremendous room for improvement. But before you think this example is unrealistic, you should do a VSM on your organization.

At this point, we are ready to calculate TAKT time. TAKT time is the time it will take to produce one unit of product in order to meet customer demand. It is calculated by dividing the Available Time by the Customer Demand (over that period of time). Looking at Chart 8.3, we see the TAKT time calculated for this example. Assuming a 7.5-hour workday, we get 27,000 sec per day. Then, in order to produce 16 pumps each day, we would need to complete a pump every 1,688 sec or 28.1 min.

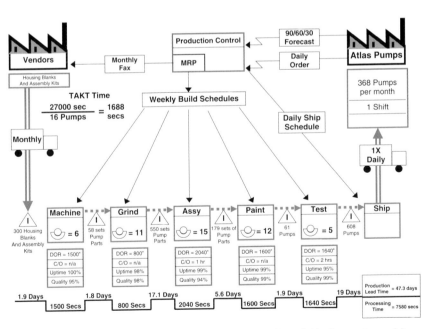

Chart 8.3 Sample VSM with TAKT. For a more detailed view of this figure, please visit our companion site at: http://books.elsevier.com/companions/0123705177

The value of the VSM process can be seen in the diagram. We now review the VSM, attempting to find the sources of the high non–value-added times. We look for the seven types of waste:

- Motion
- Processing
- Transport
- Excess inventory
- Defects
- Delays
- Overproduction

For the pump example we see an enormous delay between grinding and assembly. This delay of 17.1 days also results in a large interim Work In Progress inventory of 550 sets of pump parts being stored. Another area of significant concern is the 19-day delay between testing and shipping. The result is an enormously large finished goods inventory of 608 pumps, which is a significant overproduction of parts. Similarly, all the delays and all the inventories in the process need to be challenged. This organization needs to get its production process to where it adds value more than just one-half a percent of the time that it is in operation. And this will require some major revamping of the current system.

For Z Base the value-added time turned out to be about 10 percent of the total part processing time. This indicates a 90 percent non–value-added time, and the Value Stream Map identified several key areas that needed detailed attention. This attention was given to each of these areas in the form of "events," which will be discussed later.

The VSM has given the team an excellent tool for understanding the materials and information flow. Sometimes, however, this is not sufficient for environments where the information flow is very complex. In these cases it would be valuable to create a systems flow chart so that more of the information process could be detailed out. The systems flow chart was needed for the Z Base process, and a very summary example of the flow chart can be seen in Chart 8.4. The actual flow chart had several dozen information flow lines in it, and about one-third of these lines were determined to be for control purposes or for error recovery purposes. The goal of one of the events was to eliminate the non–value-added information flow lines that existed.

Another mapping tool is needed in order to show the travel time of the materials and/or the people involved in the process. The tool for this analysis is referred to as the *Spaghetti diagram*. This is simply a floor plan of the area under consideration with lines showing the people movement or the materials movement for a particular process. With this diagram we can calculate travel time per part produced, and we can look at ways to reduce this travel time.

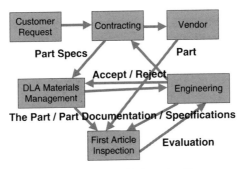

Chart 8.4 Detailed Information Flow

The Spaghetti diagram for Z Base is shown on Chart 8.5. This shows the people travel time both before the Lean process and after the Lean changes were implemented. The reduction in movement is obvious. A similar diagram can be made for materials movement or any other type of physical movement that occurs in any area under consideration.

IDENTIFYING IMPROVEMENTS

At this point the three key movements—materials, people, and information—have been mapped, and we are ready to identify opportunities for improvement. The process for identifying improvements has the following steps:

- Create a future state Value Stream Map.
- Develop an action item list of improvement opportunities.
- Classify the action item list.
- Select improvement events based on the highest priority areas of improvement.

CREATE A FUTURE STATE MAP

The objective behind developing a future state Value Stream Map (FS-VSM) is to identify a target goal for our improvement effort. We start by throwing away the current state VSM and redrawing an ideal VSM. How would the perfect system operate? Next, using the ideal VSM, we come down to reality, realizing that we have limited resources. For example, the ideal VSM may require a new building, but the FS-VSM requires us to remodel and renovate the existing location. We use our ideal VSM to create our FS-VSM. From this we can take our current state VSM and identify changes that will need to be made in order to

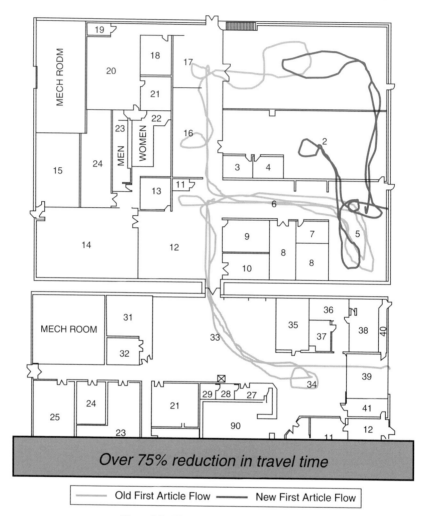

Over 75% reduction in travel time

——— Old First Article Flow ——— New First Article Flow

Chart 8.5   First Article Spaghetti Diagram

bring out current operating state to the desired future state. If we look at Chart 8.6 (taken from MainStream Management's training program) we see three versions of any value stream:

- What we think it is
- What it actually is (which is the current state value stream that we develop during the VSM process)
- What is achievable (which is the FS-VSM)

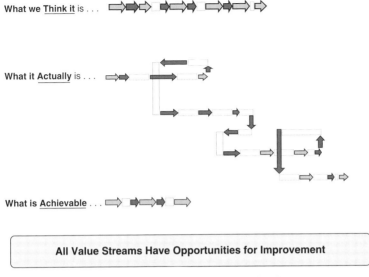

What we Think it is . . .

What it Actually is . . .

What is Achievable . . .

All Value Streams Have Opportunities for Improvement

Chart 8.6 The Three Versions of Any Value Stream

Using the VSM of Chart 8.2, we develop an FS-VSM, which can be seen in Chart 8.7. The differences between Chart 8.2 and Chart 8.7 define the improvement gaps. These are the opportunities for improvement, and the process of identifying these gaps is often referred to as the gap analysis.

IMPROVEMENT PLAN — DEVELOP AN ACTION ITEM LIST OF IMPROVEMENT OPPORTUNITIES

Using Chart 8.2 as the current state and Chart 8.7 as the future state, we can now generate an action item list of improvements. In some Lean activities, this list is referred to as the Lean Newspaper. These improvements are highlighted in Chart 8.8 where we see the specific areas that are targeted for change.[3]

CLASSIFY THE ACTION ITEM LIST

We should now have an action item list of improvements. We need to classify each item on the list by assigning it a priority based on issues such as:

[3]Most of the slides from this chapter are taken with permission from the MainStream Management Consultants training program.

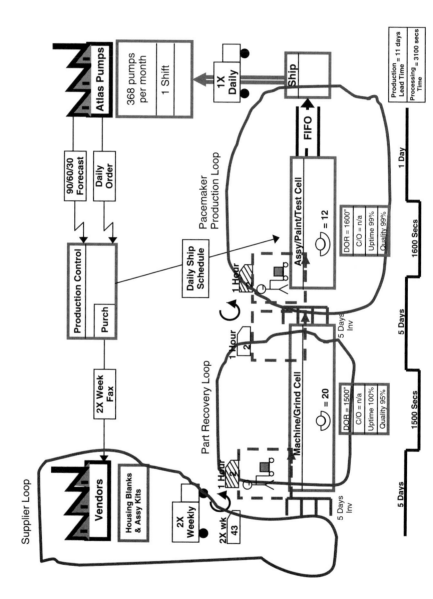

Chart 8.7 FS-VSM

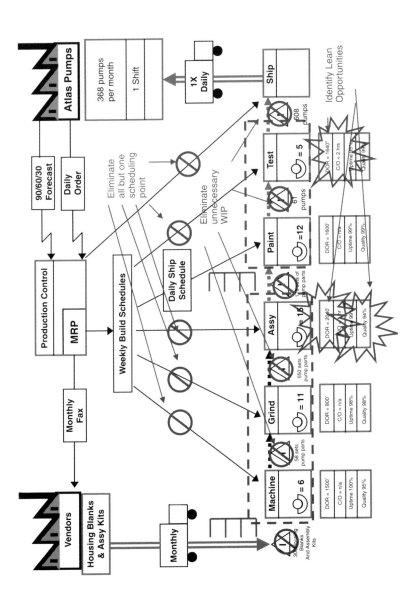

Chart 8.8 VSM Improvements. For a more detailed view of this figure, please visit our companion site at: http://books.elsevier.com/companions/0123705177

- How hard is this change to implement?
- What is the overall impact of this change on the process?
- What is the cost?
- What is the time span for implementation?
- How does this relate to top management's priorities for this Lean activity?

We use these priorities to rank each of the change items. Then we use this ranking to identify Lean "events" around each of these areas of change. These recommendations are brought before the steering team for their approval or modification, and the facilitator moves forward with the planning process for the first event.

SELECT IMPROVEMENT EVENTS BASED ON THE HIGHEST PRIORITY AREAS OF IMPROVEMENT

An improvement event goes through a process that is very similar to the organizing of any team activity. First the team is selected based on the recommendations of the steering team. The team receives a cultural assessment using the tools of Chapter 7. Then, with an appropriate team structure in place, the team meets for the first time where they

- Receive direction by having the steering team come to the kickoff of the event and describing their goals and vision for the event.
- Receive appropriate training of any tools that will be used during the event.
- Set team rules.
- Identify team leaders and scribes.
- Set goals for the event.
- Study the current state of the process thoroughly.
- Identify a future state.
- Perform a gap analysis and develop a list of action items specific to this event.
- Assign team members to work each of the action items.
- Monitor and measure the improvement process.

The event starts off with all-day meetings running for about one week. After that, the complexity of the change needs to be reviewed. The activities of the event may be concluded at this point. However, an event can run for one week or it may run for years, depending on the complexity of the event. If the event goes beyond the initial week, then regular weekly or biweekly meetings need to be arranged so that the team can ensure continuing progress on the event action items.

On the last day of the first week, the event team reports their progress to the steering team. It is important for the steering team to stay in the loop regarding the team's activities. The event team should also debrief the steering team at regular intervals, for as long as the event team remains organized.

Z Base performed a VSM and then theorized a FS-VSM. From these they identified some major areas of improvements and made a recommendation for future events to the steering team. Then they proceeded to schedule events in:

Communications and Customer Relations. This event focused on the communication gaps that were occurring and that had resulted in several reporting control systems and several follow-up systems that could be completely eliminated. This event created two lengthy action item lists— one for their main customer, the DLA, and one that reflected the needs of the remainder of their customer base.

Staffing and Training. There was some question as to whether the correct staff was in place and whether this staff was properly trained. This event focused on identifying what the correct mixture of staff should be and what the training program should look like. Two action item lists came out of this event, one for staffing recommendations and one for training.

Facilities. This event was triggered by the poor organizational flow within the lab. As we saw in Chart 8.5, the differences in the before and after flows were dramatic.

Supply Chain Management. The movement of the materials to and from the first article area was somewhat sporadic, and the team needed to look for ways to smooth out the flow and eliminate errors, like parts that should be tested ending up on aircraft prior to going through the appropriate tests.

Systems. There were numerous overlapping information systems that resulted in multiple data entry activities. These needed to be integrated and simplified.

6S. As you will see later in this chapter, 5S (referred to as 6S in the military) is a workplace organization and cleanup activity that was also important for this organization. This event was performed after the remodel was complete and after everyone was situated into their new work areas.

SUSTAINMENT

It is not enough to run a Lean activity where we do the cultural (Chapter 7) and technical processes, and then just brag about our successes and go away. True success in Lean is found in the sustainment of the process. What this means is that the "events" do not stop just because the facilitator leaves the scene. The steering team remains in place and continues to organize events around newly identified opportunities. And the Lean process continues forever.

For the facilitator, sustainment means that as many people as possible should be involved in the process and should find ownership in the Lean process. This allows a maximum number of people to be familiar with the Lean process and to want to keep it operational. In addition, this means training for as many people as possible. The more people that understand the objectives and workings of Lean, the greater the chance of continued success.

SOME SUCCESS STORIES

The Z Base Lean activity lasted about one year under the guidance of the facilitator and achieved phenomenal results that included:

- *A 75 percent reduction in travel time*
- *A reduction in QVC queue levels from 200 jobs to 14 jobs, with a goal of moving to below 10 jobs*
- *A reduction in flow days from 141 days down to 81 days before the remodel and 45 days after the remodel*
- *A reduction in first article "jobs on hold" from 14 jobs down to 1 job*

Other Lean activities achieved dramatic actual results in military bases throughout the United States, such as:

- A 64 percent lead-time reduction for forecast development
- A 75 percent lead-time reduction for kitting
- A 90 percent reduction in non–value-added time
- A 93 percent front office research time reduction
- A 93 percent reduction in order processing time
- A 70 percent reduction in part lead time from the DLA
- A 99 percent reduction in maintenance flow days
- A 400 percent improvement in reducing the number of parts that are "on the maintenance clock"
- A 50 percent reduction in work-in-process fuels
- Brake maintenance support of 200 percent over the forecasted goal
- For overhauls a 90 percent reduction in overtime in the targeted improvement areas
- For overhauls, 7 jets overhauled in the time once needed to overhaul 2.7 jets

And the stories go on and on in all areas of industry, including manufacturing, service, maintenance, logistics, and the front office.

REVIEWING A FEW ADDITIONAL EXAMPLES OF THE TECHNICAL TOOLS

Different technical tools fit different events, and not all of them are useful in any particular situation. Space does not allow us to discuss each of these tools in much detail. However, they need to be discussed so that the reader knows what is available.

1. Value Stream Mapping (see earlier in this chapter)
2. Systems Flow Chart (see earlier in this chapter)
3. Spaghetti Chart (see earlier in this chapter)
4. Future State Value Stream Map (see earlier in this chapter)
5. TAKT Time (see earlier in this chapter)
6. Lean Action Item List or Lean Newspaper (see earlier in this chapter)
7. Lean Events (see earlier in this chapter)
8. 5S. The objective of a 5S activity is to create an organized, safe, and productive work environment. This requires some reorganization of how current activities are performed. The 5Ss are:

   - Sort—separate the needed from the unneeded items.
   - Set in Order (Straighten)—physically rearrange the layout; organize the work area.
   - Shine—clean and remove reasons for contaminants.
   - Standardize—implement procedures and signaling systems that ensure worker understanding of the process.
   - Sustain—set up systems to ensure open and complete communication.

   The 5S process begins with a scan of the current workplace. The objective of the scan is to document current operating conditions. We start by clearly defining the target area that is under consideration. Then we try to define the purpose and function of each of these target areas. We use our maps (VSM, Spaghetti chart, and system flow chart) to show the physical flow between equipment and people. We look for problem areas, such as inconsistent or intermittent flow, quality failures, or bottlenecks. We record current problems on a checklist. We photograph and document these problem areas and put them on a display board so that the entire team can review and evaluate these areas. The team then searches for alternative solutions to these problems.

   Once the scan has been finished, the team goes on to complete the Workplace Scan Diagnostic Checklist (shown below). Each 5S step is then analyzed using questions similar to the ones on the checklist.

Sort

For the Sort phase, we start by identifying a reject area where we will place all the "tagged" items. Then we go through and question every physical item in the target area, including all equipment, inventory, tools, and so on.

		# Problems	Rating
		5 or more	Level 0
Workplace Scan Diagnostic Checklist		3 - 4	Level 1
		2	Level 2
		1	Level 3
		None	Level 4

Step	Item Date:				
	Determine what is and is not needed				
	Unneeded equipment, tools, etc. ...are present				
Sort	Unneeded items are on walls (bulletin boards etc.)				
	Items are present in aisleways, stairways, corners, etc.				
	Unneeded inventory, supplies, parts, materials are present				
	Safety hazards (water, oil, chemicals) exist				
	A place for everything...				
	Correct places for items are not obvious				
Straighten	Items are not in their correct places				
	Aisleways and equipment locations are not identified				
	Items are not put away immediately after use				
	Height and quantity limits are not obvious				
	Cleaning and looking for ways to keep it clean				
	Floors, surfaces, and walls are not free from dirt				
Shine	Equipment is not kept free from dirt, oil, and grease				
	Cleaning materials are not easily accessible				
	Lines, labels, and signs are not clean				
	Other cleaning problems are present				
	Maintain and monitor the first three categories				
	Necessary information is not visible				
Standardize	All standards are not known and visible				
	Checklists don't exist for all cleaning and maintenance jobs				
	All quantities and limits are not easily recognizable				
	How many items can't be located in 30 seconds or less				
	Stick to the rules				
	How many workers have not had 5-S training				
Sustain	How many times last week was daily 5-S not performed				
	Number of times that personal belongings were not stored				
	Number of times job aids are not available or up to date				
	Number of times last week 5-S inspections were not done				
	Total				

We "red tag" (see Chart 8.9) all tools or equipment that have not been used in the production process for more than one year, and we question all inventory items that have been in inventory for more than three months (these time periods are general and need to be adapted to the specific work environment). We need to question the existence and purpose of everything in the target area. We look for all items that are currently not in use or that simply do not belong in the target area. We also look for potential safety hazards. The

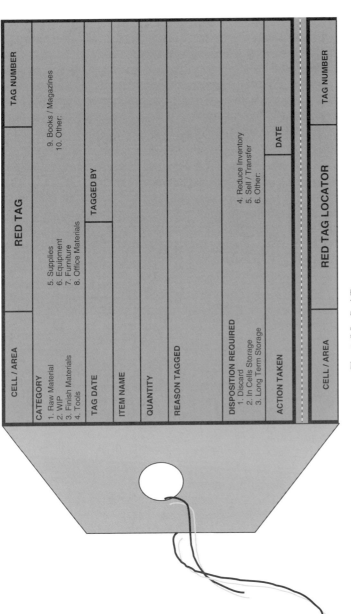

RED TAG

CELL / AREA		TAG NUMBER

CATEGORY

1. Raw Material
2. WIP
3. Finish Materials
4. Tools

5. Supplies
6. Equipment
7. Furniture
8. Office Materials

9. Books / Magazines
10. Other:

TAG DATE	TAGGED BY

ITEM NAME

QUANTITY

REASON TAGGED

DISPOSITION REQUIRED

1. Discard
2. In Cells Storage
3. Long Term Storage

4. Reduce Inventory
5. Sell / Transfer
6. Other:

ACTION TAKEN	DATE

RED TAG LOCATOR

CELL / AREA	TAG NUMBER

Chart 8.9 Red Tags

slogan for this phase of 5S is: "When in Doubt, Move it out." The list of areas to inspect includes:

Search

- Floors
- Aisles
- Operation areas
- Workstations
- Corners, under equipment
- Small rooms
- Offices
- Loading docks
- Inside cabinets

Look for unneeded equipment

- Machines, small tools
- Dies, jigs, bits
- Conveyance equipment
- Plumbing, electrical parts

Look for unneeded furniture

- Cabinets
- Benches, tables
- Chairs
- Carts

Search these storage places

- Shelves
- Racks
- Closets
- Sheds

Search the walls

- Items hung up
- Old bulletin boards
- Signs

Look for unneeded materials

- Raw material
- Supplies
- Parts
- Work-in-process
- Finished goods
- Shipping materials

Look for other unneeded items

- Work clothes
- Helmets
- Work shoes
- Trash cans

As we identify items that need to be tagged, we "red tag" them (see Chart 8.9) and log them on the unneeded items log (see Chart 8.10). The tagged items are then removed to a "5S reject / removal area" where each of the items is evaluated and a disposition decision is made. The disposition of each item is then recorded using the item disposition list (see Chart 8.11), and the item is no longer a distraction to the current targeted process.

SET IN ORDER (STRAIGHTEN)

The motto for the Straighten phase is "A place for everything and everything in its place!" The process requires that we decide where we are going to keep items and then organize ourselves so that we keep these items in their appropriate locations. We need to organize not only a location, but also a methodology or a "how" we are going to keep them there. We use visual techniques for the proper identification of each work area. Once we have made these decisions, we focus on implementing the changes that will make this process effective. As we proceed with the change process, we need to evaluate and document the "before and after" effects of the changes we are making.

Needless Items (describe)	# of items	Date	Reason for Tagging	Notes / Disposition

Chart 8.10   Unneeded Items Log

Use this list to help determine the disposition of each red tagged
item, then transfer the information onto both the red tag and the
Needless Item Log

Category	Action
Obsolete	• Sell • Hold for depreciation • Give away • Throw away
Defective	• Return to supplier • Throw away
Used about once per week	• Store in area
Used less than once per month	• Store where accessible in plant
Seldom used	• Store offsite (or in distant place) • Sell • Give or throw away
Use unknown	• Store until information is found

Chart 8.11   Item Disposition List

For the straighten phase we work to identify specific locations for each
item that is used in a process. We accomplish this by

Making it obvious where things belong

Drawing Lines

- Divider lines
  - Aisle ways
  - Operations areas
- Marker lines
  - Position of equipment
  - Inventory
  - WIP
  - Finished product area
- Range lines
  - Range of motion for doors
  - Range of motion for equipment
- Tiger lines—safety
- Outlines or shadows
  - Tool or equipment placement
- Arrows—direction

Making Labels

- Color coding
- Item location (tools, parts)
  - Storage location of tools
  - Storage location of parts/inventory

Creating Signs

- Equipment-related information
- Indicate location of areas
- Visualize processes and functions
- Show location, type, and quantity of inventory
- Scrap or trash area
- Provides direction in the factory

For the straighten process we look at:

Equipment

- Machines
- Small tools
- Dies
- Jigs
- Bits
- Conveyance equipment
- Cleaning equipment

Furniture

- Cabinets
- Benches, tables
- Chairs
- Carts
- Shelves
- Racks

Materials

- Raw material
- Supplies
- Parts
- Work-in-process
- Finished goods
- Shipping materials
- Cleaning supplies

Other items

- Charts, graphs, bulletin boards
- Books, paperwork

- Pens, pencils
- Work clothes
- Trash cans

SHINE

In the Shine phase, we focus on preventing dirt and contamination from occurring. The objective is to create pride in the workplace, to provide a safer environment, to set an environment for fewer breakdowns, and to promote a higher level of product quality.

The implementation of the Shine phase starts, as always, by analyzing the current situation. We develop a shine cleaning plan (see Chart 8.12) where we list all the areas that need cleaning. Once the team has identified the areas that need cleaning they will:

- Identify all needed cleaning materials.
- Build a cleaning cart.
- Clean everything, inside and out.
- Inspect the thoroughness of the cleaning process.
- Replace worn wires, hoses, tubing, filters, and so on.
- Compare "before and after" results.

During the shine process we look at everything. For example, our inspection list should include:

- Ceilings
- Aisles
- Workstations

Task	Location	Who	When	Materials/ tools needed

Chart 8.12   Shine Cleaning Plan

- Corners, under equipment
- Loading docks
- Walls
- Doors
- Pillars, posts
- Floors
- Machines
- Conveyance equipment
- Plumbing, sinks
- Cabinets, shelves, racks
- Carts, racks
- Drawers, storage bins
- Fixtures, power boxes

STANDARDIZE

In the Standardize phase, we focus on documenting all the 5S standards and making them visible to everyone involved in the process. We also make sure that a system exists which will maintain and monitor the work conditions to make sure that 5S standardization is continually maintained. This would include systems like the following for each of the 5S phases:

Sort

- Amount of inventory
- Tools that belong in the area
- How often to remove scrap

Set in Order

- Location of pathways
- Location of tools, equipment

Shine

- Cleaning schedule
- Maintenance tasks
- Checklist of what to look for as cleaning is performed

With the systems in place to monitor the performance of each of these items, we can develop workplace display boards that are updated regularly with photos, maps like Spaghetti charts, data, and graphs. This would give everyone in the workplace a visual representation of the 5S performance improvements as they occur.

SUSTAIN

In the Sustain phase, we focus on committing everyone involved in the work environment to adhere to the 5S standards. This includes everyone from production employees to top management. We want to establish a 5S culture of total employee involvement where 5S becomes a habit. We want 5S to become part of the corporatewide communication plan. To accomplish these objectives we need organizationwide training and methods of communication. And we need to standardize these throughout the organization.

A SIXTH "S" — SAFETY

In the United States, especially in the military and in military-related industries, a sixth "S" has been added: Safety. They refer to this process as the 6S process (not to be confused with Six Sigma). In the safety activity you would:

- Look for unsafe conditions.
- Look for potentially unsafe acts.
- Look for difficult tasks (are they ergonomic?).
- Try the jobs yourself . . . where could you get hurt?
- List the opportunities.
- Resolve them.

When performing a 6S activity at a workplace, be sure to investigate, identify, and correct possible hazards associated with the following:

- Ergonomics
- Environment
- Fire protection
- Machine and tool guarding
- Preventive maintenance
- Housekeeping
- Training

Baxter Healthcare engaged in a 5S project that focused on cost reductions of office supplies. They had initially set a goal of reducing spending by 30 percent by changing the ordering process and by making supplies more readily available so that individuals did not feel the need to stockpile their own set of supplies. After a six-month effort they were able to reduce office supply spending by a surprising 60 percent. In addition, on-hand inventory was reduced by 50 percent, and space that was previously wasted on inventory storage has now been made available for other functions.

9. Cell Design. In cell design we are trying to optimize the flow of a work area using Lean techniques. A cell is the arrangement of equipment, people, machines, and methods in such a way as to facilitate continuous flow production. A cell allows for "one-piece flow" whenever possible, where one operator can process the entire part if needed, or where work content can be balanced between operators. This will facilitate quicker response and help to meet customer demand. Cells are usually grouped by either product family or process family. One popular configuration of the cell is the U-shaped design.

   The cell minimizes inventory staging between work steps and therefore results in a significant reduction in overall inventory levels. It also reduces the amount of workspace required to perform the production process by reducing part staging and transfers.

   In order to cover this topic adequately, it would require a book all by itself. I will leave it to the reader to choose one of the hundreds of sources on cell design and cell balancing for further reading and understanding.

10. JIT. Just-in-Time (JIT) systems have the fundamental objective of bringing in only what is needed when it is needed and in the amount it is needed. JIT does not believe in stockpiling anything; it attempts to minimize materials, equipment, labor, and space. In the production process, JIT wants workers to have only the one piece they are working on, and nothing else before their process or after it. JIT utilizes the pull system whereby nothing is introduced into the process until it is requested. For example, we produce nothing until the customer requests it, and we buy nothing until the production process begins and materials get requested from the vendor. Therefore, materials are "pulled" from their source and are never "pushed" into the process because some schedule says it should be there. The pull system works on feedback from the user before parts are introduced into the process; they are not automatically introduced. As a result, we see that the three to four months of production lead time (the time it takes to produce a car from start to finish) for a typical American auto manufacturer can be reduced to four hours at Toyota.

    A typical JIT company will utilize small, inexpensive machines in the process, not large, multiproduct producing ones. It will have one-piece production flow, not batches of parts. It will have standing operators who move around between machines and workstations. It will be intolerant of production abnormalities. It will continually look for waste reduction opportunities in the production process.

11. Poka-Yoke. *Poka-Yoke* is a Japanese term meaning "mistake proof." It is a method of redesigning processes in a way so as to prevent errors. It is one

of the foundational quality improvement tools in any Lean process. Some everyday life examples of Poka-Yoke tools include:

- Computer diskettes that can only be inserted in the drive one way
- Automatic seat belts
- Auto-shut-off irons
- Automatic sinks in public restrooms
- Low clearance barriers in a parking garage

In our production environments there are four different levels of quality (see Chart 8.13). Unfortunately, we find that most of U.S. industry falls into one of the first two levels, where inspection and quality certification occur with the customer or at some other point at the end of the production process. This is unfortunate for many reasons. With level one and two, we often find that an extensive amount of unnecessary effort has been used to produce parts, and this effort could have been saved if the error had been caught earlier in the process. In addition, catching the problem late often means that the cost of rework is much higher. This failure to catch the problem earlier may also cause extensive customer dissatisfaction or frustration.

The third level of quality is the basic level of quality for all JIT (Just-in-Time) systems where inspection becomes part of the production process. Inspection occurs at each production step, at the end of each step.

The fourth level of quality is the level that Poka-Yoke strives for where inspection is not a separate step but rather an unnecessary step. We redesign the production process so that it will validate and eliminate quality errors.

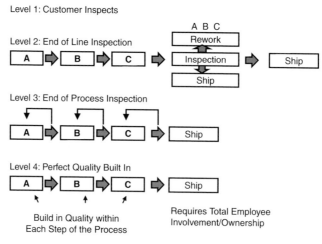

Chart 8.13 4 Levels of Quality

12. PQ (Product/Quantity) Analysis. The PQ analysis is the tool used to identify the products (P) and the quantities (Q) that will be going through the production cell. We are attempting to forecast the volume of activity that the cell will need to manage. To accomplish this, we need to collect data by product family on

- The date of the data collection process
- The person doing the data collection
- The time period covered by the data
- The part identification information (name and number)
- The quantity of the part used
- The cumulative total of all the parts going through the cell during this period of time
- The percent total that each of the part types contributes to the overall total of parts
- The cumulative total of the percents (totaling to 100 percent)
- Comments added about each part in case specific characteristics of that part need to be documented

A bar graph is made showing the individual contribution and the cumulative contribution of all the parts going through a specific cell. This graph is later used to facilitate the design and development of the cell.

13. Six Sigma (6σ).[4] The term *Six Sigma* (6σ) is a performance measure that was developed in order to accurately measure quality. Using Six Sigma, we can set process goals in parts per million (PPM) in all areas of the production process. Since its origin, 6σ has evolved into a methodology for improving business efficiency and effectiveness by focusing on productivity, cost reduction, and enhanced quality.

Six Sigma has its roots in the efforts of Joseph Juran and W. Edwards Deming. Their programs for Zero Defects and Total Quality Management in Japan led to the adoption of the 6σ philosophy by Motorola. Motorola was able to achieve a 200-fold improvement in production quality and saved a reported $2.2 billion using this tool. General Electric has also become a strong proponent of 6σ. It claims extensive successes. GE used it during the reign of Jack Welch, generating global recognition. Jack Welch made 6σ the biggest corporate initiative in GE's history. Other users include Texas Instruments and Allied Signal. Allied took 6σ to an even higher level not only by incorporating it in production but by making it a system of leadership. Other current users include JP Morgan Chase, Sun Microsystems,

---

[4]Some of this material was developed by the author for an article in the *Encyclopedia of Management*, 5th Edition, Edited by Marilyn Helms, Gale Group, Detroit, MI, 2005.

American Express, and Lloyds TSB. Today 6σ has evolved to become a management methodology that utilizes measures as a foundational tool for business process reengineering.

The name Six Sigma comes from the statistical use of the sigma (σ) symbol, which denotes standard deviations. The six identifies the number of standard deviations around the mean. Hence, in Six Sigma we are saying that you have to go out beyond six standard deviations around the mean before you find failure. With a high enough number of sigmas (beyond six), you would approach the point of "zero defects." The sigma levels step changes, for example, moving from 3σ (93 percent accuracy) to 4σ, require quantum leaps of improvement. A move from 3σ to 4σ is an 11 times improvement. From 4σ to 5σ is a 27 times level of improvement, and from 5σ to 6σ it is a 69-fold change. Hence, moving from 3σ to 6σ is a 20,000-fold level of improvement.

At the Six Sigma level, the product failures (number of parts beyond the allowable limits) would be 3.4 parts per million. This equates to a 99.9997 percent accuracy. In today's world, 98 or 99 percent accuracy is considered excellent. However, 6σ has now become the universally recognized standard of quality.

A guiding principle of Six Sigma is that if you want something to happen, you had better measure it. Unfortunately, that also means that if you measure the wrong things, you will get the wrong results. For example, measuring throughput may speed up production but at the cost of quality. Measuring quality may increase quality but decrease customer service. So one of the toughest challenges in Six Sigma measurement is to identify the measurement system that will trigger the correct collection of responses.

A second key principle of measures in the Six Sigma environment is that all the measures should be openly visible. Openly displaying all measures on charts and graphs is a primary motivator toward the correct response.

A third principle to remember is that the change curve applies (see Chapter 7). When change happens, performance will initially go down before it recovers and goes back up. This drop in performance is often scary, but a little patience will soon see its recovery.

A principle of success or failure in the Six Sigma world is the requirement for cultural change or change readiness. If the organization is not primed for change, then an environment for change must be instilled prior to starting Six Sigma, or the project is doomed to failure. This requires training, team bonding, and team-based goal setting. The resistance that exists because of a lack of understanding of what the Six Sigma process is attempting to achieve can be avoided with proper training.

Six Sigma concentrates on measuring and improving those outputs that are critical to the customer. The tools to accomplish Six Sigma include a range of statistical methodologies, which are focused on continuous improvement using a statistical thinking paradigm. This paradigm includes the following principles:

- Everything is a process.
- All processes have variations that are inherent within them.
- Data analysis is a key tool in understanding the variations in the process and in identifying improvement opportunities.

It is in the management methodology that the key, underlying benefits of 6σ, can be found, which includes a problem-solving and process optimization methodology. Six Sigma creates a leadership vision utilizing a set of metrics and goals to improve business results by using a systematic five-phased problem-solving methodology. There are two common problem-solving project management methodologies that are commonly associated with 6σ. The first is DMAIC (Define, Measure, Analyze, Improve, Control), and the second is DMADV (Define, Measure, Analyze, Design, Verify). We will discuss the most common, DMAIC.

Six Sigma is a measurement-based strategy that focuses on reducing variations through monitoring and measurement tools. It is based on a philosophy which holds that every process can and should be repeatedly evaluated and significantly improved, with a focus on time required, resources, quality, cost, and so on. The philosophy prepares employees with the best available problem-solving tools and methodologies using the five-phased DMAIC process. Explaining each of the steps in the process in more detail we have:

- *Define.* At the first stages of the process we look for and identify poorly performing areas of a company. We then target the projects with the best return and develop articulated problem and objective statements that have a positive financial impact on the company.
- *Measure.* At this stage we are trying to tie down the process under consideration. Where does it start and end? What should we be measuring to identify the deviation? What data characteristics are repeatable and identifiable? What is the capability of the process? We use tools like process mapping, flowcharting, and FMEA (Failure Model Effects Analysis). We develop a baseline for the targeted area and implement an appropriate measurement system.
- *Analyze.* Having identified the who and what of this problem, we now target the where, when, and why of the defects in the process. We use appropriate statistical analysis tools, scatter plots, SPC and SQC, Input/Output matrixes, hypothesis testing, and the like, and attempt to accurately understand what is happening in the process.
- *Improve.* At this point we should have identified the critical factors that are causing failure in the process. And through the use of experiments,

we can systematically design a corrective process that should generate the desired level of improvement. This improvement will then be monitored to assure success.

- *Control.* In the control phase, we implement process control tools that can manage and monitor the process on an ongoing basis. The DMAIC process is now in full operation, but it does not stop here. The continuous monitoring of the process will not only assure the success of this change process, but it will also identify future opportunities for improvement.

Some excellent and highly recommend web sites include onesixsigma.com and qualitydigest.com; they present several informative articles.

14. Statistical Process Control (SPC).[5] Statistical Process Control (SPC) and its companion, Statistical Quality Control (SQC), are tools utilized by a 6σ improvement process. The original objective of SPC is to provide productivity and quality information about a production process real time. The focus was on process control and continuous improvement. The operators become their own inspectors and control their own processes.

The SPC process should collect data and report results as the process is occurring, so that immediate action can be taken. This should help a process, and its quality measures, avoid straying beyond acceptable limits and would avoid the production of bad parts. When appropriately applied, SPC can virtually eliminate the production of defective parts. In addition, SPC creates visibility of the cause of the failure. Since an operator is able to immediately recognize that a failure is occurring, he would be able to react to that failure and observe the cause of the failure, and then take corrective action.

Because of its success, SPC has found application in other industries, including service industries, transportation industries, and delivery services, and can even be found in fast-food and baggage handling. For example, on-time delivery performance can be monitored on an SPC chart.

Within the SPC process there are several tools, including a Change Management process, the collection of data, and the display of the data. In the Change Management process we find the use of PDCA (Plan-Do-Check-Act) whose objective is to solve problems by trial and error. The process includes (P) planning a work change, (D) executing the change, (C) monitoring the effects of the change to assure that the desired results are occurring, and taking corrective (A) action in the event that the desired results are not occurring—in effect repeating the PDCA cycle. The PDCA cycle is repeated until the error is reduced to zero.

---

[5]Some of this material was developed by the author for an article in the *Encyclopedia of Management.*

In the SPC data collection process, the objective is to collect the data that will be needed to validate that a specific process is occurring correctly. The methodology for measurement is established at the point where the appropriate data is collected. Only the data required for monitoring the process is collected. An analysis of the specific reasons for collecting the data is important because any additional, unnecessary data collection is considered to be a waste. The accuracy of the measurement process is also confirmed.

The tools available for the display of SPC data include:

(1) Graphs and charts—used to display trends or to summarize the data. These tend to be bar on-line graphs that report on a specific parameter of performance.
(2) Check sheets or tally sheets—used to take the raw data and reorganize it into specific categories that are being observed.
(3) Histograms or frequency distribution charts—used to translate raw data into a pictorial display showing the performance of specific quality characteristics.
(4) Pareto principles—used to prioritize the contribution effect of specific quality problems. This tool assists in identifying which problems have the largest impact on a specific quality problem under study.
(5) Brainstorming—used to generate ideas by taking advantage of the synergistic power of a team of people.
(6) Ishikawa diagrams (Fishbone Charts)—used to create problem and solution visibility by grouping problem causes into branches. Often this is referred to as a cause-and-effect diagram. Using this tool in conjunction with the PDCA process helps to narrow down the root cause.
(7) Control charts—used to validate that the variation of measurement of a specific parameter is kept within a set of control limits.

In SPC, the most critical part of the process is the validation that you are measuring the right thing and are thereby motivating the correct response. In addition, if one measure can take the place of several measures, then that one measure should be identified, thereby simplifying the measurement process. Once a measurement has been selected, we are ready to set up the data collection process and to establish control charts that will monitor the performance of this data.

The control charts are built around a specific product parameter that requires monitoring because of its impact on the overall quality of the product. The following discussion is an extremely basic overview of the SPC process and should not be considered to be sufficient for implementing an SPC process. Rather, this discussion is simply intended to give the reader a basic overview of the process.

The next step in the SPC process is to establish a set of control variables, which includes an average (X) and a range (R). These can be established by going to the drawings and reviewing the initial part specifications using the expected value as X and the tolerance range as R. Or these variables can be established using historical values and calculating the historical average (X) and range (R) for the data.

Having established an X and R value, we can calculate an Upper Control Limit (UCL) and a Lower Control Limit (LCL).

$$UCL = X + R$$

$$LCL = X - R$$

From these values, a pair of control charts is created. These charts are used to plot the SPC data as it occurs. They are used as a visual tool to monitor the process. Chart 8.14 is an example of the X-Bar SPC chart that monitors a process. For this chart we will use $X = 1.23$ and $R = .45$.

From Chart 8.14 we can see how the measurement data is recorded on the chart at the time each measurement occurs. The objectives behind this data collection process are several. One is to catch outliers in the data (anything above the UCL or below the LCL). These outliers are quality failures and must immediately stop the process. Another purpose of the measures is to identify trends. For example, data points 1 through 5 indicate a strong trend to failure approaching the LCL. Corrective action should be taken immediately to avoid the possibility of producing bad parts. Another objective can be seen in data points 7 through 13, which indicates that perhaps our LCL and UCL are too far and need to be brought in tighter, thereby giving us a higher level of performance and a higher level of quality.

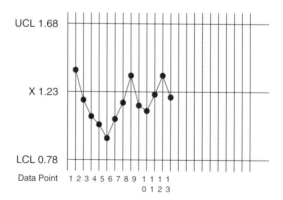

Chart 8.14   X-Bar Chart

Another methodology for applying SPC processes is by collecting data, not on every event but on a random sampling of the event. This occurs when there is a large volume of activity and the time required to measure each event is too burdensome. A statistical sample is taken, and from that sample the average of the sample data (X_1) and the range of that sample $(R_1 =$ highest minus lowest measure) are calculated. For example, if our random sample size was 5 data points and our sample included the measures of 1.4, 1.45, 1.2, 1.3, and 1.65, then $X_1 = 1.4$ and $R_1 = 1.65 - 1.2 = .45$. This X_1 value would then be the first data point plotted on Chart 8.14.

Using the statistical random sample, we would also need to create a range chart. Chart 8.15 is an example of a range chart and the first data point of this chart would be the plot of the data corresponding to the example given. For this example, the lower limit is zero, which states that there is no deviation between each of the data points of that sample. The center point is R (.45), and the UCL is equal to 2 times R (.90).

In the example of the range chart (R chart), the lower the value the better. A lot of vibration all over the chart suggests that the process may be going out of control. Also, a trend moving upward as we see from data points 5 through 10 would indicate that a process is starting to go out of control and corrective action should be taken immediately.

With the X-Bar and R charts, we can now create summarized reports, like the histograms and frequency distributions discussed earlier. This allows a long-term, summarized perspective of the process, rather than the chronological timeline that the X-Bar and R charts offer.

15. Total Productive Maintenance (TPM). TPM is a system designed to help attain and maintain competitiveness in quality, cost, and delivery. TPM

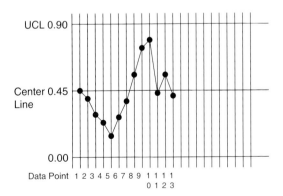

Chart 8.15 R Chart

is utilized to alleviate manufacturing wastes associated with equipment (improving the effectiveness and longevity of machines). Examples include:

- Minor, medium, and major stoppages (breakdowns)
- Long setup times
- Rework, defects, abnormalities, and low yields
- Planned downtime
- Incomplete 2S application
- Overproduction by large equipment
- Equipment problems at production startup

TPM is an attempt to eliminate minor work stoppages. It focuses on zero defects. It is accomplished by

- Understanding the current changeover process
- Clarifying the problem areas in changeover, adjustment, and test runs
- Checking the precision of the equipment and replaceable parts
- Improving your positioning methods
- Taking care of the remaining adjustments
- Carrying out P-M analysis
- Creating changeover standards
- Maintaining and managing

A list of other Lean technical management tools would include:

- Visual Workplace—helps identify abnormalities through nonverbal communication
- 7 Wastes—involves the areas that need to be thoroughly investigated when searching for improvements
- *Kaizen*—is a quick Lean event methodology often referred to as a Blitz; I prefer to run more sustained events that will have ongoing results long after the facilitator has dropped out of the process
- Design for Manufacturing—is an engineering design methodology that focuses on "ease of manufacturing" rather than "ease of design"
- SMED—Single Minute Exchange of Die
- TQM—Total Quality Management, a change management methodology out of Toyota
- TQC—Total Quality Control, a quality improvement methodology focused on control systems that enforce quality
- Business Process Improvement (BPI)—a rapid and radical change methodology
- Kanban—is a mechanism for inventory and materials flow control within a Just in Time system
- Jidoka—is detection and prevention of abnormality with the goal of reducing downtime and improving quality

- Standard Work—is a tool for standardizing and documenting the work process
- Brainstorming—generates ideas without criticism

WRAP-UP

It is difficult to say whether one particular tool is more important than another. It is quite possible that the tool that would best fit any particular reader's environment may be a one that was just brushed over in this discussion. I had to make some hard choices when determining which tools to list in detail. But with these tools you can learn the Lean process and begin facilitating the improvement opportunities within your organization.

REFERENCES

Antony, Dr. Jiju, and Mukkarram Bhaiji, "Key Ingredients for a Successful Six Sigma Program," onesixsigma.com.

Bothe, Keki R., *World Class Quality*, AMACOM, New York, 1991.

Drucker, Peter, "The Emerging Theory of Manufacturing," *Harvard Business Review*, May/June 1990, p. 95.

Kullmann, John, "An Introduction to Six Sigma," onesixsigma.com.

Plenert, Gerhard, *The eManager: Value Chain Management in an eCommerce World*, Blackhall Publishing, Dublin, Ireland, 2001.

Plenert, Gerhard, *International Operations Management*, Copenhagen, Denmark, Copenhagen Business School Press, 2002. (Republished in India by Ane Books, 2003.)

Plenert, Gerhard, and Shozo Hibino, *Making Innovation Happen: Concept Management Through Integration*, DeRay Beach, FL, St. Lucie Press, 1997.

Pyzdek, Thomas, "Cargo Cult Six Sigma," Quality Digest, qualitydigest.com.

Robustelli, Peter, and John Kullmann, "Implementing Six Sigma to Affect Lasting Change," onesixsigma.com.

Ross, Joel E., *Total Quality Management*, St. Lucie Press, Del Ray Beach, FL, 1995.

Chapter 9

What Are the Measures
of Lean Success?

WHY ARE THE LEAN IMPROVEMENTS
SO DRAMATIC?

In Lean management, the improvements are often so dramatic they are unbelievable. For example, we have seen improvements like:

- Aircraft Gearbox Rebuild cost reductions of $17.5 million annually
- Aircraft Rebuild Time reductions from 132 days down to 51 days with a 90 percent reduction in overtime
- Aircraft Wing Overhaul Time reduction from 213 days down to 109 days with a 47 percent reduction in overtime
- Engine Rebuild cost savings of $8.3 million annually with a 73 percent production capacity increase
- Guns Rebuild's 35 percent reduction in lead time and 53 percent reduction in WIP (work-in-process)
- Service Parts Requisition Process's 90 percent reduction in office labor, 69 percent reduction in handoffs, and 93 percent reduction in flow days

And these are just a few examples; the list of examples is quite lengthy.

At Z Base we experienced a 40 percent reduction in flow days, a 75 percent reduction in travel time, an 84 percent reduction in in-process jobs, and a 93 percent reduction in the backlog in the verification lab, while at the same time experiencing a reduction in the workforce.

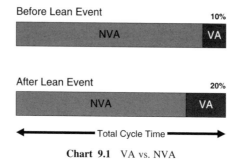

Chart 9.1   VA vs. NVA

How is all this possible? Let's start by looking at a typical example of value-added (VA) and non–value-added (NVA) time. As noted in the previous chapters, value-added time is where we have a direct impact on the finished item. Non–value-added time is waste time that is spent on activities such as batching, sorting, stopping, scrapping, walking, moving, watching, searching, approving, controlling, reworking, and waiting.

If we study a process thoroughly, we can compare the VA with the NVA times. The best tool for this analysis is the Value Stream Mapping (VSM) process discussed in the last chapter. It is extremely common for the VSM to come up with numbers where over 90 percent of production time is NVA.

At Z Base, the first article processing time had 90 percent NVA.

Using this information, we can study the comparison of VA and NVA time in Chart 9.1. Through this chart we can demonstrate how Lean does not attempt to make people work harder. Lean does not try to push the VA time to be more productive; rather, Lean attempts to reduce NVA time in order to provide more productive time. As shown in Chart 9.1, NVA time can be reduced from 90 to 80 percent and then, simultaneously, VA time can be increased from 10 to 20 percent. The result is obvious. By merely taking 10 percent out of NVA time, we have effectively doubled our output; we have twice as much time available to directly produce product. This would be reported as a 100 percent increase in output. Repeat this process and you can easily see how 200 or even 300 percent increases in output and similar corresponding increases in capacity are possible.

Another way to look at Chart 9.1 is to observe that if we cut NVA time from 90 to 80 percent and we maintain VA time at 10 percent, then we end up gaining 10 percent of unused capacity. We now do the same amount of work in 90 percent of the time that it took us before. And we can use the newly gained capacity for other productive functions.

I applied this principle to an office of attorneys and their assistants through-out the state of Texas. In some cases (in offices that were receptive to these principles) I was able to triple the amount of output of the office within two weeks, without making any change in staff and without having anyone work harder.

MEASURES

Throughout this book we have encountered measures that "motivate." Key among these measures are those based on time, including cycle time, flow time, lead time, and processing time. If we can have an effect on time, then we have an effect on inventory levels (materials move through the process quicker and do not wait around as much), capacity (see the example in the first part of this chapter), customer satisfaction (review the Z Base example), and on and on. Time reduction is what we want to motivate with the Lean process. And the key measure of time is cycle time.

CYCLE TIME

Time has become a key success measure in business, often even more so than many of the other measures of performance.[1] For example, in marketing, *time to market* is a measure of how quickly a new product becomes available to the customer and will often determine the success or failure of the product. Time to market is one of many cycle time measures that we use in management. Cycle time is the measure of a business cycle, from the start of the cycle to its conclusions. The term is used to refer to activities in production, like the total time required to produce a product or the *production cycle time*. It is also used in the front office to determine the total time required to process an order, which is the *order processing cycle time*. From a financial perspective we find terms like *cash-to-cash cycle time* where we determine the amount of time a company takes to recover its financial investment. From a management perspective, cycle time is used to evaluate performance in all aspects of a business.

Cycle time improvements have been linked to reduced costs, reduced inventories, and increased capacity. The resource areas that are measured by cycle time include the measurement of financial flow, materials flow, and information

---

[1] Many of the pieces of this discussion come from an article that the author wrote for the *Encyclopedia of Management.*

flow. In each case, a delay or failure of any of these measures would indicate a failure of the entire business process.

Cycle time is best illustrated by a few examples. In marketing, the time to market cycle time is the critical measure of success in industries like the fashion, apparel, or technology industries. If you are not the quickest to get your product to market, you may find yourself completely washed out of the market. So the measure of time from idea inception through idea development, design and engineering, pilot, and finally production and customer availability is the measure of time to market. For example, the United States led the world in the idea phase of automotive air bags, but their design and engineering process was so slow that the Japanese had the air bags generally available in their vehicles a couple of years ahead of the United States.

Another example of cycle time is the production cycle time—the time extending from release of a production order on the production floor through completion of the product, ready to ship to a customer. For the American automobile manufacturer, this time is measured in weeks and in some cases in months. For Toyota, this time is approximately *four hours*. The repercussions of this stark contrast in time are found in the staging of enormous amounts of work-in-process inventories. The actual "hands-on" production time in both cases is about the same. However, since the United States produces in large batch quantities, they are in effect producing hundreds and thousands of cars at the same time; therefore there is a lot of staging of inventory and a lot of work space requirements for the staged inventory. This example shows us the direct relationship between cycle time and inventory.

Still another example of cycle time is order processing time. Unfortunately, in far too many factories, the paperwork time needed to process an order is longer than the time required to produce the product. Order processing time starts when the phone call or fax initiating the order is received, and ends when the order is sent to production scheduling. This cycle time includes all the paperwork steps such as credit verification and the filling out of order forms.

In finance the measure of cash-to-cash cycle time reflects the cash performance of a company. This measure is the amount of time it takes from the time money is spent on a customer's product for the purchase of components until the time the "cash" is recovered from the customer in the form of a payment. For example, in the computer industry, the industry average cash-to-cash cycle time is 106 working days. For the "best-in-class" companies, this cash-to-cash cycle time is 21 working days, and for Dell, it is a negative 7 days. From this example you can see that the average company in the computer industry needs to finance its inventory investment for 106 days, whereas Dell has the advantage of being able to utilize the customer's cash to earn interest. Dell can then use this advantage to offer its customers price incentives that the other computer manufacturers cannot.

In its more general usage, however, cycle time is how long it takes from when a material enters a production facility until it exits. Depending on the industry, this definition is appropriate with slight modifications. For example, in the automobile collision repair industry, the term *cycle time* refers to the time a car enters the facility for repair until the repair is completed.

OTHER MEASURES

Time is the most important measure, but a large number of supporting measures should become part of the motivation system. Some examples include:

- Shortened customer lead time
- Increased customer satisfaction
- Improved quality of products and services
- Reduced cost of quality
- Reduced processing cycle time
- Reduced cost of inventory
- Increased capacity for other needed tasks
- Increased employee satisfaction
- Reduced cost of forms and paperwork
- Reduced cost of administrative processes
- Reduced cost of manufacturing
- Increased level of competitiveness

In summary, with Lean we will experience increased levels of quality and delivery and reduced costs. In addition, we will have established a continuous improvement culture.

RESULTS

In the Lean process of eliminating waste, reducing non–value-added time, and increasing quality to where it becomes integrated with the process, we will find a dramatic shift in our organizational structure. For example, the traditional factory, as seen in Chart 9.2, will be reorganized and will become the factory seen in Chart 9.3, where the entire production process will now fit into the space of the superintendent's office. In the process, the factory will experience an increased level of output and capacity.

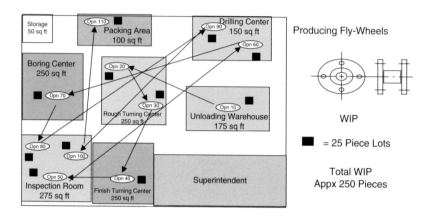

Waste of Walking, Moving, Excessive Inventory, & Miscommunications

Chart 9.2   Traditional Factory

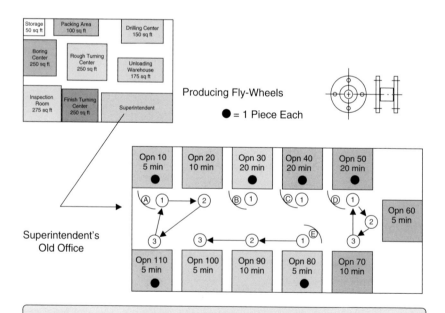

Cell Streamlines Value Stream - Reduces Waste

Chart 9.3   Lean Factory

SUMMARY

Lean management principles have demonstrated dramatic improvement results. These same improvements can be implemented throughout the supply chain, as we will see in the next chapter. For an additional resource on Lean management, see the appendix which presents a glossary of Lean terms.

REFERENCES

Blackstone, John H., *Capacity Management*, Cincinnati, Ohio: South-Western Publishing Co., 1989.

Cox, James, F., John H. Blackstone, and Michael S. Spencer, *APICS Dictionary*. 9th ed. Falls Church, VA: American Production and Inventory Control Society, 1998.

Plenert, Gerhard, *International Operations Management*, Copenhagen, Denmark, Copenhagen Business School Press, 2002 (490 pages). (Republished in India by Ane Books, 2003.)

Stevenson, William J., *Production Operations Management*, 6th ed., Boston: Irwin McGraw-Hill, 1999.

Appendix 9-A

Glossary of Terms[2]

Andon: A system of flashing lights used to indicate production status in one or more work centers; the number of lights and their possible colors can vary, even by work center within a plant. However, the traditional colors and their meanings are:

> green—no problems
> yellow—situation requires attention
> red—production stopped; attention urgently needed

Andon Board: A visual control device in a production area, typically a lighted overhead display, giving the current status of the production system and alerting team members to emerging problems.

Annual Inventory Turns: A measure that is calculated by dividing the value of annual plant shipments at plant cost (for the most recent full year) by the total current inventory value at plant cost. Total current inventory includes raw materials, work-in-process, and finished goods. Plant cost includes material, labor, and plant overhead.

Autonomation: Automation with a human touch. Refers to semiautomatic processes where the operator and machine work together. Autonomation allows man-machine separation. Also referred to as Jidoka.

---

[2]These terms were taken from the MainStream Management Consulting database and from the Lean Training Program and were primarily the work of Scott Larkin.

Balanced Production: All operations or cells produce at the same cycle time. In a balanced system, the cell cycle time is less than TAKT time.

Batch-and-Queue: Producing more than one piece of an item and then moving those items forward to the next operation before they are all actually needed there. Thus, items need to wait in a queue.

Benchmarking: The process of measuring products, services, and practices against those of leading companies.

Best-in-Class: A best-known example of performance in a particular operation. One needs to define both the class and the operation to avoid using the term loosely.

Blitz: A blitz is a fast and focused process for improving some component of business—a product line, a machine, or a process. It utilizes a cross-functional team of employees for a quick problem-solving exercise, where they focus on designing solutions to meet some well-defined goals.

Bottleneck: Any resource whose capacity is equal to, or less than, the demand placed on it.

Capacity Constraint Resources: Where a series of nonbottlenecks, based on the sequence in which they perform their jobs, can act as a constraint.

Catch-Ball: A series of discussions between managers and their employees during which data, ideas, and analysis are thrown like a ball. This opens productive dialogue throughout the entire company.

Cells: The layout of machines of different types performing different operations in a tight sequence, typically in a U shape, to permit single-piece flow and flexible deployment of human effort.

Chaku-Chaku: A method of conducting single-piece flow, where the operator proceeds from machine to machine, taking the part from one machine and loading it into the next.

Change Agent: The catalytic force moving firms and value streams out of the world of inward-looking batch-and-queue.

Changeover: The installation of a new type of tool in a metal-working machine, a different paint in a painting system, a new plastic resin and new mold in an injection molding machine, new software in a computer, and so on.

Constraint: Anything that prevents a system from achieving higher performance or throughput.

Continuous Flow Production: Process whereby items are produced and moved from one processing step to the next, one piece at a time. Each process makes only the one piece that the next process needs, and the transfer batch size is one. Also called single-piece flow or one-piece flow.

Continuous Improvement: A never-ending effort to expose and eliminate root causes of problems; small-step improvement as opposed to big-step or radical improvement.

Covariance: The impact of one variable on others in the same group.

Cross-Functional Team: Teams of employees representing different functional disciplines and/or different process segments who tackle a specific problem or perform a specific task, frequently on an ad hoc basis.

Current State Map: Helps visualize the current production process and identify sources of waste.

Cycle Time: The time required to complete one cycle of an operation.

Dependent Events: Events that occur only after a previous event.

Design Approach (to management improvement): Effort to build a better approach through predetermined goals.

Error Proofing: Designing a potential failure or cause of failure out of a product or process.

Five S: Five terms utilized to create a workplace suited for visual control and Lean production. *Sort* means to separate needed tools, parts, and instruction from unneeded materials and to remove the latter. *Simplify* means to neatly arrange and identify parts and tools for ease of use. *Scrub* means to conduct a cleanup campaign. *Standardize* means to conduct Sort, Simplify, and Scrub at frequent intervals to maintain a workplace in perfect condition. *Sustain* means to form the habit of always following the first S's.

Flow: A main objective of the Lean production effort and one of the important concepts that passed directly from Henry Ford to Toyota. Ford recognized that, ideally, production should flow continuously all the way from raw material to the customer and envisioned realizing that ideal through a production system that acted as one long conveyor.

Functional Layout: The practice of grouping machines or activities by type of operation performed.

Future State Map: A blueprint for Lean implementation. Your organization's vision, which forms the basis of your implementation plan by helping to design how the process should operate.

Heijunka: A method of leveling production at the final assembly line that makes Just-in-Time production possible. This involves averaging both the volume and sequence of different model types on a mixed-model production line.

Hosin Planning (HP): Also known as Management by Policy or Strategy Deployment; a means by which goals are established and measures are created to ensure progress toward those goals. HP keeps activities at all levels of the company aligned with its overarching strategic plans. HP typically begins with the "visioning process," which addresses the key questions: Where do you want to be in the future? How do want to get there? When do you want to achieve your goal? And who will be involved in achieving the goals? HP then systematically explodes the what, who and how questions throughout the entire organization.

ISO 9000: An international quality process auditing program, based on a series of standards published by the International Organization of Standardization in

282 Reinventing Lean - Introducing Lean Management into the Supply Chain

Geneva, Switzerland, through which manufacturing plants receive certification attesting that their stated quality processes are adhered to in practice.

ISO 14000: A series of generic environmental management standards developed by the International Organization of Standardization, which provides structure and systems for managing environmental compliance with legislative and regulatory requirements and affect every aspect of a company's environmental operations

Just-in-Time (JIT): Principles that are fundamental to Time-Based Competition. Waste elimination, process simplification, setup and batch-size reduction, parallel processing, and layout redesign are critical skills in every facet of the lean organization. JIT is a system for producing and delivering the right items at the right time, in the right amounts. The key elements of Just-in-Time are Flow, Pull, Standard Work, and TAKT Time.

Kaizen: The philosophy of continual improvement, which states that every process can and should be continually evaluated and improved in terms of time required, resources used, resultant quality, and other aspects relevant to the process. When applied to the workplace, *Kaizen* means continuing improvement involving everyone—managers and workers alike. *Kaizen* is not limited to manufacturing systems; it also means continuing improvement in one's personal life, home life, social life, and working life.

Kaizen Event: A concentrated effort, typically spanning three to five days, in which a team implements a major process change to quickly achieve a quantum improvement in performance. Participants generally represent various functions and perspectives, and may include nonplant personnel.

Kanban: A signaling device that gives instruction for production or conveyance of items in a pull system; can also be used to perform *Kaizen* by reducing the number of Kanban in circulation, which highlights line problems.

Kanban Signal: A method of signaling suppliers or upstream production operations when it is time to replenish limited stocks of components or subassemblies in a Just-in-Time system. Originally a card system used in Japan, Kanban signals now include empty containers, empty spaces, and even electronic messages.

Karoshi: Death from overwork.

Lead Time: The total time a customer must wait to receive a product after placing an order. When a scheduling and production system is running at or below capacity, lead time and throughput time are the same. When demand exceeds the capacity of a system, there is additional waiting time before the start of scheduling and production, and lead time exceeds throughput time.

Lean: Business processes requiring less human effort, capital investment, floor space, materials, and time in all aspects of operation.

Manufacturing Cells: The layout of machines of different types performing different operations in a tight sequence, typically U shaped, to permit single-piece flow and flexible deployment of human effort.

Mistake Proofing: Any change to an operation that helps the operator reduce or eliminate mistakes.

Muda: Waste; anything that interrupts the flow of products and services through the value stream and out to the customer.

Natural Work Team: A team of employees, often hourly personnel, who share a common workspace and have responsibility for a particular process or process segment.

Non-Value Added: Activities or actions taken that add no real value to the product or service, making such activities or action a form of waste.

Operating Expenses: The money required for a system to convert inventory into throughput.

Overproduction: Producing more, sooner or faster than is required by the next process.

PDCA

PLAN: Senior management should use the visioning process in the context of its Business Plan. HP translates the Business Plans to action plans, which is meaningful to all levels of the organization.

DO: Answer the whats, hows, and whos for the total number of tiers for your organization; remember: the fewer the number of tiers, the better. Also, this is the time to bring management together and to provide them with a basic understanding of HP mechanics.

CHECK: On a periodic basis, review the measurements and note what you have learned that can help in the future.

ACT: Make the necessary adjustments to plans and priorities in order to ensure the success of the strategy breakthroughs.

Perfection: Always optimizing value-added activities and eliminating waste.

Poka-Yoke: A mistake-proofing device or procedure to prevent a defect during order taking or manufacture. An order-taking example is a screen for order input developed from traditional ordering patterns that question orders falling outside the pattern. The suspect orders are then examined, often leading to the discovery of inputting errors or buying based on misinformation. A manufacturing example is a set of photocells in parts containers along an assembly line to prevent components from progressing to the next stage with missing parts. A poka-yoke is sometimes called a baka-yok.

Process: The flow of material in time and space. The accumulation of sub-processes or operations that transform material from raw material to finished product.

Queue Time: The time a product spends in a line awaiting the next design, order processing, or fabrication step.

Quick Changeover: The ability to change tooling and fixtures rapidly (usually minutes), so that multiple products can be run on the same machine.

Re-engineering: The engine that drives Time-Based Competition. To gain speed, firms must apply the principles of re-engineering to rethink and redesign every process and move it closer to the customer.

Resource Utilization: Using a resource in a way that increases throughput.

Sensei: An outside master or teacher who assists in implementing Lean practices.

Sequential Changeover: Also sequential setup. When changeover times are within TAKT time, changeovers can be performed one after another in a flow line. Sequential changeover assures that the lost time for each process in the line is minimized to one TAKT beat. A setup team or expert follows the operator, so that by the time the operator has made one round of the flow line (at TAKT time), it has been completely changed over to the next product.

Seven wastes: Taiichi Ohno's original catalog of the wastes commonly found in physical production. These are overproduction ahead of demand, waiting for the next processing stop, unnecessary transport of materials, overprocessing of parts due to poor tool and product design, inventories more than the absolute minimum, unnecessary movement by employees during the course of their work, and production of defective parts.

Single-Piece Flow: A situation in which products proceed, one complete product at a time, through various operations in design, order taking, and production, without interruptions, backflows, or scrap.

Six Ss:

  Sort—Clearly distinguishing the needed from the unneeded

  Straighten—Keeping needed items in the correct place to allow for easy and immediate retrieval

  Shine—Keeping the workplace swept and clean

  Standardize—Consistency applying 6S methods in a uniform and disciplined manner

  Safety—Identifying dangerous and hazardous conditions

  Sustain—Making a habit of maintaining established procedures

SMED: Single Minute Exchange of Die. All changeovers should be less than one minute.

Standards: These involve comparison with accepted norms, such as those set by regulatory bodies.

Standard Work: A precise description of each work activity specifying cycle time, TAKT time, work sequence of specific tasks, and minimum inventory of parts on hand needed to conduct the activity.

Sub-Optimization: A condition whereby gains made in one activity are offset by losses in another activity or activities, created by the same actions creating gains in the first activity.

System Kaizen: Improvement aimed at an entire value stream.

TAKT Time: The available production time divided by the rate of customer demand. For example, if customers demand 240 widgets per day and the factory operates 480 minutes per day, TAKT time is two minutes; if customers want two new products designed per month, TAKT time is two weeks. TAKT time sets the pace of production to match the rate of customer demand and becomes the heartbeat of any Lean system.

Theory of Constraints: A Lean management philosophy that stresses removal of constraints to increase throughput while decreasing inventory and operating expenses.

Throughput Time: The time required for a product to proceed from concept to launch, order to delivery, or raw materials into the hands of the customer. It includes both processing and queue time.

Total Productive Maintenance (TPM): A series of methods, originally pioneered to ensure that every machine in a production process is always able to perform its required tasks so that production is never interrupted.

Value: A capability provided to a customer at the right time at an appropriate price, as defined in each case by the customer.

Value-Added Analysis: With this activity, a process improvement team strips the process down to its essential elements. The team isolates the activities that in the eyes of the customer actually add value to the product or service. The remaining non–value-adding activities ("waste") are targeted for extinction.

Value Chain: Activities outside of your organization that add value to your final product, such as the value-adding activities of your suppliers.

Value Stream: The specific activities required to design order and provide a specific product, from concept to launch, order to delivery, and raw materials into the hands of the customer.

Value Stream Mapping: Highlights the sources of waste and eliminates them by implementing a future state value stream that can become reality within a short time.

Visual Control: The placement in plain view of all tools, parts, production activities, and indicators of production system performance so that everyone involved can understand the status of the system at a glance.

Visual Workplace: A work area that is self-explaining, self-regulating, and self-managing. In this workplace, what is supposed to happen does happen: on time, every day.

Characteristics of a Visual Workplace:

Physical impediments to effective processing are removed.
Processes are tightly linked and logically ordered.
Tools and fixtures have homes—no searching.
Information and material travel together.
Standards are clear and self-explaining. There is a clear baseline for continuous improvement.

Waste: Anything that uses resources but does not add real value to the product or service.

Work-in-Process (WIP): Product or inventory in various stages of completion throughout the plant, from raw material to completed product.

Yield: Produced product related to scheduled product.

Part III

Creating a Lean Supply Chain Management Environment

Chapter 10

How to Create an Integrated World-Class Lean SCM Environment

An efficient supply chain is one that everyday, day in and day out, succeeds at selling to customers what we currently own, and having those customers be extremely pleased that that's what they bought.

Paul Gaffney, EVP of Supply Chain, Staples
CSCO: Insights for the Supply Chain Executive,
May 2005, Vol. 1/No. 2, p. 13.

Staples Inc. is running a supply chain transformation initiative called Summit, which has a strong focus on transforming both culture and process. Over three years they were able to reduce inventory turns from 4.9 to 5.6 by applying Lean initiatives to their supply chain process. In addition, sales increased by 11 percent. Thirty percent of their inventory moved directly to distribution centers and bypassed the warehouses. The Summit Initiative is characterized by:

Clearly defined and simple goals
Improved communication within and without the organization
Integration and involvement at all levels
Integrated multichannel approach
Sustainability
Incentives/measures/motivators

The goals of the Summit Initiative are to

Drive greater coordination among supply chain participants
Improve supply chain reliability and costs
Increase effective service

Improve selling effectiveness

Improve return on marketing investment[1]

HOW DO THE PRINCIPLES AND GOALS OF LEAN AND SCM ALIGN?

Let us start by reviewing the principles and goals of Lean and SCM and comparing them with each other. For SCM we have:

- SCM desires the optimized movement of resources from supplier to customer.
- SCM has us analyze the current and future state of our organization.
- SCM has us perform a gap analysis that identifies areas for improvement.
- SCM wants us to define "motivation"-based measures.
- SCM requires a plan of operation for implementing the identified changes.
- SCM desires a participative style of management.
- For SCM, education and training are critical.
- SCM has a collection of tools, and when SCM is implemented, the tools are selectively chosen and customized to fit the environment.
- Control systems add complexity and delays to the SCM process.
- The measures of SCM performance are cycle time, on-time performance, and quality.

For Lean we have:

- Lean focuses on the elimination of non–value-added activities (the elimination of waste).
- Lean's primary goals include the reduction of cycle time and optimization of quality.
- Lean's secondary goals include the reduction of inventory, increased capacity, increased customer satisfaction, and the elimination of bottlenecks.
- Lean focuses on an organizationwide cultural change.
- Lean requires a Change Management process.
- Lean stresses that change can be accomplished only if an acceptance process occurs which requires buy-in from all employees.
- Lean has an extensive set of acceptance and technical implementation tools that facilitate the Lean change process.
- Lean is a participative, team-based change process.

---

[1]Barney, Doug, "How Staples Is Making It Easy to Do Business," *CSCO: Insights for the Supply Chain Executive*, May 2005, Vol. 1/No. 2, pp. 11–17.

- The proper implementation of Lean would require a significant amount of training so that sustainment occurs and the process lives on long after the facilitator has left the building.

If we put the SCM and Lean principles and goals side by side, we find a dynamic synergy of opportunity. SCM is the big picture environment that requires integration and optimization, whereas Lean is the optimizer that offers the tools that will accomplish the optimization. The accompanying table illustrates the obvious fit between the two environments.

TOPIC	SCM	LEAN
Purpose of the System	Optimize movement of resources from supplier to customer.	Elimination of non–value-added activities (the elimination of waste).
Primary Goals	Minimize cycle time, improve on time performance, and optimize quality.	Reduction of cycle time and optimization of quality.
Secondary Goals	Avoid control systems.	Reduction of inventory, increased capacity, increased customer satisfaction, elimination of bottlenecks.
Culture		Organizationwide cultural change
Change	Analyze the current and future state of our organization and perform a gap analysis. Plan of operation for the implementation of the identified changes.	Change Management process—current and future state VSM.
Participation at all levels	Participative style of management.	Acceptance process requires that we get buy-in from all employees—participative, team-based change process.
Tools	Collection of tools that are selectively chosen and customized to fit the environment.	Extensive set of acceptance and technical implementation tools.
Education and Training	Education and training are critical.	Training so that sustainment occurs.
Performance Measures	Motivation-based measures.	Time-based measures.

When we merge the two environments, we end up with the characteristics in the following table. This give us a Leaned out and optimized Supply Chain Management environment.

TOPIC	SCM and Lean Integrated
Purpose of the System	Optimize movement of resources from supplier to customer by eliminating all non–value-added (waste) activities in the supply chain.
Primary Goals	Minimize cycle time, improve on time performance, and optimize quality.
Secondary Goals	Avoid control systems, focus on reducing inventories in the supply chain, manage the capacities of the supply chain, and optimize the supply chain flow so as to maximize customer satisfaction.
Culture	Create an organizationwide Lean-based change culture.
Change	Analyze the current and future state of our organization using step charts and Value Stream Mapping, identify a future state of the organization, and perform a gap analysis, thereby creating a plan of operation for implementing the identified changes.
Participation at all levels	Acceptance process requires that we get buy-in from all employees—participative, team-based change process.
Tools	Extensive collection of SCM and Lean tools that are selectively chosen and customized to fit the environment—many of the tools, like JIT, are in both environments.
Education and Training	Education and training are critical in order to establish the process and for sustainment to occur.
Performance Measures	Motivation using time-based measures.

The integration is obvious. The two systems merge together nicely, and a synergy occurs whereby they optimize each other's performance.

By integrating the SCM and Lean models, we end up with something like Chart 10.1. In this model we see Lean at the heart of the SCM environment. Through the use of acceptance and technical tools, the performance of Lean will optimize the performance of the supply chain, which is the ultimate goal of any Supply Chain Management environment. Lean makes the supply chain move optimally.

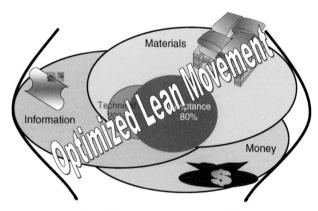

Chart 10.1   Integrating Lean into SCM

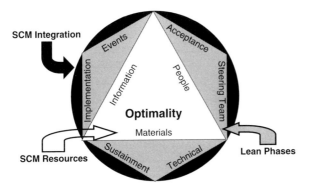

Chart 10.2 Integrated SCM/Lean Model. For a more detailed view of this figure, please visit our companion site at: http://books.elsevier.com/companions/0123705177

Another way to visualize the integration between Lean and SCM can be seen in Chart 10.2, where Lean is an integral part of the supply chain, not just an add-on.

MORE EXAMPLES

We have seen numerous examples of SCM and Lean in a production environment, but additional examples of the effectiveness of this integration can be found in service environments. For example, if we examine offshore IT development or call centers, we find that many IT firms are looking to India to outsource calling centers and back-office services. The statistics that are driving this transfer show that 44 percent of the market for software and back-office services are currently being outsourced to Indian firms. But this has triggered less than a 3 percent layoff rate of American workers over the past five years, which has resulted directly from companies relocating operations overseas. The average annual entry-level salary for Indian information technology graduates is about $5,400. This reduced labor rate has generated a projected $17 billion in revenues by 2008 by offshore IT services worldwide. Nonetheless, 40 percent of the U.S. firms that are undertaking outsourcing projects have failed to produce satisfactory work results or savings. This is an obvious Supply Chain Management/Lean optimization concern. Perhaps if Lean tools had been implemented earlier, and if the old working environment in the United States had been Lean optimized, the jobs would never have gone offshore to begin with.[2]

[2] *Sources*: Gartner Inc., Global Insight, Datamonitor, ComputerWorld, neoIT, International Monetary Fund, University of California/MERCURY NEWS, IDC, Service Excellence Research Group, Associated Press, *Wall Street Journal*, Janco Associates.

INDUSTRY'S MANDATE

We are being bombarded with articles like "Using Lean and Six Sigma in Project Management"[3] and "Unlimited Visibility."[4] Such articles demonstrate that industry is rapidly waking up to the integration of SCM and Lean. Additional articles support the use of Lean tools in the supply chain, notably the article "Manufacturing Shifts from Push to Pull"[5] or the article "A Bigger 'Pop' at Levitz."[6]

A successful supply chain environment requires the optimization tools that Lean provides. Hopefully, this book will start you down that path of Lean and SCM success.

Where domestic companies can compete is on response time. I
can manage my supply chain 10 times better with domestic
companies in a weekly replenishment model.

                      Sandeep Chugani, COO, Levitz Home Furnishings[7]

---

[3] James, Darrell S., "The Tools from These Methodologies Can Help Build a Better Project Manager," *Quality Digest*, August 2005, pp. 49–55.

[4] Quinn, Paul, "A Major Electronics Provider Collaborates with Its Suppliers to Keep Inventory Levels Lean throughout the Supply Chain" *Supply Chain Systems*, January 2005, pp. 34–36, 39.

[5] Navas, Deb, "Manufacturing Shifts from Push to Pull: Shifting to Demand-based Manufacturing Decreases Inventories and Provides Companies with a Competitive Edge," *Supply Chain Systems*, June 2005, pp. 18–24.

[6] Terreri, April, "A Bigger 'Pop' at Levitz: For Levitz, excellent customer service is all about a successful supply chain. A weekly replenishment cycle will reap huge paybacks for the company." *CSCO: Insights for the Supply Chain Executive*, August 2005, pp. 34–36, 39.

[7] Ibid, p. 36.

Chapter 11

Summary and Conclusions

SUPPLY CHAIN WOES

"Crisis after Katrina; Supply Chain Woes Mount; Gulf Coast port closures may mean tighter supplies and higher prices of some goods." That was the front-page headline for the Sunday, September 4, 2005, *Sacramento Bee* newspaper. Then the article went on to discuss higher prices and tighter supplies. But the real question was not whether the hurricane caused this new threat to the supply chain, but rather:

- Was the supply chain ready for abnormalities like disruptions in flow?
- Wasn't this crisis really the result of a poorly managed supply chain being stressed out?
- Would improved supply chain performance have minimized the disruption?

If Supply Chain Management was doing its job properly, then the supply chain would have rapidly diverted its attention to alternative transportation methodologies and alternative sources, and the flow would have experienced minimal disruptions. So how do we optimize this supply chain flow? After reading this book, the answer should be obvious. Lean methodologies are structured in such a way as to search out optimal opportunities for improvement that will make the supply chain

Perform better on a day-to-day basis.

Manage abnormalities and disruptions with minimal pain to the end user.

Identify alternatives for optimal performance so that if one process does not work correctly, a secondary alternative will pick up the flow.

Supply Chain Management can achieve peak performance through Lean tools. The only question remaining is "Will you beat the competitive rush and optimize your supply chain ahead of your competitors?"

Imagination is more important than Knowledge.
                              Albert Einstein

About the Author

Gerhard Plenert, Ph.D.
President, Institute of World Class Management
6624 Penney Way, Carmichael, CA 95608
cell (916)233-9758, home (916)536-9751, fax (916)536-9758,
e-mail: tiowcm@aol.com

Dr. Gerhard Plenert has over 25 years of professional experience in quality and productivity consulting and in manufacturing planning and scheduling methods. He also has 13 years of academic experience. He has published over 150 articles, and eight books: *International Management and Production: Survival Techniques for Corporate America* (1990); *The Plant Operations Deskbook* (an APICS series book) (1993); *World Class Manager* (1995); *Making Innovation Happen: Concept Management Through Integration* (1997); *Finite Capacity Scheduling* (an APICS/Oliver White Series Book) (2000); *EManager: Value Chain Management in an eCommerce World* (2001); *International Operations Management* (an MBA textbook) (2004); and *Operations Management* (A United Nations Training Manual for Developing Country factories) (2005).

Dr. Plenert has extensive industry experience.

Private sector

- Food—Kraft Foods, Smart and Final, Davis Lay, Ritz-Carlton, Hewlett-Packard, Seagate, Motorola, PPI, Clark Equipment, NCR Corporation, and AT&T
- Consulting companies—AMS, IBM, SCI, SAS
- Corporate "guru" on Supply Chain Management for AMS

Government sector

- California—DCSS, DHS
- Federal—DSS
- International—United Nations
- Texas—OAG
- New York—City of New York warehousing system

He also has extensive academic experience.

- Ph.D. in Mineral Economics at the Colorado School of Mines, which is their Operations and Business Management degree (under Gene Woolsey)
- Eleven years as a full-time faculty member (BYU and CSUC)
- Currently teaching SCM at the University of San Diego
- Teaching operations, manufacturing, and Supply Chain Management as far away as Malaysia and England

Dr. Plenert has

- Worked in senior management
- Generated up to triple the office productivity with the same staffing
- Worked as an industry consultant implementing SCM, ERP, and eBusiness systems and designing a Next Generation Enterprise model
- Literally "written the book" on leading-edge Supply Chain Management concepts like Finite Capacity Scheduling (FCS), Advanced Planning and Scheduling (APS), and World-Class Management
- Taken an over 14 percent defect rate down to 2 percent
- Reduced setup times from 20 minutes to as low as 6 minutes
- Reduced facility-wide inventories by 40 percent

Dr. Plenert's ideas and publications have been endorsed by Steven Covey and many companies including Motorola, AT&T, Black & Decker, and FedEx.

Index